TOP SECRET EXECUTIVE RESUMES

BY
STEVEN A. PROVENZANO, CPRW

CAREER
PRESS

Franklin Lakes, NJ

TOP SECRET EXECUTIVE RESUMES
Cover design by David Fiore
Typesetting by Eileen Munson
Printed in the U.S.A. by Book-mart Press

To order this title, please call toll-free 1-800-CAREER-1 (NJ and Canada: 201-848-0310) to order using VISA or MasterCard, or for further information on books from Career Press.

The Career Press, Inc., 3 Tice Road, PO Box 687, Franklin Lakes, NJ 07417
www.careerpress.com

Library of Congress Cataloging-in-Publication Data

Provenzano, Steven.
    Top secret executive resumes / by Steven A. Provenzano.
        p. cm.
    Includes index.
    ISBN 1-56414-431-3 (paper)
    1. Resumes (Employment) 2. Executives. I. Title.

HF5383 .P7387 2000
808'06665—dc21   99-051919

Contents

Today's Executive Resume

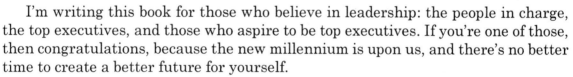

I'm writing this book for those who believe in leadership: the people in charge, the top executives, and those who aspire to be top executives. If you're one of those, then congratulations, because the new millennium is upon us, and there's no better time to create a better future for yourself.

The keyword here is leadership, because that never goes out of style. As an executive, you already know that every single company, from Intel and Honda to UPS and Kraft, relies on effective leadership to deliver quality products and services, expand, and stay competitive. Top-quality people are always in demand, because with the explosion of the Internet, e-commerce, and e-mail, business decisions are made more quickly than ever, and it's tougher for companies to stay competitive. The world is a much smaller place, and information travels at the speed of light.

Keeping up with new technologies and beating the competition to the punch have become essential to survival for thousands of companies. That's why they're constantly on the lookout for highly qualified people just like you. Even with unemployment below 5 percent at the time of this writing, there are plenty of employed executives looking for better work: more money, more challenge, a better geographic location, or all of the above. That's why it's essential to create a high-impact resume that markets you with impact and precision and that helps you stand above the crowd.

Many of the best leaders are already employed and are in greater demand than ever before. They in turn are demanding—and getting—higher pay and better benefits.

At my resume service, I get calls every week from top executives looking for feedback on their resume or someone to write it for them. Some of these very talented people head large companies; others are vice presidents, directors, or sole proprietors.

But there's a catch. Employers are now looking for people with wider skill sets to work longer hours, and they expect higher quality work and devotion to their companies. Just like the customers they work for, they want more bang for their buck.

Many expect a focused, hard-working leader to have well-rounded skills in finance, team-training, communications, marketing, and sometimes even the latest computer systems. At least one of these attributes, communication skills, will be directly reflected in your resume and will give a first impression to someone you may want to work with—so it better be good!

But that's not all. Fred Wackerle is a recruiter who only fulfills CEO and Board searches. Here is his top 10 list of leadership skills. How do you stack up?

1. Unquestioned integrity.
2. High work ethic.
3. Ability to handle failure (and quickly learn from it, I say).
4. Leadership and motivational skills.
5. High personal values and an ability to motivate yourself.
6. Appropriate balance between work and family.
7. Ability to focus and prioritize.
8. Straight talker.
9. Self-confidence.
10. Willingness to make tough and unpopular decisions.

A new philosophy

Because my staff and I write resumes just about every day for executives all over the world, I talk with a wide range of people looking for better jobs. After writing more than 4,000 resumes, I'm still amazed at the variety of work that people do. But all those who come to me have one thing in common—they all want a better position. They can't, however, get that position without an interview—and they often can't get an interview without a great resume.

People still walk into my office and give me a stack of handwritten notes on scratch paper. They scribble out a basic history of where and when they worked and a short outline of their daily duties. I tell them that's a start, and then I ask "The Question":

What do you really want to *DO* in your next position?

I figure this is the most basic question I can ask of a new client, and some are surprised by it. You'd be surprised at the answers I get. Many people assume they will keep doing the same exact work they were doing for their previous or current employers (which, of course, they don't have to), until they really start to think about the question.

But no two jobs, even if they have the same job title, are exactly the same. That's why it's essential to look at the *types* of skills you would like to use, and then to create a resume that will help get you a position that uses them—with the right kind of product or service.

Your resume is one of the few aspects of your job search over which you have complete control, and it is one of your most valuable assets. During my career seminars, I tell people that their resume can be the most important document they will ever have—more important than their driver's license, their passports, or even their birth certificates. No other document can have such an impact on income and, most importantly, on where and how they spend 40 to 50 hours of each week.

A new approach

Even some of the most qualified executives think a resume is just an outline of old jobs and educational background (that's what I call a "job list," a history of your working life). To some extent that's true, because your work history is an essential part of your resume (more on this later).

But done correctly, resume-writing can help open doors to the really *good* positions, increase your income, and help you enjoy what you're doing every day. To do this, your resume must:

Develop and market your skills and abilities.

This may sound like a simple concept, but think about it: Does the average "job list" resume really highlight your skills, your talents, and what you can bring to your next position? Usually not, and for one important reason: When you send out a "job list" resume, you're telling people what you've *done* for your previous employers, but not what you *can do* for your next employer.

And that's really what this book is all about—helping you identify and *sell,* on paper, your most relevant skills, knowledge, and training. With so many people looking for new jobs (even with low unemployment, competition for the *best* executive jobs is still tough; many companies hire from within).

Simple and basic? Or ineffective?

From time to time, I get top executives calling my office who say they want a "simple" or "basic" resume, and I cringe. They think there's something magical about those words, bringing me brief descriptions of their work history and education. They want it typeset so they can run off 100 copies at the local office supply store.

But when I hear the words "simple" or "basic," I stop them in their tracks and tell them: "We'll make it *effective*." Never underestimate the power of a few "basic" words.

What you're up against

With the advent of the Internet, job postings can be viewed by thousands of executives all over the world, generating hundreds of responses the very same day. Web sites, such as CareerPath.com, offer high-speed access to job advertisements nationwide. Did you know that a display advertisement in the Sunday paper can draw more than 100 resumes? And that was *before* the Internet took off. Research tells us that most resumes have only a few seconds to grab the reader's attention, so yours must quickly rise above the rest. Here's a chilling statistic:

> A survey of 150 executives from the nation's 1,000 largest companies was conducted by Accountemps/Robert Half. Can you believe that 70 percent said they spend two minutes *or less* reviewing an applicant's resume? That's why your resume must become an attention-getting *advertisement,* and not just another job history.

The resume screening process

So there you have it: years of experience and you may get just a few seconds to market yourself. Let's face it. Resumes are often used as a tool for weeding out potential candidates. No matter how many job openings a company may have, it simply doesn't have the time or staff to interview every single applicant.

When I worked in human resources as a corporate recruiter, I did what many of my peers did—I sifted through the day's resumes and made three piles. I labeled them "Great," "Possible," and "Never," and called people from the "Great" stack for interviews. Often, I ended up throwing out not just the "Never" pile, but the "Possible" one, as well.

With the advent of new computer software, your executive resume may be scanned as quickly as any other resume, either by a screener in the human resources department (who may pass it on to the hiring executive) or electronically by a computer.

In both situations, employers are looking for essential keywords that relate to their job requirements, including, but certainly not limited to: project management, budgeting, international marketing, team leadership, staff training, finance, CEO, COO, CFO, and so on. Computers and people may also be turned on to see particular certifications, software brand names, or an overall knowledge of a specific industry.

Assuming this is found, readers may then check for a steady work history (not too many jobs in too short a time) or educational background and training.

If the initial glance passes muster, the HR representative may pass along your resume, with several others, to the hiring executive. Typically, that manager is the direct supervisor over the open position, and will make the final decision about whom to call for interviews. The initial interviews are often conducted by the HR department, and a short list of candidates is created.

Finally, three to five candidates will be interviewed by the hiring manager (sometimes with other department managers present) and a decision is made to offer the position to the candidate who best suits their needs and their payroll budget. Clearly, there are plenty of opportunities throughout the process to eliminate resumes and candidates. You don't need to be perfect, you just need the chance to interview.

The need for accuracy

As noted earlier, research shows that the average resume has only a few seconds to catch the reader's interest. For the same reason, brevity, accuracy, and overall appearance are key to a successful resume. If you're not sure how to spell a word, look it up. If you don't know how to type accurately, hire a professional typist.

┌

Job Search Facts

Proofread, proofread, proofread!!! OfficeTeam conducted a survey of 150 managers from the nation's 1,000 largest companies. The survey revealed that 76 percent said they would not hire candidates who have one or two typographical errors on their resume, and 45 percent said it would take only one typo to eliminate a candidate from consideration. Be careful what you send—have family and friends proofread your resume from top to bottom, and bottom to top.

└

Accuracy and quality of writing are essential. I've seen thousands of resumes from top executives, many of which had basic typing and spelling errors. Nothing turns off an employer more quickly. The impression is, "If this person can't even produce a decent resume, how could he or she possibly perform this job well?" Later on in this book, we'll offer proofreading suggestions and tips for designing and creating an attractive and readable resume.

You can choose to present yourself through your resume in an average way—or in an outstanding way. The difference between a good resume and a *great* resume may just be the foot in the door you need to land those job interviews—which will lead to more opportunities for *better* job offers.

Interview yourself

You must now become your own professional writer. Because I can't sit across from you and ask questions about your experience and education, you must do it yourself. This requires honesty and objectivity. Are you really proficient at *everything* you do? Of course not. On the other hand, don't take any of your applicable experience for granted. It can be a mistake to assume an employer knows what you can do simply because she or he is already in that particular business.

I truly believe that writing an effective resume is a process of self-discovery, so I try to create personal advertisements for the people who walk into my office. I assume they have certain abilities, skills, and training that will be useful in their next jobs. It's my job to identify their best talents and then to *develop* those talents on paper—otherwise they're not much use in the job-hunt process.

You must take stock of your knowledge and accomplishments in your chosen field and decide what to develop, what to downplay, and what to leave out. It's easier than you might think, and the worksheets in Chapter 1 should help.

This discovery process will prove even more valuable when you start to go on job interviews. It can help prepare you for interview questions and can actually create new career choices, when you see that your skills may be applicable to entirely new industries.

Job Search Facts
   Market studies show that 60 to 80 percent of professionals get their jobs through informal referrals. About 15 percent are filled through search firms, 10 percent through mass mailings, and only about 5 percent through published advertisements. Although it may be who you know that matters, you will always need a great resume to pass on, even through a personal contact.

Some new perspectives

Remember, your resume will not get you a job—only you can do that—but it certainly can prevent you from getting one. If your resume does *not* effectively sell your skills and showcase your experience and achievements, you can bet that there are plenty of others on the hiring manager's desk that do.

Everyone defines a great resume differently, given the particular situation and job market. That's why there are very few hard and fast rules about the "perfect" resume. In fact, top executives may appear overqualified (that is, overpriced) for certain positions. What's perfect is what will work best for you given your situation and the income level of the position you're shooting for. Just because a resume style or format seems to work for someone you know doesn't mean it'll work for you.

Tips on professional services

Consider a free resume analysis by a Certified Professional Resume Writer. There are only about 230 CPRWs nationwide, and they must pass a challenging test and meet rigid criteria before receiving certification from the Professional Association of Resume Writers (PARW).

As a CPRW, I've created resumes for top executives and even for some great technical writers who were amazed at the results. That's because I make resumes my specialty. If I needed written documents on integrated circuit design or computer programs, I'd hire a technical writer. If I needed someone to run a company, I'd hire the best executive I could find.

A good CPRW may be able to write better about you simply because he or she is *not* you. The best ones know what employers want to see, and may even have experience in human resources departments of major businesses. The writer can take an objective look at your background, ask you numerous, in-depth questions, and create a marketing piece that has a better chance of impressing an employer and generating an interview than your own would.

When considering a professional resume writer, ask about CPRW certification, years of experience, and whether that person can give you references. Make sure the person works out of a regular, full-time office, and that this isn't just a sideline business. Additional experience in human resources, recruiting, or top management is a plus.

If the resume writer offers you a flat fee over the phone, remember it can easily change when you walk in the door, or after a look at your old resume materials. The writer should offer a free resume analysis and not even try to quote prices without seeing what kind of work is involved for your resume.

For a free resume review and price quote, you may fax your resume to me directly at (630) 582-1105 or send it via e-mail at Advresumes@aol.com. You may also visit our Web site at TopSecretResumes.com, or call me personally at (630) 582-1088.

Making the most of this book

This book was designed to help you develop your skills and abilities, then market them to employers with the goal of landing interviews.

Use my ideas about effective resume writing, then sift through your entire work history, extract and develop key points about your talents, and sell them to the reader.

I'll try to outline the entire process we use for the top executives we write for, including evaluating past work experience, education, and skills, and then translating and developing them into powerful selling points. I'll also go over essential points of format and organization of your achievements, as well as designing and printing the finished product, writing and using a cover letter, making job contacts, and acing the interview.

Additionally, this book includes more than 100 sample resumes, all of which produced interviews for my clients. Their names and company names have been changed, but the circumstances of each resume represented in this book are real-life. Read through them and study the different formats, designs, and phrasings to help create your own masterpiece. Although not every industry could be represented, I've tried to include a good cross section of resumes from our executive clients.

Make the most of this book: make notes in the margins, fill out the worksheets, and circle phrases and ideas that apply to you—as long as this isn't a library book.

The more you involve yourself in the writing process, the better you'll understand what makes a successful resume—and the better your final results will be.

Chapter 1

Assessing Your Skills

Whenever I write an executive resume, I think about what runs through the minds of other executives when they read it:

Why should I interview this candidate?

Employers must find reasons to consider you (and keep reading) as soon as they pick up your resume. Obviously, the more reasons you give them, the better. Put yourself in their shoes, and pretend you're reading your own resume: Is it enough to write that you are skilled in new business development? Or do you need to be specific? ("Skilled in strategic planning, turnarounds and the hiring, training and motivation of high-impact sales teams in major national markets").

Every line you write on your resume must answer the question: *"Why should I interview this candidate?"*

In the following pages, you'll find worksheets that will help you identify your skills, achievements, and experience in detail. This may be the most important step in developing your resume. Not only will it help you extract the accomplishments that will answer the questions of prospective employers, it will help *you* learn more about yourself and make you more confident as you pursue new opportunities and walk into job interviews.

If necessary, review performance evaluations from previous jobs and ask co-workers for honest assessments of your skills and strengths. Give some thought to which aspects of your work you are best at and, most importantly, really enjoy doing. What would be the ideal position for you? What turns you on at work?

For many executives, it's being in charge of a wide range of functions: from staffing and budget planning to writing procedures, product development, or creative marketing. It's time to choose any or all of these areas, and then develop and market the skills you have in each of them.

Begin with the Personal Inventory on page 15, then use the Skills Assessment to brainstorm your favorite skill areas for your Profile or Experience summary, which will be at the top of your resume.

The Personal Inventory includes the standard nuts and bolts about your work history and education: company names, job titles, achievements, and so on. The Skills Assessment sheet is really your wish list. Here's where you can write about and develop your most important skills and abilities, extracted from your entire working life. This is where you interpret your past, and highlight the skills and knowledge you would most like to use in your next position. This is the material you'll use for your Profile (summary) section at the top of your resume. I'll talk more about how to write your Profile in the next few chapters, so you may want to skip completing the Skills Assessment page until then.

YOUR PERSONAL INVENTORY

Name

First _____

Middle_____

Last _____

Address

Street _____

City_____ State_____ Zip_____

Telephone: Area Code _____/_____

E-mail Address: _____

Desired Position or Industry: _____

_____

_____

_____

_____

_____

_____

_____

_____

_____

EMPLOYMENT (List most relevant jobs first)

From _____ Company _____

City/State _____

To _____ Type of Business _____

Product or Service _____

Positions or Titles _____

Responsibilities and Duties _____

_____

_____

Supervisory Duties _____

_____

Accomplishments or Major Achievements _____

_____

From _____ Company _____

City/State _____

To _____ Type of Business _____

Product or Service _____

Positions or Titles _____

Responsibilities and Duties _____

_____

_____

Supervisory Duties _____

_____

Accomplishments or Major Achievements _____

_____

EDUCATION
(Most recent first)

College _____

City/State _____

Degree _____ Year _____

Major _____ Minor _____ GPA _____

Course work _____

_____

Achievements/Activities _____

_____

College _____

City/State _____

Degree _____ Year _____

Major _____ Minor _____ GPA _____

Course work _____

_____

Achievements/Activities _____

_____

Awards/Scholarships _____

_____

Seminars and Special Training _____

_____

_____

_____

_____

_____

_____

Vocational/Trade School _____

City/State _____

Certificate _____ Dates Attended _____

Awards/Achievements _____

_____

Special Jobs/Equipment _____

_____

Vocational/Trade School _____

City/State _____

Certificate _____ Dates Attended _____

Awards/Achievements _____

_____

Special Jobs/Equipment _____

_____

High School _____

Dates Attended _____

City/State _____

Achievements/Activities _____

_____

Military Service _____

Dates Enlisted _____

Special Skills/Training _____

_____

_____

Awards/Achievements _____

_____

Honorable Discharge? _____ Rank _____

PROFESSIONAL MEMBERSHIPS

Organization _____ Dates _____

Offices Held _____

Duties/Responsibilities _____

_____

Skills Acquired _____

_____

Organization _____ Dates _____

Offices Held _____

Duties/Responsibilities _____

_____

Skills Acquired _____

_____

Organization _____ Dates _____

Offices Held _____

Duties/Responsibilities _____

_____

Skills Acquired _____

_____

Organization _____ Dates _____

Offices Held _____

Duties/Responsibilities _____

_____

Skills Acquired _____

_____

COMMUNITY SERVICES & VOLUNTEER ACTIVITIES

Organization _____

Offices/Titles Held _____

City/State _____ Dates _____

Specific activities in which you were involved and skills utilized

_____

_____

Organization _____

Offices/Titles Held _____

City/State _____ Dates _____

Specific activities in which you were involved and skills utilized

_____

_____

Organization _____

Offices/Titles Held _____

City/State _____ Dates _____

Specific activities in which you were involved and skills utilized

_____

_____

PERSONAL INTERESTS, SPORTS & HOBBIES

_____

_____

_____

_____

References

Business:

Name _____ Title _____

Company Name _____

Company Address _____

_____

Telephone, Office _____ Home (optional) _____

Name _____ Title _____

Company Name _____

Company Address _____

_____

Telephone, Office _____ Home (optional) _____

Name _____ Title _____

Company Name _____

Company Address _____

_____

Telephone, Office _____ Home (optional) _____

Personal:

Name _____ Profession _____

Telephone, Office _____ Home (optional) _____

Name _____ Profession _____

Telephone, Office _____ Home (optional) _____

Name _____ Profession _____

Telephone, Office _____ Home (optional) _____

SKILLS ASSESSMENT

Transferable / Marketable Skills & Abilities	Specific Job Duties and Achievements
Write down the specific skills you'd like to use most in the ideal position. This is the basis for the Profile bullets at the top of your resume:	*Write about daily duties at positions, beginning with your most recent or relevant position:*
1. Skill Group: A big picture of talents in general areas, such as research and development, production, etc.	1. Duties and achievements at present, or most recent company, such as type and size of operation supervised (products, operations, or finance, etc.) and services produced, etc.
2. Skill Group: Expand on the first group, such as loan acquisition (for M&As), strategic planning, more specific types of operations, etc.	2. Duties and achievements at previous position:
3. Skill Group: Expand on the second group: types of leadership skill, such as staff hiring, training program development, procedure planning, etc.	3. Duties and achievement at previous position:
4. Skill Group: Expand on entirely different areas: technical skills in your industry, and/or specific, related hardware and software knowledge, used for what purpose?	4. Duties and achievements at previous position:
5. Skill Group: This can be a final wrap-up bullet, with items such as knowledge of specific foreign markets, foreign languages, or other unique talents.	5. Duties and achievements at previous position:

Chapter 2

Organizing a High-Impact Resume

A resume is the one part of your job search over which you have total control. It's your chance to sell yourself and create a positive first impression.

Because each of us has different experiences, skills, and achievements, there isn't one perfect way to organize a resume. In this chapter, we'll take a look at the three most common resume formats to determine which may work best for you.

1. Chronological format. The *chronological* format is one of the most commonly used resume formats (although my least favorite). It emphasizes your work history, positioning it either first on the resume or following the Job Objective section or Title. The employment history is listed in the order of the most recent job first.

Many people use this format because it's simple to write, and its main emphasis is work history. If you've had a steady work history and you've gained skills and achievements as you have progressed, this may very well work for you.

The main problem with this format, however, is that it emphasizes work history but doesn't interpret that work history for the reader. If you're applying for a position with a company that's very different from your most recent one, your resume might get tossed in the reject pile before the reader learns more about your marketable skills and abilities.

The chronological format may also be troublesome for the person who has had an erratic job history—gaps in employment are made apparent by the chronological listing of jobs, and may raise questions in the reader's mind. Most troublesome: This resume puts the entire emphasis on your past, and is therefore not a future-oriented document. In essence, the chronological resume makes it easier for the reader to take you out of the running for the position.

2. Functional format. A functional format consists of a summary of job-related information (past information). It emphasizes various key skills and certain job-specific achievements *out of context*. This summary actually *replaces* specific job descriptions under company names and job titles. The Employment section is then reduced to only company name, city/state, dates of employment, and job title. Although I've seen people actually omit any company names or dates, I don't recommend this unless you've really got something to hide about your past which you think will immediately knock you out of consideration.

For example, if you were seeking a CEO position, you might list in your functional summary that you had full P&L responsibility for a $500 million operation with more than 200 employees. However, you would omit that this was six years ago and that you've been a director of marketing since that company closed down.

Job seekers may use this format to downplay gaps in work history or the fact that they're jumping into a new career or type of position. But many recruiters and hiring executives are aware of this (hey, they have resumes, too).

Now you see why I rarely recommend this format. A functional resume can send up red flags to readers who may suspect that you're hiding something. Remember that many employers don't enjoy reading resumes and see it as a weeding-out process. Any perceived negative may be all they need to not call you in. Avoid as many potential negatives as possible, and in most cases, use my favorite format, the combination, instead.

3. Combination format. Here's the format I like the most, and the one we use most often for our executive clients. Just about all of the resume samples in this book are in combination format. It combines the best of a *modified* functional summary and a chronological format. It usually begins with a short Title or Objective (explained later) followed by a strong Profile/Experience (summary) section to sell your most relevant and marketable skills, abilities, knowledge, and training acquired throughout your career.

> **The Profile is the heart of your resume:** *your transferable skills, what you can and really want to do for the employer, and what you want the employer to notice about you.*

After a hard-hitting Profile section (drawn from items listed in your Skills Assessment sheet) you then write a high-impact Employment (chronological) section. Here's where you emphasize daily duties and achievements—*in context*—at specific companies. Notice I used italics to emphasize that your daily duties and accomplishments are in context. That's because it's essential that employers know where, when, and how you applied your skills and what you achieved at specific jobs.

This is the format that typically works best for my clients. It showcases their applicable skills and accomplishments and reassures the reader that the candidate has nothing to hide by offering details about work history and job-specific accomplishments. You may also incorporate volunteer jobs and non-paid experience into your Employment section. This is fine, but don't try to lead the reader into thinking they were paid positions.

You may even leave out shorter jobs in certain cases, provided they don't show long gaps between employment. Consider leaving out months and using only years to hide short gaps. For example, you could place a job dated 1997-1998 underneath a position dated 1998-Present. Never mind that you left the older job in February of 1998, had a meaningless temporary assignment for two months, and didn't begin your current job until May of 1998.

Remember that you don't want to lie on your resume, but there are instances when we feel it's okay to omit irrelevant positions. In this type of situation, be prepared to tell interviewers, in person or over the phone, that you didn't think listing that short assignment was relevant to your job search, or to give other reasons. I'm giving you some options here, but when all is said and done, it's *you* who must be able to back up everything you include in, or leave out of, your resume, and it's *you* who must feel comfortable answering questions about how you've developed—or downplayed—items about your prior employment, education, or transferable skills.

Potential results:
My staff and I have found that the combination format works well for most of our clients. Many people have told us they received a 20- to 40-percent positive response rate (requests for interviews). Of course, the exact response rate you'll get depends on a variety of factors: relevant skills, recent training on new systems or procedures, how you customize your cover letter, whether you call and/or research the company, and whether you follow up your resume with a phone call or letter.

Distinguishing yourself

When I was an HR manager and reviewing resumes, my requirements were simple—the candidate had to do what most applicants fail to do:
1. Demonstrate on paper that he or she had truly considered at least some of the key requirements of the position.
2. Effectively pre-sort experience and information in terms of relevance to my needs.
3. Identify his or her most relevant and transferable skills and abilities.
4. Clearly develop those skills and abilities.

Because time is tight during a job search, and the competition can be intense, the trick is to get as much *relevant* information across to the reader as quickly as possible. In most cases, the best ways to do this are:
　▹　Match your skills and abilities to those demanded by the job.

> ▸ Clearly spell out what those skills and abilities are at the very top of your resume.

> ▸ Back this up with evidence: your job-specific duties, achievements, and accomplishments.

Keeping your resume honest

Remember that hiring managers may be in a rush to get someone on the job. When they come across too many adjectives, or get a sense that the applicant is trying too hard to sound perfect (rather than communicating tangible skills and qualifications), they may just assume you don't have relevant skills. They'll go on to the next resume in the stack and look for essential items.

If you find yourself embellishing too much, look closely at what your talents really are. When employers come across too many fluff words, such as "self-motivated," "computer literate," or "hard working," they may simply not read the Profile section, and just quickly scan your jobs. Then all that expensive paper and typesetting was for nothing. That's why I always remind people that *content* matters most.

There's another reason for leaving out the fluff: If employers think you're trying to embellish too much in your writing, they may wonder, "What is this person trying to cover up? A lack of genuine skill? A rocky job history?"

Never lie on your resume. Someday your boss may ask you to do something you can't, and there goes your credibility and possibly your job. You must be able to back up everything on your resume during an interview. It's easier to develop your most important skills for the work you're seeking when you give yourself credit for your real talents, spell them out simply, and then position them to your (and the employer's) best advantage.

Job Search Facts
    Starting to feel underqualified? Don't worry, because here are four more reasons why your Profile section can be so helpful. According to a survey by the American Society of Training and Development, the top four qualities employers are looking for today are:
    1. The ability to learn.
    2. The ability to listen and convey information.
    3. The ability to solve problems in innovative ways.
    4. The knowledge of how to get things done.

Resume essentials

I know most of us don't like to fill out forms, but by now you should have filled out the worksheets in the previous chapter. If you haven't done this yet, do so now, because those sheets will provide the primary content for your resume.

Let's review the definitions and importance of the different pieces of information your resume may include:

1. Name, address, phone number. Hard to believe, but I've actually received resumes without phone numbers! Needless to say, those applicants didn't get far with our company. Be sure you've listed your contact information correctly, and include an e-mail address if you have one.

2. Job titles. These can be changed to be understood by as many employers as possible. For instance: "Marketing Manager: Northeast Sector" can become "Marketing Manager" followed by an explanation that you were "responsible for a team of 12 in the marketing of X products throughout the Northeastern United States." Don't, however, give yourself a promotion, listing a title that implies more responsibility than you actually had, such as "Director of Marketing."

3. Company names and dates. Unless you've had four or five jobs shorter than one year and are writing a purely functional resume, include company names and locations (city *and* state, unless they're local). Use months as well as years or, as mentioned previously, omit months if it helps you leave out jobs or cover your tracks. However, be consistent and be able to back everything up in an interview. Note different ways of listing dates throughout the resume samples in this book.

4. Job duties. Identify key duties in your jobs, then develop and highlight your achievements and how you exceeded job expectations. Include part-time employment when it applies to the position desired. You may also include part-time jobs or volunteer work that shows initiative, self-motivation, leadership, and organizational or communication skills.

5. Licenses and certifications. Obviously, include licenses and certifications, such as ISO 9000 Certification. Also include civil service or government agency licenses, grades, and classifications when appropriate for the type of job you're seeking, for example: Series 6 and 63 license holder, CPA, or CFP. You should also spell out these acronyms if you think there's a chance they won't be understood, for example: MCSE: Microsoft Certified Systems Engineer, and so on.

6. Education. List the highest level reached first. Avoid listing high school if you have a college degree. Education becomes less important as work experience and abilities expand. Place your Education section following Employment when you have several years of applicable work history.

You should also include college attendance and course completions even if no degree was earned.

Additional professional training should be included, especially if it was sponsored by an employer—it shows the firm had confidence in your ability to learn and succeed. List which firms sponsored the seminars or college courses.

If you have no applicable work experience, develop any relevant education or training right after your Profile/Experience section.

7. Languages. Knowledge of a foreign language may be extremely valuable. List your level of proficiency: "Speak conversational French," "Fluent in Spanish," "Read and write Italian," "Familiar with Russian." These can be mentioned in a communications bullet in your Profile section, or near the bottom in a Personal section as shown in some of the resume examples that follow.

8. **Professional memberships.** You should list trade and professional groups if they're relevant to your future position. This demonstrates an active interest in industry developments and that you share ideas with others in your field. These affiliations can prove very valuable when you get to personal networking.

Eliminate from your resume

1. **Salary requirements/history.** When employers want to know your salary requirements, they generally want to know if they can afford you—or how cheaply they can get you. They also want to make sure they don't end up paying more than they need to fill the position. If this is requested in the job posting or advertisement, you may include it, but on a separate salary history sheet and never on the resume itself. On the other hand, consider the following survey, and you may wish to omit salary information all together:

> In a survey of more than 200 employers who posted job openings stating, "Resumes without salary history will not be considered," a full 94 percent of respondents said they would *still* call a candidate if they thought he or she was right for the job, even if salary history or requirements were not included.

> If salary information is not requested, then do not offer it; you could be knocked out of consideration for being over- or underpriced. Another option is to mention a salary range in a cover letter. ("Although I am seeking an income in the range of $95,000, this number is negotiable depending on the potential for advancement, benefits, type of position, and geographic location.")

> It's best, however, to avoid discussion of salary until you've hooked the employer. Once you get an offer, or at least have a phone conversation, *then* you can negotiate compensation.

2. **"Resume" at the top of the page or "References Available Upon Request" at the end.** If the person reading your resume can't tell it's a resume, do you really want to work for him or her? As for references, create a separate References sheet, with three or four names, titles, and phone numbers of previous supervisors and personal contacts, if you are sure they will give you a positive reference. (See the example after the cover letters in Chapter 11.)

Print these on the same paper stock as your resume and bring this page along with your resume to the interview to complete job applications if necessary.

The personnel representative or hiring manager may want to contact a former employer, but usually someone will check with you before doing so. Double-check this at the interview if you are concerned about keeping your job search confidential.

3. **Reasons for leaving a job.** For the most part, don't include this information on your resume—you want to highlight positives, not negatives. The only exception

to this is if you were promoted or transferred within a company. Why? Because this shows continuity and growth—*positive* reasons.

During the interview you may be asked why you left a particular position—and you should be prepared to answer such a question then. Rehearse a concise response with a positive a spin. Until you're confident about this, check your library or bookstore for books on interviewing, or consult recruiters or career counselors in your area.

4. Religious or political groups. This type of information has a chance of working against you, so don't offer it unless you know it will be perceived in a positive manner. Try to put business considerations first. What do these associations have to do with the position you're seeking? Like anything else, if it won't help you get in the door, leave it out.

If you have volunteer experience with schools or service groups (Kiwanis, the Rotary Club, Boy Scouts, etc.), then you should develop and include this experience on your resume in a Personal or Volunteering section. You may also leverage the communication, organizational, and leadership skills acquired with these groups and paraphrase them in your Profile section.

5. Any negative information. Remember that resume reading is often a process of elimination, so don't give the reader any reason to take you out of the running. Never mention lawsuits or a bad experience with a former supervisor, and avoid including any item that could be seen as affecting your performance on the job—for example, the fact that you were unemployed for two years because of an illness. You may disclose this to the employer if asked when you get the chance to explain yourself directly, but no one's asking you to spill your guts up front in your resume.

6. A photograph. Unless you're applying for a job as a model, don't include a picture or other physical description of yourself. You may briefly list excellent health in a short Personal section, but when you provide a photo you open yourself up to being considered based on your appearance. Don't subject yourself to the personal biases of an HR department or hiring executive.

Optional items

1. Title. Titles are explained in Chapter 4. If you're applying at a large company that may be hiring for many positions at the same time, this component will help quickly match your position to the job you're seeking. Whenever possible, modify the Title to match the actual job description: "Chief Financial Officer," "Director of Marketing," and so on. If you don't have the time or resources to constantly update the Title, simply rely on the first paragraph of your Profile/Experience section to show readers what you can do for them and where, in general, you're coming from.

2. Objective. Also explained in Chapter 4, this element helps define and summarize your job goals so the reader can quickly determine what type of position you're seeking. It also focuses on what *you* want, which is fine as long as you know it's in sync with what the employer wants. Objectives are best when they're specific and focused rather than broad and vague. Just like Titles, they may also be omitted completely, in which case the first paragraph of the Profile section takes over.

3. **Military service.** You may include any positive experience in the military, especially leadership experience. If you're seeking a position with a firm involved in defense contracting that hires former military personnel, then your military background may prove invaluable. Include highest rank attained, supervisory experience, and applicable training. For technical positions, include systems and equipment operated, repaired, or maintained.

If your only applicable work experience was in the military, then it must be developed like any other job. On the other hand, if you're looking for work that's completely unrelated to skills gained during your time in the military, it may be best to list only highest rank attained and city and state of deployment.

4. **A Personal or Interests section.** If you need to fill room at the bottom of the page, include two to three lines outlining your interests. But make sure the interests you choose can help lead to interview discussions or are related to responsibilities demanded by the job. You could mention that you're an avid golfer or subscribe to certain trade journals in your industry.

The interests you list may also represent indirect skills that can reflect positively on your potential. For example, playing on a recreational sports team may indicate that you work well with others—you're a team player. Your involvement in a Big Brother or Big Sister program shows you can be a good role model and that you have leadership potential.

Of course, omit items that have no connection to tackling the job—especially pastimes that might be considered controversial or in conflict with the company's goals.

5. **Age and marital status.** Legally, these two items have no bearing on whether you're called in for an interview. But let's face it, some employers still discriminate based on age and marital status. Revealing your age can label you as too young or too old. What if you're twice as old as the president of the company, or half as old as the average manager? You may be perfect for the job, but prejudice can run deep. Leave out your age altogether, and get the reader to focus on your relevant skills and abilities.

If you're happily married, you may mention that here. You may also mention how many children, if any, you have. (Omit their names!) It demonstrates a certain stability that some executives like to see.

One page or two?

Contrary to popular belief, one page is not always best. Two-page resumes earned a bad reputation years ago because people were including too much useless information. They were writing long, irrelevant job histories or expanding too much on their personal likes and dislikes, hobbies, and so on.

Try to think in terms of *relevance* rather than number of pages. I write plenty of two, and even three-page resumes for my clients. Unless you have an extensive *and* *relevant* work history, or a detailed technical background of more than five years, try to keep your resume to two pages—but don't leave out important skills simply to force your resume into two pages.

Once again, it's *content* that drives the length of your resume. Imagine that you're writing a pro-active advertisement of you as a person and of your most relevant skills. The Profile section lets you make sense of your background for the reader, even before he or she picks up your resume. Grab that person's attention by spotlighting the benefits your experience and skills will bring to the company. Whether that takes two pages or three depends upon how many benefits you have to offer.

Job Search Fact

An Accountemps survey polled 150 executives from the nation's 1,000 largest companies. A full 64 percent of respondents said they prefer two-page resumes from candidates for executive positions, and 73 percent said staff-level applicants should stick with one page.

Chapter 3

The Pro-Active Executive Resume

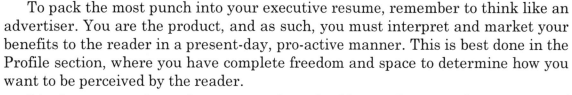

To pack the most punch into your executive resume, remember to think like an advertiser. You are the product, and as such, you must interpret and market your benefits to the reader in a present-day, pro-active manner. This is best done in the Profile section, where you have complete freedom and space to determine how you want to be perceived by the reader.

It's always tempting to focus too much on the *history* of your work experience, of which you may be proud, rather than interpreting the *value* of that history to the reader (your marketable skills and abilities).

The language you use must add strength to your descriptions of work experience, skills, and training, but should not be so business-like as to seem like just another memo, business letter, or outplacement-style resume. As advertising executives would say, "Don't just talk about the steak, make it sizzle." Avoid run-on sentences; use semicolons, commas, and periods to let the reader breathe between phrases. We live in a sound-bite world, and your statements and listings should be written in short, concise, digestible sentences.

Go for strong, action-oriented words when describing your experiences. Avoid passive-sounding verbs such as "did," "was," and "used." And employ more powerful descriptors like "exceeded," "increased," "accomplished," and "directed" when possible. Try to vary your use of words; while "achieved" is a terrific word to describe your accomplishments, it loses its impact if you repeat it in every bulleted listing.

A Professional Resume Writer's Tip

It's okay to use sentences that take "I," "we," "he," "she," and other pronouns for granted. Omit these words altogether. Use the abbreviated third-person form shown in the Profile sections in this book. This is more direct. It helps you get straight to your qualifications and *sell* them. When space is tight, however, or if you must have all of your qualifications on two pages, you can reduce the Profile section to two or three short paragraphs with bullets.

When developing your resume, keep a dictionary and perhaps a thesaurus by your side. A thesaurus will help you find synonyms for commonly used words when you're searching for a fresh way to describe an experience. Another flaw I've been seeing lately is too many sentences starting with "responsible for." Avoid doing this more than once per page, although you can sprinkle it within text. Alternate sentence starters for job descriptions include: manage(d), direct(ed), in charge of, supervise(d), control(ed), and so on.

The following list features some powerful, high-impact words you may find helpful.

Power Words

Achieved	Demonstrated	Introduced	Reinforced
Adapted	Designed	Investigated	Reorganized
Administered	Developed	Maintained	Researched
Advised	Drafted	Managed	Restructured
Amended	Eliminated	Modified	Reversed
Analyzed	Established	Monitored	Reviewed
Approved	Evaluated	Motivated	Revised
Assigned	Expanded	Organized	Saved
Assisted	Expedited	Participated	Scheduled
Budgeted	Focused	Performed	Screened
Built	Forecasted	Planned	Solved
Collected	Formulated	Prepared	Spearheaded
Compiled	Generated	Processed	Streamlined
Computed	Guided	Produced	Strengthened
Conducted	Implemented	Promoted	Structured
Controlled	Improved	Proposed	Supervised
Coordinated	Increased	Provided	Supported
Created	Initiated	Purchased	Taught
Cut	Innovated	Recommended	Trained
Decreased	Instituted	Recruited	Trimmed
Delegated	Interpreted	Reduced	Updated

Chapter 4

Using a Title or an Objective

Resume-writing professionals argue about the value of including job Objectives or Titles in resumes. Some claim that the two elements are unnecessary and only take up space. Others believe they add focus to the resume and quickly tell a busy employer exactly what type of position you are seeking. I lean toward the second school of thought. Let's define each element, and then examine its merits and its weaknesses.

The Title

The more straightforward of the two elements is the Title, and its purpose is pretty self-explanatory. It's two or three words defining the exact position—or overall *type* of position—you're seeking, centered at the top of your resume, typically presented in all caps, bold, and/or italics.

When you are applying for a specific position, the Title should read exactly the same as the job title presented in the want ad or job posting.

If you are interested in working for a company in any capacity, and would be interested in other job openings, then you may want to omit the title completely, and let the first bullet of your Profile section do the talking. You also have a chance to personalize and target your presentation in your cover letter, which will be discussed in Chapter 11.

If it's not possible to constantly change your Title as you come across new job listings, simply use an overall Title that describes your area—or level—of expertise. Some examples are:

> EXECUTIVE MANAGEMENT

> MARKETING / MANAGEMENT

> HUMAN RESOURCES

> MANAGEMENT / OPERATIONS

> PRESIDENT / CEO

The Title is easily changed with every resume you send out. However, because it stands alone at the top of your resume, a Title should never consist of just one word, but of two to four words.

The Objective

The Objective is a short statement that comes directly after your name and contact information that describes the job you want. It may even work in tandem with a Title as a one-line expansion of the type of person you are or the type of work you're seeking.

As you read this definition, you may already see what the weakness of such a statement might be. Remember that a resume is supposed to focus on what the prospective employer wants. The Objective tends to focus on what *you* want.

Still, there are times when the Objective can enhance your resume. For example, if you know exactly what you want to do, and it matches perfectly with the position you're applying for, then by all means introduce your resume with a targeted Objective that zeroes in on the job.

However, if you're not sure about the job responsibilities of the position you're applying for—or you're applying at a company where you'd be willing to consider other openings just to get in, then don't waste resume space by including an Objective. Instead, rely on the first paragraph of your Profile section to develop relevant skills and abilities pulled from your education and work experience.

It's best to customize the Objective for each resume you send. Short and sweet, the best Objectives are specific and indicate a clear focus.

Here's an example for someone who's very sure about what she or he wants:

OBJECTIVE: A position as President or CEO where profit-building skills with a Fortune 500 firm would be utilized.

Note the open-ended approach of this Finance professional:

OBJECTIVE: A position in Finance where proven abilities as Controller and CPA would be of value.

Also open-ended, but more demanding:

OBJECTIVE: A position utilizing comprehensive experience in Marketing and new business development, and offering the potential for career advancement.

Completely open-ended, and only to be used as a last resort:

OBJECTIVE: A position where solid leadership skills would be utilized in challenging new business environments.

Be sure to review the resumes in this book for more examples of Objectives and Titles. Because a company may be hiring for many different positions, an Objective or Title will quickly help the reader understand what you're shooting for.

Again, if you are interested in a broad range of jobs within a given company, you may consider omitting these components. That's when a Combination format works especially well: the first Profile bullet gives the reader a big picture of the type of skills and knowledge you can bring to the job. This puts even greater importance on the Profile section of your resume, discussed in the next chapter.

Chapter 5

Market your Skills in the *Profile*

In the Profile section you develop your key skills, abilities, knowledge, and qualifications. Although I sometimes use the word "summary" to describe a Profile section, I use it only as shorthand. (To me, a summary implies a re-hash of your past.) A Profile section should fit you, like a key into a lock, into the ideal position you're seeking right now.

Here's where you actively interpret and sell your most transferable and relevant qualifications. It's what you can really bring to the table, and why the reader should call you in.

The Profile section is a key component of the combination format; other sections, such as Employment or Education, support it with job-specific details. You may also include a shortened Profile section at the top of a chronological format, where it provides a nice development of your work experience and training.

The Profile section consists of skills or training derived from work history and education. In a functional resume, it consists of a detailed work history, without reference to when and where that history occurred. The Profile section in a functional resume may include dollar amounts, percentages, numbers of people supervised, and so on. Because a functional resume provides this out of context for the reader, it's my least favorite format.

Here's an example of how effective the Profile can be: I once wrote a short Profile section—only six lines of text—for a client of mine. He sent out 20 resumes and received four job offers in just the first two weeks. He also received compliments on the writing and design of his resume from employers. I told him to act as if he wrote it himself!

The Profile section gives you control over marketing yourself. You choose which skills to emphasize, which to downplay, and which key words to include. Without a Profile, you're at the mercy of your job history.

It's important to note that your Profile section may contain marketable skills and abilities, *whether or not you've used them on the job.* You can list just about any skill, aptitude, or training with the right qualifying words. Start with the skills that are most valued by the prospective employer *and* that are your strongest. You can then follow those with weaker skills, as long as they are still relevant.

Using data from the worksheets in Chapter 1, think about how best to extract your skills and abilities from your actual work experience and training and how best to present them.

Your Profile should be kept to two to five bulleted paragraphs for a two- or three-page resume.

A Professional Resume Writer's Tip

The first bullet or paragraph of your Profile section acts as an umbrella over the other items. It provides a "big picture" of where you're coming from, and gives the reader reasons to keep reading.

Begin the first Profile paragraph with a few words about the type and level of skills you have that would best match the job, keeping in mind what you really *like* to do. These might include three or four top executive items, such as experience in startup operations, new business development, market penetration, and/or mergers and acquisitions.

In the next paragraph, begin to break down and expand upon the major items listed in the first paragraph. Which skills did you use to give you success in your key areas? The skills might be strategic planning, market research, competitive analysis, budget development, and forecasting for multiple locations (or international, or Fortune 500 accounts).

In the summary paragraphs that follow, get even more specific: Proficient in (or knowledgeable in): the setup and management of multiple operations, the management of multimillion dollar budgets, ISO 9002 standards, OSHA or EPA requirements (in what industry?), production line setup and/or scheduling, CAD/CAM systems, Windows NT, and so on.

Following is a list of present-tense sentence starters to get you going on your Profile section. Note that in this section, the *I am* or *I have* at the beginning of each section is not included, and only implied. I normally keep these items present tense because you still have the skills, don't you?

- Proficient in...
- Experience in...
- Skilled in...
- Perform...
- Plan and implement...
- Utilize...
- Familiar with...

- Comprehensive experience in...
- Extensive knowledge of...
- Proven abilities in..
- Plan and conduct...
- Train and supervise staff in...
- Knowledge of...
- Trained in...

Note how these differ from sentence starters for actual job descriptions, which may include:

- In charge of...
- Direct...
- Coordinate...
- Effectively lead...

- Manage...
- Control...
- Supervise...
- Responsible for...

Develop your qualifications into phrases your prospective employer would appreciate. Imagine yourself already in the position and think of the actual, hands-on skills you would need on a daily basis. Write down everything you think of on a blank sheet of paper or the Personal Assessment sheet, then narrow it down and make a short list of items you feel would be most useful in your dream job.

Keep it relevant

The main goal here is to keep your Profile section relevant to both your needs and the employer's. This section is about overall ability, and it's one of the best ways to take control of your resume and your future.

If you're still having trouble starting this section, simply think of the type of work you've done that would be useful or relevant, or that shows an aptitude for the next job—then extract those skills and develop them. Here are some examples:

▷ Skilled in long- and short-term strategic planning and business development in major national markets.

▷ Coordinate logistics, inventory control, and vendor relations, as well as contract negotiation and cost-reduction in the "X" industry (if desired).

▷ Plan and conduct training programs for staff and managers in new product lines, sales presentations, and account tracking procedures.

Combined with your education and knowledge of the field, these skill sets will help project you as able to walk in, tackle the responsibilities, and succeed in your new position.

The first paragraph = the first impression

The first paragraph (bullet) of your Profile section must give the reader a big picture of who you are. Avoid beginning with heavy adjectives. Give employers at least three strong, no-nonsense reasons to keep reading. Avoid starting this important section with subjective phrases, such as "highly motivated executive" (I hope so!) or "seasoned executive." What are you, a salad?

Rather than stating that you're great, motivated, or seasoned, tell them *why* you think you are, using specific, honest business language.

The one to four paragraphs that follow then expand on that first bullet. Group like skills together, and check out these examples. Notice how each paragraph works to build on the previous one:

Examples of first paragraphs:

Emphasis on M&A activity, banking, and finance:

- Skilled in mergers and acquisitions with Fortune 500 companies; coordinate banking procedures, loan acquisition, and effective, long-term business relationships.

Emphasis on all key aspects of new startups:

- Comprehensive experience in startup operations, including long- and short-term planning, staffing, budget administration, and international marketing.

Emphasis on the creative:

- Proficient in team leadership and the direction of major national organizations, with a proven ability to penetrate international markets through high-impact advertising and promotions.

Examples of corresponding supporting paragraphs:

- Effectively hire, train, and supervise accounting staff and management in accounts payable/receivable, payroll, and general ledgers for multiple operations.

- Plan and implement procedures for production line setup, assembly operations, quality control, packaging, and import/export activities.

- Coordinate market research, strategic planning, and competitive analysis for new product introduction, with successful experience in European and Asian markets.

Get the idea? Once again, avoid overused, general statements, such as, "Excellent communication skills" and instead give the reader specifics. Without details and tangible skills backed up elsewhere in your resume, your statements could read as fluff. For instance, in the following example, the writer offers specific applications for good communication skills, both written and oral:

Communication skills:

⊳ Plan and conduct written and oral presentations in a professional manner

⊳ Manage staff training, performance reviews, and written documentation.

⊳ Compile (or oversee the preparation of) financial statements and annual reports to the SEC and IRS, as well as other federal and state agencies.

⊳ Proficient in cost reduction through detailed monitoring and reporting on quantities, parts, components, component/finished good prices, labor cost, and quality.

⌐

Still think communication skills aren't so important? An Accountemps survey of more than 1,400 CFOs found that 96 percent of those who responded believe communication abilities are a key success factor for accountants. In other words, if you're a genius but can't communicate your knowledge and work well with others, why would anyone hire you?

⌐

I consider the Profile section a great way to distinguish yourself from a stack of chronological resumes. It quickly communicates to the reader that you are a candidate worth getting to know. Take the time to carefully craft this section, but be careful not to oversell yourself. At executive levels, you may come across as too much for a small company to handle; you may have twice the experience of the company's president.

A constantly changing document

If you're not satisfied with response rates from the first draft of your resume, don't be afraid to downplay or omit some higher-level leadership skills from your Profile section. The key is to get readers to pick up the phone (or send an e-mail) and ask more about you. That's when you can have a personal, interactive conversation about mutual interests.

When your resume is on computer, save several different versions emphasizing or downplaying top leadership skills to suit different positions. Just like customizing your cover letter, this takes extra time and effort, but in the long run it's well worth it.

Chapter 6

Developing Your Career History

Let's briefly review the three most common resume formats. In the traditional chronological format, the Employment section is the focal point of the resume. Your career history comes right up front, following the name and contact information, and the Objective or Title, if used.

In a purely functional resume, the Employment section may be absent, replaced by an expanded summary section that summarizes experience, including job-specific duties and achievements out of context.

My definition of a modified, combination format includes the best of both worlds: a Profile section of transferable skills (what you *can do* for the new employer, extracted from work, education, etc.), followed by the Employment section (what you *have done,* or are doing for past or present employers, along with a list of college degrees, etc.).

In any case, the Employment section is a listing—and development of—actual work events, and is a fairly structured element. Tell the reader what you've done or achieved at other companies, and back up and verify the statements about skills and abilities in your Profile section. Almost always, your previous jobs are listed in reverse chronological order—that is, your most recent work experience is listed first, followed by the previous job, and so forth.

A Professional Resume Writer's Tip

Here's a great little excerpt from an article that appeared in the National Business Employment Weekly (NBEW): *"An easy method of quantifying your experience in a resume is to follow the SMART approach: Results need to be Specific, Measurable, Action-oriented, Realistic, and Time-based. When a result includes each point, it will have impact, say recruiters."*

Each job listing in the Employment section of your resume should include the following components:

Company name. Use the complete name, avoiding nicknames or abbreviations that may not be familiar to the reader. You may omit this in rare cases where confidentiality may be compromised, as when posting your resume on large, non-exclusive Internet databases.

Company location. Use city and state only, and don't list the company phone number—you want the employer to call *you* first.

Your job title. You might consider translating your title to a more universal title if the internal label is unusual or unfamiliar to other work environments. Just don't promote yourself to a job level you didn't really have.

Dates of employment. Typically, use year *and* month. However, you may omit the month, particularly if you have a history of longevity—staying with employers for many years. In this case, as long as the years are correct for the jobs you're listing, you could leave out irrelevant jobs lasting only a few months.

Job descriptions. Most employers will have some idea about your responsibilities by your job title, but spell them out anyway. That's because a CEO at a $1-million company has far different responsibilities than a CEO at a $1-billion firm. What's the size and scope of the company (if you want to stay with that size company)? What departments do you oversee, if any? Check the resume samples for ideas. Develop or downplay product lines and daily duties to match future career goals. In other words, if you really want to get out of the service sector and into managing tangible products, you may want to spare details of what type of services your company provides.

Try to include specifics. If you supervise people, indicate how many employees report to you directly and how many indirectly. If you're in charge of a budget, include the amount (if you think it's substantial and will interest readers at the size company you're shooting for; otherwise, omit this, or write "multimillion dollar budget").

If there is anything unique or unusual about the job that the title or general description doesn't reveal mention that as well. For example: "Travel to offices in Mexico six times annually."

Also, consider whether your general management skills include researching and writing (or producing) status reports. If so, on what topics: product or material costs, finished goods, labor costs, or quality? Do you think this will be a valuable talent at the position level you're targeting, or too menial a function?

Even after years of resume writing, I've found there are few hard and fast rules for what to include in an Employment section, except this one: Include any and all information that you feel is most *relevant to your current career goals,* and that will present you in the best light at the size and type of company you would like to work for.

Keep this in mind and you will avoid appearing like a $200,000 executive going for a $75,000 job, and vice-versa.

Achievements at each position. Employers love to see achievements, accomplishments, and results that demonstrate excellence on the job. Here you can list awards, percentage increases, and any other raw data to support your image of success. Typically, this information will appear in a list or bullet format, which sets it off and catches the eye of the reader. For example:

◆ Ranked #1 in quality control since promoted to this position.

◆ Analyzed and streamlined sales and marketing efforts; expanded annual sales from $500,000 to $750,000 in the first six months since joining the company.

◆ Increased profit margin from 18 percent to 25 percent through cost reduction and more effective staff training.

Check the resumes in this book for achievements and quantifiable, verifiable results. Did you increase the efficiency of operations? Reduce downtime? Speed turnaround or inventory turns? How much money did you save the company by introducing a new maintenance procedure, operation, computer system (what type?), or other piece of equipment? Of what value was this to your past or present employer? Did you win awards? Get promotions? How did you improve conditions?

Try to give the reader a scope and perspective to understand your achievements: What percentage of overall revenues? How many others were you competing with for the top sales award? Again, try to do this without misrepresenting yourself or using generic language or vague wording.

When you proofread your resume, ask yourself whether your descriptions of achievements could apply to anyone or only to you. Step back and look deeper into your skill sets. What *measurable* results did you bring about in your previous jobs—in terms of dollars saved or earned, time saved, or production increased?

If you find yourself trying to stretch the truth, then maybe you're not right for the position you're shooting for. It's time to reassess, and look at yourself more objectively.

Are your talents transferable to other fields or markets? Someone with strong marketing or leadership skills should be able to apply them to a wide range of products, markets, and industries. That same person could leave actual sales and marketing behind and be very effective in training and developing staff and management. We've all heard of top executives entering academia and conducting MBA courses or specialized training programs, seminars, and workshops, or breaking out on their own.

Following is an example of a high-impact job description. Note the overall layout, including placement of dates off to the right (to de-emphasize) and the company name emphasized with an underline. This creates an "umbrella" effect over the job title and description. Also note that bullets are used sparingly and only for emphasis of various key achievements. The first sentence gives an overall *big picture* of daily duties, followed by a more specific breakdown of those duties:

EMPLOYMENT: <u>Strong Brothers Health System, Inc.</u>, National Corp. Ofc., New York, NY

Chief Administrative Officer / Executive Vice President   6/94–Present
In charge of virtually all operations for this $259 million, multi-institutional healthcare system with multiple sites, including two hospitals and four elder-care facilities.
Plan and implement national polices in tandem with the Corporate Compliance Officer and VP of Mission Services.
Design, implement, or oversee virtually all policies for legal services, human resources, treasury functions, and financial planning.
Directly supervise three hospital CEOs and three VPs; indirectly responsible for more than 2,800 employees.

→ Established all strategic direction and financial structures.
→ Maintained performance levels that achieved an A2 Moody's rating.
→ Determined all strategic, financial, and operating objectives for this tax-exempt corporation.
→ Effectively centralized strategic planning, while decentralizing operations.
→ Involved in selecting facility and system trustees, as well as agenda design, resulting in a professional board process.

Remember that bullets add white space, give the eye a focal point, and help break up gray blocks of type. You may repeat some skills that appear in the Profile section, but here you'll show exactly *how those skills were applied* and what they produced.

A note about dates: I sometimes recommend moving descriptions of jobs that occurred 18 or more years ago into a section labeled "Prior Experience." Employers are most interested in your most recent experience anyway, and if your "ancient" work history is irrelevant or adds nothing to your credentials, you may want to leave it off entirely. If those experiences enhance your overall value, you may still mention them, but minimize them so you have space to focus on more recent experience.

So far I've focused on skills and abilities and where you've applied them, but employers will also want to know about your education, special training, certifications, and other credentials. So let's move on to the Education section, covered in the next chapter.

Chapter 7

Education: Play Up Your Best Credentials

Just as with skills and work history, how you list your formal education, training, special courses, and required certifications depends on their relevance. Because this is your personal advertisement, you want to lead with the information that will put you in the best light and play up your strengths. In fact, in rare cases when education is both very recent and your strongest suit, you may place it right under the Profile section and just above the Employment section. However, I usually reserve this technique for those with MBAs or PhDs from prestigious schools.

For example, if you just earned an MBA in finance and you're seeking a position in that arena, you may list that degree above your current position (let's say, Director of Marketing) if it's less relevant to your career goals.

For most executives, however, work history will be more relevant or recent than education. That's why most samples in this book place the Education section toward the end of the resume.

Here are some examples of Education sections I developed for clients. Note that the layout is consistent with the Employment sections illustrated in the previous chapter in that the name of the institution is underlined and acts as an umbrella over titles of degrees and coursework. Whatever format you choose to present your work history and education, consistency is essential.

EDUCATION: <u>Judson College</u>, Elgin, IL   Graduated 12/96
                 Bachelor's Degree: Marketing   Minor: Accounting
                 Courses included studies in market research, strategic planning, creative product
                 development, and business-to-business selling.

Even if you didn't earn a degree at a certain college, it may still be to your advantage to indicate that you have taken or are taking courses, perhaps listing the specific classes that may be relevant to your job goals.

                 <u>Elgin University</u>, Elgin, IL   Spring, 1995
                 Completed various liberal arts courses.

                 <u>Bergen Community College</u>, Paramus, NJ   1/93
                 Completed courses related to Business Management.

                 <u>Plaza School of Technology</u>, Paramus, NJ   7/92
                 Trained in CAD (Computer-Aided Drafting) versions 11 and 12

                 <u>National Education Center</u>, Rets Campus, Nutley, NJ   4/90
                 Associate Degree: Electronics Engineering

CERTIFICATE: HAZMAT Certified by the State of Illinois   1999

Some clients ask me, "Should I include my high school information?" I tell them yes if there's no other indication that you have graduated from high school. In other words, if you list that you've earned a bachelor's or associate's degree, it's assumed that you graduated from high school.

As for dates, I sometimes advise leaving off date of graduation—whether for high school or college. Age discrimination still exists, and often older workers are the targets of this bias. But remember, if you omit the dates for one listing under Education, then leave them off for all. If you choose to list that you earned an associate's degree, but leave off the fact that you did so in 1962, then you should also leave off the date for your recent completion of a certification program.

I recommend listing certifications and training programs following such formal education listings as college. But you may also highlight your most relevant certifications in the Profile section.

If you have a minimal amount of formal education, your certifications, as well as workshops, seminars, and other professional training experiences you've gathered become more important. When you list these, be sure to point out any pertinent subjects covered in the training, and make note that you completed or graduated from the course.

EDUCATION: Successful completion of an Executive Leadership seminar by Hewlett Packard
                 Corporation.
                 Completed seminars by Anthony Robbins and Zig Ziglar on communication, sales
                 and self-motivation.

Give yourself credit for any kind of training, formal or informal. This communicates a lot more than the fact that you have acquired a certain knowledge. It also conveys to the reader that you are self-motivated, have a desire to keep informed about changes in your field, and are eager to grow and advance—traits that all savvy employers are looking for.

Chapter 8

Designing an Executive Resume

If you ask a dozen people about resume design and layout, I can promise you one thing: you'll get a dozen responses. Here are some key points of resume design culled from what seems to work best for our clients. Use these tips and check the resume examples for a variety of ideas to personalize your layout.

The initial appearance of your resume—or any advertisement for that matter—is of course very important. Whether we know it or not, we all make snap judgements about everything we see or choose to read. Is it attractive, does it draw the eye in, do you feel good about reading further? There must be something about your resume that makes the reader *want* to read further.

Just like an Armani suit or a pair of blue jeans, the appearance of your resume will create, or at least slant, the first impression you'll make on the hiring authority. Because you may only have a few seconds of the reader's attention, it must appear inviting, lightweight, and clean. It must prod the reader to *continue* reading and to pay attention to you long after the first few seconds when their attention is at its peak.

I find resume formatting easier and more fun than content development. Here's your chance to be creative and to *sparingly* use a variety of elements, including type (sizes and styles), white space, margins, and such special treatments as bullets, indenting, and boldface type. You can greatly enhance the overall appearance of your resume just by how you design and print it.

Laser printer or professional typesetter?

First determine how you'll create your resume. On your old manual typewriter? On your neighbor's or secretary's computer? Maybe you're a two-finger typist and would rather write something longhand and have a professional design and typeset the information.

Putting yourself in the hands of a professional resume writer will be your easiest course of action. But if you want to develop your own resume, a computer and laser printer (or deskjet printer) are essential. Not only will you be able to get a much more professional look, you'll have a greater choice of type styles and design elements to develop a more readable look than with any typewriter. You'll be able to store your resume, modify it, update it, and customize it for each job you apply for. If you don't own a computer, check your local library or copy shop to see if you can rent time on one.

What typeface? What size?

Typefaces used for text are either *serif* or *sans serif*. Serifs are the "hands" and "feet" at the top and bottom of letters. Serif typefaces include fonts such as the one you're reading now, (Century Schoolbook, 11.5 pt.), while sans serif typefaces include those without these flourishes.

This is an example of a sans serif type face. (Arial, 11.5 pt.)

Which should you use? Serif types are recommended for most printed materials. Just about every major newspaper and book uses serif type. Why? Serif is easy to read. The theory is that the serifs help the eye move along from word to word more easily. If you are in a creative or high-tech field such as advertising or leading-edge package design, or your resume copy is pretty spare, you might consider a sans serif face such as Arial, Helvetica, Kent, or New Gothic. For a more conservative, executive approach, stick with Times Roman or Bookman.

Keep your type size between 10 and 12 points—11 or 11.5-point type is best. Anything smaller is hard for the eye to scan and anything bigger can seem excessive. Fill the page with essential information, then adjust the size of type and the margins and tabs to make it all fit.

Bullet points and white space

One of the best ways to make your resume attractive and readable is to use white space, space without type. Break up blocks of text and add white space with bulleted text, and healthy margins and indents. Compare the block-style of the page you're reading right now to the much lighter look of the resume samples in this book. Which would you rather read at first glance? White space gives readers a break and helps them quickly scan the page for key points.

Bullet points of many shapes are common in resumes. When not used on every line, they're a great way to make achievements, or anything else you want to highlight, jump out at the reader. I usually indent (tab) after each bullet. Most word processing software will give you a wide selection of arrows, large circles, diamonds, or boxes to choose from.

Another method of adding white space, used in just about every resume in this book, is to indent each paragraph after the appropriate heading (such as Experience, Employment, and so on). I prefer an indent of 1.5 to 2 inches from the left margin.

Yet another trick we use is to leave blank spaces between groups of text, as seen in the following resume examples:

PROFILE: ✦   Comprehensive experience in information technology and management systems, including full responsibility for projects, schedules, and performance for a multibillion dollar organization.

→   Skilled in needs assessment, problem identification/resolution, process reengineering, and cost analysis, as well as price structuring, order expediting, inventory tracking, and budget administration.

▪   Formulate and interpret financial and statistical data to facilitate critical decision-making; well-versed in import/export procedures and distribution logistics; hire, train, and supervise teams to meet project goals.

You may also use a simple dash or asterisk for a more subdued, conservative look. These don't stand out as well as the computer-generated bullets:

—   Successfully implement innovative programs to increase profits, enhance market position, reduce operating costs, meet strategic goals, and ensure client satisfaction.

*   Skilled in departmental/facility startup, call center management, process re-engineering, staff mentoring, and information technology transfer.

Use frills like boldfacing, underlining, italics, bullets, or dashes only now and then, and not on every line. They quickly lose their impact when overused. They should only be used to make major points stand out or to set items apart and break up type. Avoid using all the elements—boldfacing, underlining, and italics—on the same line of type. Choose a combination of any two. My personal favorites are bolding and underlining, but pick whichever you like.

Some of these techniques may seem trivial, but it's the little things that make up a great resume. Without attention to detail, you end up with yet another data-sheet resume like those sent out every day by the thousands. These techniques will help distance you from the pack and win the resume game.

Line length

The resumes I design for my clients follow a simple format. Because the body copy is usually indented about 1.5 inches from the left margin, I end up with shorter lines, which makes the resume easier for the eye to scan. (That's why newspaper columns are so narrow.) This also gives more white space and an excellent place to put your section headings (Objective and Profile, for example). Outside margins should be 1 inch all around, but they may be shortened to .75 inch or widened up to 1.5 inches as needed to fit your information on one or two pages. Again, don't be afraid to use three pages if that's what it takes to really develop and market your skills!

If you still need more or less space than margin shifting allows, change your type size by one-half point, but try to keep it within half a point of 11 points.

Avoid violating your margins or hyphenating words at the end of a line. You can make an exception to this rule for compound words such as self-employed, when the line ends after "self."

Don't worry about squaring off (fully justifying) your lines unless space is really tight. Most resumes in this guide are fully justified, in order to pack more information on each page, but we almost always place a return at the end of each individual sentence. This automatically adds white space between lines and your resume avoids that "tombstone" look, with big blocks of gray type.

Placement of dates

I recommend placement of dates directly across from job title or company name, flush right. An assistant director for alumni career services at a major university said she liked to see dates placed immediately after the company location: "Chicago, IL, 8/93-1/94." I agree with this if you'd like to hide or mask dates of shorter positions.

Printing your resume

If you're creating your resume on a computer, chances are you have access to a printer that will produce good-quality copies as you need them. Be sure to use a laser or inkjet printer—never use a dot matrix printer.

As for photocopying your resume, remember that no copy machine can reproduce the print quality of a genuine laser-typeset original. Avoid printing more than 20 resumes at a time because your resume should remain flexible: you may want to make updates and changes to it the very next day.

If you don't anticipate wanting to customize your resume for different job opportunities, visit a printer or the copy department of a major office supply store. They use high-quality photocopiers, and you can typically choose to do it yourself or to have it done for you. Either way, run a sample before you print the entire order—you want to make sure there are no marks on the glass, which may show up as spots or black or gray streaks. This also gives you the chance to adjust the lightness or darkness of the final copies.

What color paper?

I advise my clients to stick to white, off-white, or ivory paper—these are good, easy-to-read colors. Avoid grays or beiges as they reduce contrast between paper and ink. Lighter paper works much better when the resume is faxed or scanned into a database. Avoid splotchy parchment papers or those with unusual textures. If you want your resume to stand out on a desk of white papers, use a natural or ivory color. Check out linen designs, such as Classic Linen Solar White, or go for a smoother paper, such as Strathmore, available in white or natural.

The executives I write for receive laser prints of their resumes on their choice of paper (I usually recommend white linen). I can also give them a laser master on plain white paper to use for economical photocopying, or they can get more laser prints on top-grade paper at three for a buck. These days, I've been e-mailing the resumes to my clients in full digital format so they can modify and print their own copies one at a time for each new opportunity. This is by far the best way to go.

Proofread, Proofread, Proofread!

As I mentioned in the Introduction: Before you print or send out a single resume, always proofread slowly and carefully. Check *everything*, including dates of employment, the spelling of company names, and your name and address. Don't trust the spellchecker in your word processing program. One trick that helps catch typos is reading your resume backwards. Start with the very last word and read to the first. This forces you to focus on the words individually. Have relatives and friends read over your resume, too. You might be too close to it to catch errors obvious to a more objective reader.

You'd be surprised at what can slip by in the finished version. This is your life, your career, your future on paper—it must be as close to perfect as possible.

Now let's talk about distributing and using your resume effectively.

Chapter 9

The Scoop on Electronic Resumes

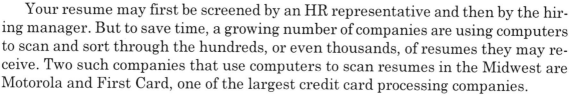

Your resume may first be screened by an HR representative and then by the hiring manager. But to save time, a growing number of companies are using computers to scan and sort through the hundreds, or even thousands, of resumes they may receive. Two such companies that use computers to scan resumes in the Midwest are Motorola and First Card, one of the largest credit card processing companies.

Your resume may be placed on a scanner and loaded onto a large computer database. Once that happens, the document becomes an electronic—or digital—resume. Employers then use special software to find certain key words for a match. When written correctly, the Profile section will contain all of your most important key words.

Examples of key words used in an executive search:

Mergers	Strategic Planning
Acquisitions	Marketing or Market Research
Profit/Loss or P&L	Team Training or Leadership
Budgeting or Forecasting	Financial and/or Analysis

Examples of key words for computer systems:

AS 400	Windows NT
Windows 98	Macintosh
Excel or Lotus	MS Office

Key words may include such operational skills as:

Accounting	Cost Reduction or Cost Analysis
Inventory control	Distribution and/or Networking

Key words may include such industry-specific terms as:

Automotive	Electronics or Computers
Food and beverage	Chemical
Mechanical	Finance or Consumer Finance

Key words may identify level of employment:

Executive	Supervisor
Manager	Assistant
Director	

Formatting tips for electronic resumes

Of course nothing is perfect, and document scanners can make mistakes. If your resume is scanned from paper into a computer system, letters and sometimes entire words may be read incorrectly. Underlining, italics, and certain type faces can be misinterpreted, and essential key words may not be picked up.

The best way around this problem is to bypass the paper-scanning procedure completely and e-mail your resume (usually text format is best, but some prefer it fully formatted in MS Word) directly to the employer. That way, the resume is already digital and there's very little chance of words being misread. You may include a disk with your resume, but make sure you also send a plain, unformatted text version on paper, in case the recipient doesn't take the time to print your resume from disk.

Note that many of the guidelines for designing traditional paper resumes (discussed in Chapter 8) will not apply to preparing an electronic resume.

Electronic Resumes, The Wave of the Future
by Wayne Gonyea

Wayne Gonyea is an electronic-career strategist and developer of numerous career-related Web sites, including Career and Resume Management for the 21st Century! (crm21.com). He is co-author of Electronic Resumes and Selling on the Internet. He's a member of PARW, NRWA, and holds a master's degree in counseling. His e-mail address is: online@resumexpress.com. Mr. Gonyea offers the following advice regarding electronic resumes.

Computer scanning is requiring a major re-engineering of the concept and process of using resumes for job hunting.

We emphasize the importance of OCR (Optical Character Recognition) in the entire process. OCR comes into play initially when the paper resume is scanned into computers. Although resumes can be received by companies electronically via e-mail and diskette, many of them are still received on paper, thus requiring scanning.

Resume-management systems scan resumes into databases, search the databases on command, and rank the resumes according to the number of resulting "hits" they receive. At times, such searches utilize multiple (10 to 20) criteria. Resume-management systems are usually utilized by major corporations and recruitment firms. The reliance upon resume-management systems, coupled with the downsizing of human resources departments in many corporations, has resulted in a situation whereby many resumes are never seen by human eyes after they enter the electronic systems!

The lesson is to make your resume as computer- and scanner-friendly as possible so that its life in a database will be extended and its likelihood of producing hits is enhanced.

In order to satisfy the idiosyncrasies of the scanning process, a new resume style using key words has developed. Key words tend to be the nouns or noun-phrases (Total Quality Management, UNIX, Biochemist), as opposed to the verbs often found in traditional resumes (developed, coordinated, empowered, organized).

Another way to look at key word phrases is to think in terms of job duties. Detailing your job duties may require a modified mindset for those accustomed to traditional resume writing. However, the words and phrases that detail your job duties are the phrases—the key words—that provide your resume with hits.

Note that the key-word resume must describe the job-seeker's characteristics and industry-specific experience in key words in order to accommodate the electronic/computer search process. These are the words and phrases that employers and recruiters use to search the databases for hits!

Use the following guidelines to enhance the processing of key-word resumes through the electronic system:

- Left-justify the entire document.
- Utilize a sans serif font (such as Arial or Helvetica) in 10-point type size.
- Avoid tabs.
- Avoid hard returns whenever possible.
- Avoid italics, script, underlining, graphics, bold, and shading.
- Avoid horizontal and vertical lines.
- Avoid parentheses and brackets.
- Avoid compressed lines of print (typesetting and proportional spacing may cram too much into one line if there's a long word near the end of the sentence).
- Avoid faxed copies, which become fuzzy.

I suggest that successful job-seekers prepare two versions of their resume. The traditional market-driven resumes will continue to be designed for the eyes of real people, to be viewed in 20 seconds or less. They will follow the formats presented by resume writers and resume-writing programs.

The key-word resume, however, should be used in any situation where computer scanning might be involved.

Most employers are changing the way they use and retrieve information. Electronic scanning into databases using the Information Superhighway is the wave of the future.

Having noted Mr. Gonyea's valuable advice, take a look at this survey:

Job Search Facts

Let's hear it for snail mail. An OfficeTeam survey of 150 executives who responded from the nation's largest 1,000 companies found that they would prefer to get your resume the old-fashioned way, through the mail. That method ranked first, at 21 percent, while fax and e-mail lagged far behind at 8 percent and 4 percent, respectively. On the other hand, some companies prefer to receive resumes by fax or e-mail, as this speeds the process—you may jump ahead of the crowd if you can deliver your resume the day of, or the day after, a job posting.

Diane Domeyer, executive director of OfficeTeam, said of her preference for traditional paper resumes received in the mail: "It shows a candidate has extended a greater effort to personalize the information. In addition, such elements as the choice of paper, quality of printing, and layout of the document give insight to overall professionalism."

If you wish to send your resume via e-mail because you know a particular employer prefers to receive and store resumes electronically, then you should modify your basic resume as recommended by Gonyea. Your fully formatted resume will probably be an MS Word or WordPerfect file. All you need to do is click "save as" and save a second version (perhaps under the name "yourname.txt") as a *text only* file, and keep it as a separate file in your computer.

When you want to respond to different job openings via e-mail, you can modify, cut, and paste it, and send it simply and quickly. If the recruiter (or database) prefers to receive MS Word files, send your fully formatted version as an attachment, but ONLY one file at a time to avoid compression of two or more files. It can be difficult for some recipients to decompress multiple files from a single attachment.

By cutting and pasting your unformatted, stripped-down text version, just like an e-mail letter, you greatly increase the chance that the resume will arrive intact and readable. Remember that you can only use this cut-and-paste technique with a *text only (.TXT)* file.

The best employment Web sites

Here's an excerpt from a BUSINESS WIRE article I found on the Internet:

"Internet recruiting services sponsored by executive search firms do not enjoy the popularity of employment Web sites, according to preliminary results of a survey recently conducted by the Market Intelligence Unit of Hunt-Scanlon Advisors. The five most widely recognized employment Web sites, according to the survey, were Monster.com (91.3 percent), CareerMosaic (79.1 percent), hotjobs.com (65.7 percent), CareerPath.com (62.8 percent) and HeadHunter.net (59.9 percent)."

Job Search Tip

When mailing your resume, be sure to use large, 9" x 12" envelopes, preferably the type that open on the long side. This creates a much more executive presentation and keeps your resume flat, avoiding the accordion look of folded resumes. More importantly, folding along a line of text can actually crack the type off certain papers and the reader can get black toner all over the place—not a very good first impression. Unfolded, your resume will stand out even before it's opened. Next to a stack of #10 envelopes, which would you open first? I always go for the largest pieces of mail first.

And don't forget the extra postage: 55 cents should do it for a two-page resume and a cover letter.

One other tip: Always keep two or three copies of your resume in the back seat of your car (or the trunk) in a firm, cardboard postal envelope. You never know when you might meet a valuable contact at a social function or drive by a new facility under construction with the sign "Now accepting applications." Don't laugh—I got my first HR job this way!

Now that your resume has been created, you need a solid plan, a job-hunting strategy that will allow you to maximize all the great information your resume contains. I'll go over some more tips in the next two chapters.

Chapter 10

Using Your Resume Effectively

Imagine for a moment that you are already employed in a top consulting position and your client is you. Your short- and long-term goals are clear: to find yourself a new and better position. Treat the job search as another position requiring motivation, common sense, diligence, and positive interaction with others. This can be hard work, but the payoffs are well worth it. By now you should have developed the most important tool in your job-hunting arsenal—your resume.

Where are the best places to find out about career opportunities? Consider these options:

Most important: build your network

What you may have always thought in the back of your mind is true: sometimes *it's who you know* that gets you the job. This is the best—if least common—use of your resume.

A network is a collection of people with whom you have relationships and can include co-workers, colleagues, industry connections, friends, and relatives. Any one of these may connect you to your next opportunity.

Some people think of networking as meeting strangers in social circumstances, shoving a business card in their hand and then calling them up to ask for a job.

Networking should *never* be a forceful action, but rather a slow building of relationships. As you build these relationships, you will share information about yourself, help your contacts when you can, and turn to them for advice and help when you need it.

It's true that one day you may turn to one of your networking contacts from a trade association and mention that you're seeking, or considering, a new position, but it's just as likely that you'll offer that contact some job leads. Your contact may introduce you to someone in the industry who provides you with knowledge that makes you do your job better, which leads to a promotion, which leads to interest from an outside employer.

Networks can be very effective. The secret is to make your network broad and inclusive. Join business organizations, volunteer in a community effort, participate in your kids' school activities, get to know others in your company better. You never know where important connections will come from. Make sure everyone you know in the industry has a copy of your resume if you are out of work. If you are still employed, maintain confidentiality and offer your resume only to people you really trust. Give copies to your family and friends, or anyone at all you think might know a company president, manager, supervisor, or influential professional in your field. Acquaintances from professional groups and associations can be extremely valuable.

You should also consider joining Exec-U-Net, one of the most successful online networking services for those at the $75,000+ income level. My staff and I have written resumes for many of their members, located nationwide. You can find them at **www.execunet.com**, and you can call them directly at 800-637-3126. Speak with Dave Opton or his staff. They've been featured in many national publications including *Business Week, Fortune,* and *The Wall Street Journal.* Here are some excerpts on networking from their newsletter:

In his article, "Savvy Job Hunters Learn to Network Nicely," author Doug Richardson sets out the basic rules for effective networking. If your networking efforts can use a little brushing up, keep these thoughts in mind:

1. Make sure each party feels that they are heard and respected and receive value.

2. Remember, the stakes are low, the risks non-existent, and communication above-board and informal.

3. It's not a sales transaction. It's about building trust, gaining visibility, gathering anecdotal information, and creating lasting favorable impressions.

4. Balance making your presentation with giving others the opportunity to share their wisdom. Don't talk too much or be too quiet.

5. A networking meeting is a favor to the networker, who has little leverage. Make sure the meeting is meaningful.

In her book *Career Intelligence, Mastering the New Work and Personal Realities,* author Barbara Moses defines career intelligence as "a way of understanding yourself and the world, and a way of acting upon the world, because you can't act effectively on the world without first comprehending it properly."

In one chapter, Moses lists her 12 new rules for career success that can help you plan your career by looking ahead. Some of these are:

> Ensure your marketability.

> Be able to communicate in powerful, persuasive, and unconventional ways.

> Keep on learning.

> Understand business trends.

> Prepare for areas of competence, not jobs.

> Be a ruthless time manager.

> Be kind to yourself.

Being a "career activist" in a demanding professional world with too little time in each day is a difficult challenge. But forcing yourself to stay focused on where your career is headed is the best way to keep ahead of the dynamic curve of constant change. *Career Intelligence* is one way to help keep that focus.

Job Search Facts

You can't network too much. Here's the results of a survey developed by Accountemps, and conducted by an independent research firm. It includes responses from 1,400 CFOs from a stratified random sample of companies with more than 20 employees. The CFOs were asked:

"How important is networking with other professionals in your field or industry in furthering your career?"

1. A full 41% said Very Important.
2. Another 39% said Somewhat Important.
3. Only 13% said somewhat unimportant, while 6% said not at all important.

Your current employer

Your next great job could be with the company you're with right now. Most companies have an HR department that posts job openings, and, typically, current employees are given priority consideration over outside candidates. Of course, this gives you a leg up on the competition. You have a chance to get your resume in and schedule an interview before the deluge of interviews and responses starts coming in by mail, fax, and e-mail.

Keep an eye out for such postings, but go further in your search for internal opportunities. Talk to co-workers in other departments to learn about upcoming changes and expansions. Seek out opportunities to work on interdepartmental projects that put you in contact with *other* managers and executives. Perhaps you can get new experience through an outside consulting position (if it doesn't conflict with your current position). If so, you'll appear much more qualified when an opportunity presents itself.

Your company's competitors

There is perhaps no better place to find job openings for positions that reflect your experience and skills than other companies *just like* the one you're at now. Unless you have signed an agreement not to work for a competitor within a period of time after you leave your company, competing firms can be a great source of job opportunities. Remember, confidentiality regarding your job search is key, unless, of course you're unemployed.

You may belong to a trade organization where you meet with others from such companies. Include some of these individuals in your network and touch base with them regularly to learn of opportunities.

Use the Internet to find opportunities at other companies (even medium-sized and small companies can have Web sites that offer information on their most recent job openings). And of course, there's always the business section at the local library, filled with directories of all types of companies, such as *Thomas' Register of American Manufacturers,* and the bible of executive recruiters, *The Directory of Executive Recruiters* (Kennedy Publishing). The directory is updated each year and available on disk for sorting—and mailing to—recruiters nationwide. There's a more complete listing of these materials at the end of this book.

Trade and industry organizations

Trade and industry groups may be organized on national or local levels. They provide opportunities for regular meetings and special events where you can meet and network with fellow executives. Most organizations have regularly published newsletters or magazines that may include job listings.

You should join at least one such organization if you haven't already, and network, network, network. If your job search is confidential, networking means just getting to know as many people as possible. Your employer may have a policy of paying for all or part of your membership, and encourage you to be active in the group. And if you're currently not employed? All the more reason to join a trade organization, so you can stay in touch with others in your industry and keep your knowledge and skills up to date.

Selecting recruiters, headhunters, and employment agencies

Some swear by them, others swear at them. Whatever you call them, don't underestimate the power of a good agency or placement professional. In a job market with less than 5 percent unemployment, the recruitment industry has really taken off.

No matter what the company calls itself, it all boils down to individual recruiters: Are they easy to work with? Do they listen well? Will they really go to bat for you or will they treat you like a number?

Recruiters often have positions that are not advertised. Register with the more established firms and avoid the sleazy operations that make promises they can't keep. Avoid paying clerical charges disguised as "out of pocket expenses." Unless you really believe the agency can help you out, let the employer pay the fees. Check

The Directory of Executive Recruiters for annual updates of employers specializing at your income level and in your geographic or industry preference.

Try to get an idea of what type of clients an agency works with before getting too deeply involved. Do they work with Fortune 100 accounts? Fortune 500, 1000, or none of the above? Also try to find out the placement rate and number of years in business.

Recruiters often specialize in a particular industry, field, or salary level. Some may specialize in placing CEOs, COOs, or CFOs, and others place their emphasis on top VPs of sales, marketing, or manufacturing. Another may focus on MIS managers or technicians, and just about all specialize in certain geographic locations.

The growth of Internet recruiting

Here's an excerpt that outlines the amazing growth of Internet recruiting. It's from BUSINESS WIRE. Recruiter's Network (www.recruitersnetwork.com), the Association for Internet Recruiting, conducted a recent poll on the Internet recruiting practices of 1,000 organizations. The study uncovered some incredible trends:

> More than 70 percent of organizations will be spending more next year on Internet recruiting.

> Almost half of the companies polled have hired 1 to 20 percent of this year's workforce as a direct result of Internet recruiting.

> Almost 35 percent of companies with more than 10,000 employees had at least one recruiter dedicated strictly to Internet recruiting.

> More than 80 percent of the organizations studied had an employment section within their company's Web site.

Be sure you understand what your financial commitment is with a recruiter. It's most common for the employer to pay any agency fees if a job match is made. However, you may be required to pay the agency for its services, and the terms of payment vary from agency to agency. You may even be required to pay an amount equivalent to one month's salary. Personally, I wouldn't do this. My rule of thumb is that it's okay to pay for help producing resume materials or job leads, but never to pay anyone for a job. As in any situation, make sure you understand all terms and conditions before signing any agreement.

Trade and newspaper want ads

You've probably read the statistics that as many as 80 percent of all job openings are never advertised. Although this may be true, it certainly doesn't make sense to ignore the classified ads in your local newspaper and trade industry publications. Sunday's edition may have numerous listings, typically categorized by field. You should also check **www.careerpath.com**, a site that offers job listings from newspapers nationwide.

Keep a few things in mind as you check off possibilities to contact on Monday morning:

Blind box ads are used by companies that don't want to be identified, and they pay extra for the privilege. Respond to blind ads if the position seems right for you, but don't expect much. Often, companies will place such an ad simply to see what the pool of available talent is like. (Be aware, too, that the blind ad you're reading *may have been placed by your current employer*.)

Also realize that newspaper want ads tend to draw the biggest deluge of resumes. Just like you, every other job-seeker is seeing the ad and will likely be preparing a resume to send off first thing Monday. Your resume may be sitting in a pile with dozens or even hundreds of others (all the more reason for an excellent resume, I say).

Advertisements in trade journals and magazines related to your field may be a little more targeted. Of course, that means the others who are responding to the ad probably have more targeted experience as well, so your competition may be stiffer.

Cold calling

Try calling companies directly to get an idea of positions available. Remember: the higher your income, the more difficult this becomes.

Alumni career centers

Yes, that old standby can prove valuable. Contact your school's alumni career center or placement office and see what's offered. Of course, some are better than others, but placement offices have some good connections with desirable employers who are looking for top-notch candidates. For example, my own alma mater, Northern Illinois University in DeKalb, has an excellent alumni career center, with job fairs, lectures, and speakers on such job-search issues as resume preparation (conducted twice by myself), networking (very important), and interview preparation.

Career and job fairs

Just as with the Sunday want ads, you'll be competing with a larger pool of candidates at major job fairs. Before putting in the time and effort to attend, try to find out what types of companies will be represented. Even if you don't think they're hiring executives or top managers, it's still another opportunity to drop off resumes and have them hand-delivered to top executives. This can save you time, travel, and postage. You won't have to provide a cover letter, and—if your timing is right—you might even have a chance for an impromptu interview on the spot with a hiring executive.

Check the Sunday classified section for listings of upcoming job fairs. They're common in college towns as well as in cities with high demand for workers. Most job fairs are free, but occasionally you may run across one that charges admission.

Pursue the job lead

Once you've learned about a job opportunity, whether it's through a networking contact, an online job board, or a trade publication, you aren't necessarily ready to zap off your resume—yet.

Before you do anything, *research, research, research!* Whenever possible, call the company to find out exactly what they do, and the name of the person who would be your supervisor. Visit your library to read up on the company, or, even better, check its Web site for the most current information and key words about their products, services, markets, and standing in their industry.

This cannot be overemphasized, because applicants who show knowledge of a company stand a much better chance of being hired—or at least interviewed—by that company. Don't forget that there may be hundreds of others applying for the same position you are. You want to do everything in your power to set yourself apart from them.

Learn everything you can about the company, the position, and your supervisor, then customize your resume and cover letter (discussed in the next chapter). Also, the hiring executive should feel like he or she is the only one getting your resume. This will also better prepare you for the interview (see the brief overview on interviews following the resume examples).

Chapter 11

Cover Letter Essentials and Examples

Following your research, it is essential to create a custom cover letter outlining what you know about the company's market, product lines, and current condition. Even changing only the first two lines of your cover letter or simply addressing it to the hiring authority helps differentiate you from the pack of applicants who send impersonal resumes to every company on earth. Of course, research isn't possible with blind ads, but you can still write a letter emphasizing key words used in the job posting.

The one thing your cover letter should *not* do is repeat too many details found in your resume. You can certainly elaborate on one or two achievements or skills applicable to the position, but you don't want to sound redundant or waste space.

The cover letter is also a good place to clarify situations that might be confusing to the reader. Let's say your resume indicates years of experience as an executive in a certain industry. Complementing the Profile section of your resume, which develops transferable *skills,* the letter allows you to explain *why* you want to work in a new industry, or with a new product line, and so on. As in your resume, avoid negatives when possible and emphasize the positive. Check the cover letter samples in this book, and always put the best spin on your motivations: you're seeking new challenges with more exciting product lines (mention up-and-coming technologies if applicable), or you want to better utilize your knowledge of changing industry trends or of fast-paced, leading-edge products and/or marketing concepts. This tells employers you're highly motivated to learn more about—and utilize—the most recent advances in products, services, or creative marketing. Employers will see obvious benefits in interviewing an executive who's in tune with the absolute latest industry trends. This is also a good place to re-emphasize recent training in new technologies or leadership skills.

You might use your cover letter to point out that the favorite aspect of your current job is "total project management, from initial staff hiring, training, and team leadership to product launch and international marketing" for example, and that you can now bring the wealth of this experience to the new company and increase its bottom line.

How long should a cover letter be? No more than one page. Lead with a catchy introduction that focuses on the needs of the employer—not just your needs. Then identify three or four points that expand upon and complement key aspects of your resume.

Close the sale

Finally, conclude with some plan of action, such as, "I'll follow up next week to see if you have any questions or would like to schedule an interview." If that's not possible, request that the reader call you to arrange an interview. If relocating, say when you'll be in town and available for interviews.

A great cover letter allows you to personalize your presentation, which is especially valuable if you omitted a Title or Objective on your resume. It also gives you the chance to write less formally about who you are, what you can accomplish in the position, and what you know about the firm. Use Internet or library resources to research companies and demonstrate your knowledge of:

1. Unique aspects of the types of products and/or services they produce.
2. Their major markets: business, general consumer, national, or international.
3. What their current hiring needs are and how you can help fill those needs.

General procedure

> Always send a cover letter with a resume. Exceptions can be made for blind box ads, but if it looks like an exceptional position, then by all means include a letter addressed "Ladies/Gentlemen:", "Dear Hiring Executive:", or "Dear Prospective Employer:". Use a colon (:) when you've never spoken to the individual and a comma when you have.

> Especially important in the executive job search: Address your letters to an individual whenever possible. If you don't have a name, call the company and get the exact spelling of the hiring authority's name and their job title. If that's not available, send it to the personnel manager, human resources representative, or corporate recruiter, with a name if possible.

> Make your letters brief and to the point so they stand a much better chance of getting read. Some employers skip the letter entirely and get to it only after they like what they see in your resume, so limit it to three or four short paragraphs.

▸ Unless you have excellent handwriting and are writing a personal note to someone you've met, cover letters should always be typed. Try to match paper colors of resumes and letters, but don't worry too much about this. White goes well with everything and doesn't look mass produced. It also looks more personal and immediate. If you honestly have no way of getting a letter typed, find someone with great handwriting!

▸ Just as with your resume, proofread your letter very closely. Proofread once for content and once for grammar and typing mistakes. Then read it backwards, and have someone else read it too.

Writing the cover letter

Expanding on the points mentioned earlier, your cover letter should contain:

▸ The exact title of the position you are seeking. If that's not possible, then the general type of work for which you are applying.

▸ Why you want to work for the company. Remember: "Why should I interview this candidate?"

▸ A dazzling sample of what you know about the company: product lines, marketing strategies, their quality and quantity of clientele, and where they stand among their competitors:

Example: "I understand you will be introducing your new robotic CNC widget assembly system in the Yugoslavian market this Fall. I have several ideas that may help you compete with Intel's established line."

▸ Whether you are willing to travel or relocate, if this is a key factor in your line of work. Omit this if it is not requested, or if you are not willing to travel or relocate.

▸ Other specifics about yourself or the job. If the posting says: "Include salary requirements," and not salary history, give them a desired salary range and avoid a specific number. For example: "upper $90s/year, negotiable." You may include this in a letter, but if they ask for salary requirements *and* salary history, include them on a separate salary history sheet and end the page with "Salary requirements are open to negotiation." However, be sure to consider the following survey:

Job Search Facts
Should you send your salary history with your resume?

Professional writer and manager Stan Wynett conducted one of my favorite surveys of all time, and it was printed in the *National Business Employment Weekly*. Wynett conducted a poll of 200 companies and found that 94 percent said they consider every cover letter and resume they receive, *whether or not salary history is included*. He found this to be true even if the company stated "resumes without salary history will not be considered," in their advertising.

Check annual reports at the library, newspaper and magazine articles, trade journals, *The Nightly Business Report* or *Wall Street Week* on television. Any and all sources can spark new ideas or bring to mind new companies to target.

Call the firm before mailing your cover letter and resume and try to speak directly with the manager or hiring authority. If that's impossible, talk to the personnel representative. Tell him or her your name and that you'll be sending a resume for "X" position. Try to strike up a conversation about your qualifications and how they're just right for the job. But don't oversell yourself if the person sounds too busy to talk.

Of course, if the advertisement or posting says "NO CALLS PLEASE," don't call—unless you can anonymously learn the hiring authority's name and/or title from the receptionist. In that case, try calling that person directly to inquire about opportunities in your field as if you've never seen the ad and heard about him or her or the company through industry contacts or a friend. Be prepared to handle yourself well if you try this!

Track your progress

Keep a detailed list or card file of which resumes you sent to whom and on what date. You should call the company three to four days after sending the resume and try to speak with the actual hiring authority. Tell them you want to confirm receipt of your resume and that you would like to arrange an interview. Again, try to speak directly with the manager or supervisor, but if that's impossible, try the personnel representative. Be sure not to make a pest of yourself! Hounding anyone on the telephone is perceived as pushy and desperate.

If the manager or representative refuses to speak with you or set up an interview, wait a few days and give it one more try. Then sit tight or send a follow-up letter. Don't be discouraged by the standard "we're reviewing the applications and will be arranging interviews as soon as we've screened them all." This is the standard "don't call us, we'll call you." And it's not without justification. Sometimes employers really do want to sift through resumes first and then decide who to meet.

The whole idea of resume follow-up is to drop your name into the mind of the executive or HR representative and distinguish yourself from the silent stack of resumes. If you can set up an interview, fine. But remember that employers have time constraints and perhaps hundreds of resumes to screen. Don't get discouraged.

Some people approach a job search with a "me against them" attitude. This can be fatal to a job search, and as hard as it may seem, you need to project yourself as an ally to all staff and managers at the target company. Rather than using an adversarial approach, act like you're already part of their operation. Try to create a "we" scenario without being presumptuous. Remember, these are people you may soon be working with.

No matter what, keep on smilin'

According to a survey by Robert Half and Accountemps recruiters, a full 60 percent of executives from the nation's largest companies said they consider their *administrative assistant's* opinions of applicants to be an important part of the selection process.

The survey found that "the interview begins from the moment you start speaking with the executive's assistant."

Assistants are seen as being increasingly skilled at gauging whether candidates will be a good fit for the company's business environment, and executives take this into account when making hiring decisions. Some assistants actually interview candidates, either formally if they serve as office managers or informally as a means of facilitating the screening process.

With all respect to the invaluable administrative assistant, I think this shows just how subjective the hiring process can become. Hiring managers may have their opinions tainted by a subjective, personal bias even before objectively considering your skills and experience. That's why a smile, a positive attitude, and eye contact may do more to win the day than you think. As management guru Tom Peters once put it, "People like to do business with people who like to do business." How true.

In the next few pages, I'll show you some sample cover letters which you should not use verbatim, but rather modify and customize for each resume you distribute. There are also sample follow-up letters, salary history and reference sheets. Again, personalization and customization are the keys to making a cover letter and resume produce the next step toward your new position: the interview.

Note: For use with Executive Search Firms.

PETER S. VICHOS

122 Tuna Can Road   Residence: 610/555-0350
Topanga, OH 10290   E-mail: peter@net.att.net

[date]

[name]
[title]
[company name]
[address]
[city], [state] [zip]

Dear [salutation] [last name]:

I am seeking senior-level positions in U.S./international corporate business development and management through your firm, and have enclosed my resume for your review.

Throughout my career, my ambition and ability to motivate others have allowed me to recruit and develop high-performance teams while managing budgets and resources for bottom-line results. Most importantly, I've proven my ability to determine and meet specific client needs.

As president at Focus Research, Inc., I met the challenge of turning the company into a profitable business and penetrated key markets worldwide. This successful turnaround and market expansion enabled the parent company, Cel Technology, Inc., to sell Personal Research in November 1996. I am now providing consulting services in strategic direction and management to the newly hired president, with a focus on market development and product innovation.

Highlights of my career include:

➢ Forging and managing distributorship alliances in Korea, South Africa, and Argentina, and immediately increasing foreign sales by 15%.

➢ Developing and launching highly competitive, technically advanced instrumentation products and techniques, including X-ray fluorescence, spectro-photometry, and bio-medical fluorometers.

Additionally, I have published and presented several scientific papers at international conferences and hold U.S. and international patents. Please contact me soon to arrange a meeting to discuss mutual interests, and thank you for your time and consideration.

Sincerely,

Peter S. Vichos
Enclosure

ANTHONY PROVENZANO
122 East 334th Street, Apt. 26G
New York, NY 10016
212/555-7492

[today's date]

[name]
[title]
[company name]
[address]
[city], [state] [zip]

Dear [salutation] [last name]:

I am forwarding my resume to you in response to your advertisement [search or announcement] for a [Title of Position]. I believe that you will find my background fits what you are seeking.

Currently, I am completing an assignment with Scream Puff, Inc. to evaluate and qualify vendor Web sites for hyperlink sales, banner advertising, and other e-commerce marketing channels. This project is one of many that I have directed as an independent consultant to major accounts such as Federated Marketing Services/Macy's, Ann Taylor, and The Rowland Company.

During the past three years of working with these businesses, I have gained practical client-oriented experience in bringing technological solutions to the rapidly changing, complex management of information vital to a business' competitive advantage. Most important, I communicate ideas well and build strong, lasting client relationships.

[*Optional:* My technical knowledge includes ....]

I am willing to travel [and relocate for the right opportunity]. Please contact me soon to arrange an interview at your earliest convenience.

Thank you for your time and consideration.

Sincerely,

Anthony Provenzano
Enclosure

ADAM R. NEPHEW
221 Palm Bay Drive
Ballwin, NE 63021

Residence: 314/555-2348   nq74A@prodigy.com   Business: 314/555-729

[date]

[name]
[title]
[company]
[address]
[city], [state] [zip]

Dear [salutation] [last name]:

I am forwarding my resume to you in response to your advertisement for **(position name)**. I would like to explore this opportunity further. Specifically, I would like to better utilize my analytical skills and extensive background in information management systems.

As EDP Supervisor at The Merchandising Corporation, I direct a staff in processing imported merchandise orders, with attention to cost analysis and pricing, for more than 200 stores nationwide. I ensure 100% accuracy of all financial and statistical data, to preserve information technology across a broad spectrum of applications.

This past year, I reengineered several processes. I reduced report generation and distribution time to within 24 hours and classified merchandise items by a Uniform Product Code. The latter change smoothed inventory levels by matching items replenished to actual items sold.

Additionally, I speak and write basic Spanish. My computer knowledge covers both mainframe and PC-based systems, including AS/400, Windows 3.1/95/NT, dBase III/IV, Lotus 1-2-3, Infomaker and MS Access, APL, Fortran, Pascal, BASIC, and Assembler.

I am willing to relocate for the right opportunity and am available for an interview at your convenience. I look forward to your response.

Sincerely,

Adam R. Nephew
Enclosure

JACK A. NICHOLS
115 Brock Road
Santa, CA 95404
707/555-8830
JA740@aol.com

[date]

[name]
[title]
[company]
[address]
[city], [state] [zip]

Dear Executive:

I am exploring senior leadership opportunities in general management with your organization. Specifically, I can bring you extensive skills in new business development, process re-engineering, and systems design and implementation. My background includes leadership in quality control, client relations, financial operations, and problem resolution, developed in the mortgage, student loan, and telecommunications industries.

[OPTIONAL: I am confident that my upper-level management background in business and government situations will ensure that your company's strategic and tactical goals will be met and exceeded.]

Throughout my diverse and highly successful career, I have proven my ability to work effectively with clients, staff, and management at all levels of experience. Most importantly, I've expanded my profit- and team-building talents, which means I can determine and meet the needs of your company with professional yet personal communication skills. In addition, I have exposure to various forms of information and telecommunication technology, such as call centers and LAN/WAN platforms.

Please let me know if there is any further information you require. I can provide excellent references upon request and would like to know when we may meet to discuss mutual interests. Thank you for your time and consideration, and I look forward to hearing from you soon.

Sincerely,

Jack A. Nichols
Enclosure

JAMES FLYER

224 Jefferson Lane
Streamwood, IL 60107
Residence: 630/555-1355

Note: *James faxed a more extensive version of this letter and his resume (the fifth resume example in this book) and received an interview in 24 hours; he sent a total of 50 resumes and received 17 interviews and a new job.*

October 25, 1999

Perry Podgorniak:
c/o The Hartford
456 Hartford Plaza
Hartford, CT 06115
Fax: 860/555-4170

Dear Mr. Podgorniak:

I am forwarding my resume to you in response to your advertisement for Director of Marketing. My experience includes highly profitable strategic planning, market penetration, and new business development. With my increasing responsibilities and success at various companies, I feel certain I can increase sales for your company significantly.

Throughout my career, I've expanded markets and bottom-line profits through:

➢ *Leadership*	Creation of high-performance sales teams in competitive markets, providing leadership in goal-setting, lead development, sales presentations, product lines, after-sale service, and total account management.
➢ *Management*	Profit-building skills in account acquisition and business development, including market research, competitive analysis, product differentiation, sales forecasting, and client relations.
➢ *Client Relations*	Direct involvement in increasing the premium volume for the division office to $130 million from $100 million over a seven-year period.

I am willing to travel extensively or relocate for the right opportunity. Please contact me as soon as possible to arrange a meeting to discuss mutual interests.

Thank you for your time and consideration.

Sincerely,

James Flyer
Enclosure

GOSHEN D. NANI
Coni 2280
Buenos Aires, Argentina
Cellular: 541/555-3907
Business: 541/636-1001
Goshen@hotmail.com

[date]

[name]
[title]
[company]
[address]
[city], [state] [zip]

Dear Hiring Executive:

I believe you will find that my experience in senior-level management fits what you are seeking. I specialize in capital investment projects and hold an M.B.A. degree.

Currently, I am Director of Operations for Sync, Inc., a company owned by Tock-Tic Investment Group. Most notably, I recently broke through a competitive barrier worldwide. I launched Sync in Argentina and Uruguay and immediately captured an unheard of 30 percent of total sales for the apparel division.

Prior to this position, I was controller of the Latin American operations for two other ventures of Tock-Tic, the Hard Rock Cafe and Planet Hollywood. During my tenure there, I opened and managed several theme restaurants new to Latin America. More important, I identified several successful new business development opportunities, such as the acquisition of a radio station and the backing of Disney's *Beauty and the Beast* theater production.

I am willing to travel or relocate to the United States for the right opportunity. Please contact me soon to arrange a meeting at your convenience to discuss mutual interests.

Thank you for your time and consideration.

Sincerely,

Goshen D. Nani
Enclosure

DAVID ROBERTSON
972 Woodsy Trail #B2
Northbrook, IL 60062
707/555-1265

Note: *The day after your interview, send a note like this or call your interviewer to restate your interest in the position and thank him or her for the interview.*

October 25, 1999

John B. Smith
National Sales Manager
ICB Corporation
228 Microchip Drive
Chicago, IL 60683

Dear Mr. Smith,

Thank you for your time and for an excellent [or very informative] interview on [Monday]. It was a pleasure meeting you. I was most impressed by the high professional standards demonstrated by your staff.

I am certain my [leadership, marketing, management, etc.] skills would prove extremely valuable to your executive team. Your product line is excellent and your company has proven its ability to penetrate both new and expanding markets.

Once again, thank you for your consideration and I look forward to new career challenges with your excellent firm.

Sincerely,

David Robertson

By the way: *an Accountemps survey of 150 executives found that 76 percent of respondents consider a post-interview thank you note of value when evaluating candidates, while only 36 percent of job applicants actually follow through with this simple courtesy.*

JOHN A. CALLER

REFERENCES

Business:

Jim E. Shields, President
Shields Southwest Sales, Inc.
1008 Brady Avenue N.W.
Atlanta, GA 30318
404/555-1133

Bruce Gin, President
Fairfield Marine, Inc.
5739 Dixie Highway
Fairfield, OH 45014
513/555-0825

Brian Krixen, Partner
Ernst & Young, L.L.P.
150 South Wacker Drive
Chicago, IL 60606
312/555-1800

Personal:

Daniel Rosati, CPA
Conklin Accounting & Tax Service
5262 South Rt. 83 #308
Willowbrook, IL 60514
708/555-8800

RickBaeson, Business Development Manager
Yamaha
P.O. Box 8234
Barrington, IL 60011
708/555-4446

Bob Redson, Salesman
Central Photo Engraving
712 South Prairie Avenue
Chicago, IL 60616
708/555-9119

STEVEN A. WRITER

SALARY HISTORY
(Annual Basis)

People Search, Inc.
Director of Human Resources $150,000

Anderson Publishing Service, Inc.
Chief Writer   Up to $85,000: commission-based

National Van Lines
Director of Recruiting $77,000

Professional Career Consultants
Writer and Branch Manager   Up to $29,000: commission-based

Notes:

In general, never include salary requirements unless requested by the employer, but also consider the following:

* You could also add: Current salary requirements are open to negotiation.

* If salary *requirements* are requested, you could add something like this in your cover letter: Currently seeking a position in the upper $90s [$80s, etc.] per year.

(Caution! This could label you as over- or underpriced for the position. That's one reason they ask for a salary history in the first place).

Remember the survey of more than 200 employers who said they would still consider you if you seemed right for the position even if you didn't include your requested salary information, so add it only if you feel it's essential, on a case-by-case basis.

Chapter 12

Executive Resume Examples

All of the following real-life resume examples resulted in interviews, and in many cases in job offers. Of course, I've changed company and job seekers' names to maintain total confidentiality.

I called all of these applicants, asked them about the results of their resumes, and included their stories at the top of each example. Most of these resumes were written in 1999, and many of these people may have received even stronger results by the time you read this.

I counted every offer of an interview as an interview. In other words, the resume had to result in at least one employer's offering to interview the applicant, usually by phone. In the vast majority of cases, clients accepted those interview offers and actually discussed the position at hand.

Eventually, many of these interviews resulted in job offers, possibly many more by the time of this printing. But remember: even high-quality resumes don't get jobs, they can only help increase the *number* and *quality* of interviews, where you have the chance to personally discuss the position. You and the employer can then square off and see if the position's right for you, but without the best possible resume (preferably modified somewhat for each position) you may never get that chance!

You may use phrases, wordings, and designs to create your own masterpiece, but keep in mind that if you use too much of any one resume, you run the risk of looking like someone else! In other words, these samples are presented with the idea that you'll use them only for help in writing your own, highly unique presentation.

Sent 60 targeted resumes; received 15 interviews and three job offers.   *(See corresponding cover letter)*

PETER S. VICHOS

122 Tuna Can Road
Topanga, OH 44290

Residence: 610/555-0350
E-mail: peter@net.att.net

CORPORATE BUSINESS DEVELOPMENT AND MANAGEMENT

PROFILE:
- ➤ Comprehensive experience in senior-level planning, administration and the direction of manufacturing operations, in advanced instrumentation technologies, with P&L responsibility for market penetration and expansion internationally.

- ➤ Skilled in strategic planning, opportunity identification, market risk analysis, venture capitalization, contract negotiation and distributor network development; recruit, train and supervise high-performance teams to meet business and financial goals.

- ➤ Effectively lead organizations through critical structuring and product rollouts; awarded U.S./international patents; conference author/presenter; proven ability to develop a pipeline of competitive products from concept to commercialization.

- ➤ Well-versed in intercultural communication and negotiation; experience working with business partners in Europe, the Pacific Rim, Israel and Latin America; fluent in English and French, conversant in Dutch and familiar with Spanish.

CAREER BACKGROUND:

<u>Focus Research, Inc.</u>, Chatsworth, IA

Consultant   11/96-Present

Provide consulting services to the president hired by the new parent company, Cel Technology, Inc. Charged with strategic planning and management, focused on market development and product innovation, for this $9 million manufacturer of photometric instruments, with worldwide distribution.

President   2/96-11/96

In charge of the planning, administration and direction of all company operations, with full P&L responsibility; turned around an $800,000 loss in profits into a $700,000 gain.
- → Transformed the company culture into a consumer-driven one from an aerospace/government-driven culture, to penetrate commercial markets.
- → Recruited and hired a Vice President of Marketing to fill a 20-month vacancy.
- → Directly managed foreign distributors representing 60% of sales and increased foreign sales by 15%; contracted distributors in Korea, South Africa and Argentina.
- → Opened a centrally located European sales and customer service center in Germany, and redesigned all products to meet EC directives to expand into European markets.
- → Launched two key products.
- → Orchestrated the sale of the company to Cel Technology, Inc., in October 1995.

General Manager and Vice President of Engineering   5/95-2/96

Recruited by the President of Kollmorgen Instruments Corporation to re-engineer the company and reverse a rapidly eroding financial position within six months.
- → Attended the fast-track AEA/Stanford Executive Institute.

<u>Biocircuits Corporation</u>, Sunnyvale, CA   1994

Independent Consultant

Spearheaded a nine-month redesign project to develop a first-to-market, low-cost physician office blood analyzer into a robust, marketable product.
- → FDA approval granted in October 1995.

<u>Xsirius, Inc.</u>, Marina del Rey, CA   1992-1994

XRF Instrumentation Manager

Responsible for the operation of a new products development and management function to produce portable X-ray detection instruments; drafted business plans for four product lines.

→ Forged three OEM relationships representing potential revenues of $5 million.

→ Designed and delivered a proof-of-concept instrument for process control to the Ford Motor Company within five months of operation.

<u>Kevex Instruments, Inc.</u>, San Carlos, CA

Research and Development Manager   1988-1992

Directed all phases of research projects to develop new products in x-ray analytical instrumentation. Provided oversight management to a staff of 26 and managed a $2.8 million budget.

→ Adopted ISO 9000 guidelines and simplified documentation procedures.

→ Ported XRF, and consequently, the micro-analysis, product line software to Windows.

→ Augmented sales revenues by $10 million solely from the x-ray analytical instrument product line.

→ Negotiated and won a multi-million-dollar contract with Intel Corporation to produce and deliver a semiconductor wafer process-control instrument to monitor metallic films on patterned wafers.

Project Group Leader   1986-1988

Led the team that invented and designed the first commercial XRF micro-fluorescence analyzer.

→ Promoted to this position from **Electronic Engineer**, 1985-1986.

<u>Pacific Scientific Company</u>, Menlo Park, CA   1984-1985

Senior Project Engineer

Designed and launched a state-of-the-art particle counter based on open cavity He-Ne lasers.

<u>Knogo Corporation</u>, Hicksville, NY   1981-1983

Electromagnetic Program Manager

Managed project teams in new product development from ideation to commercialization.

→ Awarded U.S./international patents for the underlying core technology.

→ This product, at 60% of total company sales, accounted for a 25% annual increase in sales revenues to $200 million by 1996 from baseline sales of $150 million in 1985.

**MILITARY
SERVICE:**   <u>Belgian Service / Developing Countries</u>, Africa   1979-1981

Professor of Physics, College Moderne, Ivory Coast

Professor of Mathematics, College Moulay Ismail, Morocco

EDUCATION: <u>IN.RA.CI.</u>, Brussels, Belgium

Ingenieur Industrial Electronique / MSEE Degree

Used one resume; hired by a former client.   *(See corresponding letter)*

ANTHONY PROVENZANO
122 East 334th Street, Apt. 26G
New York, NY 10016
Residence: 212/555-7492   E-mail: anthony@yahoo.com

INTERNET AND E-MULTIMEDIA TECHNOLOGIES

PROFILE: Corporate and entrepreneurial experience in the management of advanced information technologies, specializing in Web configuration and systems integration, with full responsibility for startup and growth strategies in highly competitive business environments.

> ➢ Advise senior management on emerging issues and industry trends. Produce business plans and proposals for electronic multimedia system projects, including design, installation, migration, conversion, product rollout, and digital asset management.

> ➢ Skilled in client needs assessment, market intelligence, product specification determination, risk analysis, change order management, budgeting, and client-vendor relations. Recruit and mobilize high-performance teams. Effectively communicate concepts and complex technical information to nontechnical personnel at all levels.

> ➢ Technical Knowledge: Mac OS, Windows NT, UNIX, Outlook Adobe Photoshop, QuarkXPress, Adobe Illustrator, MS Office, DNS, TCP/IP, AppleTalk, Ethernet, WinFrame, Reflections, Cyclone, Rumba, HTML, TCL/TK, PERL, Remote Access Software; hardware includes SGI, Raid storage solutions, 10/100Base-T Hubs and ISDN; expert in Internet/intranet protocols and client-server technologies.

CAREER BACKGROUND:

A. Provenzano & Sons, New York, NY   1995-Present

Consultant / Owner

Provide consulting services and project technical assistance to major corporate clients, specializing in advanced information technologies, including Web design layout and configuration, system integration, network administration, strategic planning, project direction, and account management.

Major clients and projects include:

⇨ *Scream Puff, Inc.*
Current Project: evaluate and qualify vendors/distributorships for Web site hyperlinks and banner advertising, working with client marketing and information technology staff.

⇨ *The Glamor-Face Companies*
Directed a group of 3-8 systems administrators and vendor consultants on a variety of projects.
- Led system migrations from Win 3.1/WFW3.11 to NT and from MS Mail 3.5 to Exchange/Outlook.
- Coordinated the installation of Mac OS 8.x for the Graphics Department.
- Evaluated software alternatives, such as WinFrame and intranets, for in-house applications.
- Processed Domain registrations of GF's trademark names and maintained MX records.
- Monitored and documented project progress, including milestones, change orders, and budgets.

⇨ *Fed Services/Stacy's*

Managed various major projects, with budgets ranging from $25,000 to $600,000, to upgrade all computer/LAN equipment and develop special multimedia services.

- Evaluated and implemented strategies to leverage emerging technologies.
- Handled all network systems administration, including design, upgrades, and troubleshooting.
- Implemented company maintenance and repair program for desktop hardware, to realize a savings of over $100,000 annually.

⇨ *The Land Company, Squish Communications, Sam Taylor*

System migration project: converted the MS Mail 3.5 e-mail system to a Novell GroupWise (PC/Mac).

- Evaluated software alternatives and selected software/hardware vendors.
- Upgraded server software and hardware to Mac systems.
- Planned, organized, and supervised interoffice relocation of staff and computer equipment.

High Octane Media Enterprises, New York, NY   1995-1996
Webmaster / Partner

Formed this startup ISP venture with two other partners, to offer Web development, marketing, and advertising services. Sold share to partners to expand consulting services.

- Invested $5,000 of personal finances in startup costs; prepared the initial business plan.
- Utilized Windows NT 3.5.1., O'Reilly's Web-site and Postoffice.
- Installed and maintained dedicated telecommunication lines, dial-up and fractional T-1.
- Performed network installation, troubleshooting, bandwidth monitoring, and resource utilization.
- Provided Web site technical support for clients and fielded consumer e-mail questions.

Microcomputer Publishing Center, New York, NY   1993-1995
Systems Analyst

Responsible for servicing 125 corporate accounts for this systems integration service company.

- Developed Macintosh based solutions for Design Studios.
- Provided one-on-one telephone support to clients, resolving network, hardware, and software problems.
- Tested prototype systems prior to each software release.

EDUCATION:

School of Visual Arts, New York, NY
Coursework toward a Master of Fine Arts degree.
Concentration: Multimedia

(See corresponding letter)

ADAM R. NEPHEW
221 Palm Bay Drive
Baldwin, NE 63021

Residence: 314/555-0109   E-mail: nq74A@prodigy.com   Business: 314/555-7291

OBJECTIVE: **INFORMATION TECHNOLOGY / MIS**
Retail, Manufacturing, or Financial Services

PROFILE:

➤ Extensive background in retail merchandising information technology and management systems, with full responsibility for project budgets, schedules, and performance for a multibillion dollar retail organization.

➤ Skilled in needs assessment, problem identification/resolution, process reengineering, cost analysis, price structuring, order expediting, inventory tracking, and budget administration; coordinate and prioritize multiple tasks.

➤ Formulate and interpret financial/statistical data to facilitate critical decision making; well-versed in import/export procedures and distribution logistics; knowledge of Spanish; hire, train, and supervise teams to meet project goals.

➤ Efficiently develop and implement EDP systems utilizing AS/400, Windows 3.1/95/NT, dBase III/IV, Lotus 1-2-3, Infomaker, and MS Access, and mainframe languages APL, Fortran, Pascal, BASIC, and Assembler.

EMPLOYMENT: <u>The Merchandising Corporation/Cray International</u>, St. Louis, MO
EDP Supervisor, Data Center, Imports   6/93-Present
Manage a three-member staff in processing orders from eight subsidiary department stores and warehouses, including Gord & Talon, Famous-Bike, Hecht's, and Foley's, and orders for imported merchandise to be distributed to stores coast-to-coast.
Administer a $745,000 departmental operating budget.
Design and generate scheduled/on-demand management decision support reports.

→ Maintain data control for merchandise ticketing including cost, duty rates, commissions, suggested selling price, classification, and insurance costs.

→ Handle purchasing functions of all computer equipment, with a $1.5 million annual capital budget; negotiate contract rates and maintenance costs with such vendors as Xerox, IBM, Cadtex, CDI, Lectra, and Silicon Graphics.

→ Reduced processing time and improved pricing, reporting, and merchandise distribution efficiencies.

→ *Ticket System Reengineering*: identified and classified each item by a UPC to replenish stock by actual item sold at POS.

→ Initiated electronic reporting for international operations and generated a savings of $3,000 in DHL courier costs.

→ Increased report turnaround time to within 24 hours and reduced the number of pages from four to one per report, to achieve a cost savings of $2,000 print time/paper per report.

Coordinator, Merchandise Analysis, New York, NY   6/89-6/93
Coordinated a variety of merchandise analysis assignments and provided technical assistance to buyers and EDP on vendor/inventory management projects, with strict attention to accuracy of financial data.

→ Monitored and interpreted business/foreign vendor trends, including foreign labor costs, merchandise availability, shipping routes, and political situations.

→ *Vendor Analysis Project*: Evaluated, prioritized, and consolidated vendors to improve quality and gain greater purchasing leverage.

→ Designed and implemented a sales/vendor tracking system to maintain inventory levels on target.

→ *Pricepoint Project*: Audited pricepoints by classification for a decision by senior management to increase specific pricepoints.

Cost Analyst, New York, NY   8/86-6/89
Analyzed costs of merchandise imported from Asia, Subcontinent (India, Bangladesh, Sri Lanka and Dubai), and Europe, for distribution to May stores throughout the U.S., including pricepoint guarantees for markup.

→ Classified items and considered routing, carriers, packing, volume, container capacity, and weight ratio.

→ Developed a cost/rate manual based on average pricepoints to eliminate inaccurate and costly rate estimations.

EDUCATION: State University of New York, Buffalo, NY   Graduated 1986
B.A. Degree in mathematics and statistics
Concentration: Computer Science and Applied Mathematics

Internship, Millers Harness Company, East Rutherford, NJ   1984-1985
Research Analyst
Conducted market research project on Western Apparel.

→ Analyzed market trends and recommended targeting female client base.

→ Sales increased by 12% on implementation of recommendations.

Posted on numerous databases; received 20 interview offers and three job offers.   (*See corresponding letter*)

JACK A. NICHOLS
115 Brock Road
Santa, CA 95404

Res: 707/555-8830
E-mail: JA740@aol.com

OBJECTIVE: **Executive Management**
A senior executive position utilizing results-driven abilities in strategic planning, team building, organization and needs assessment.

PROFILE:

- Comprehensive profit-building experience in turnaround functions, new business development, financial operations and systems administration, including organizational development and extensive customer service in the mortgage and wireless communications industries.

- Effectively coordinate P&L, budgeting, due diligence, contract negotiations, software design and installation; skilled in vendor selection, purchasing, regulatory compliance, accurate documentation, file updating and computerized business correspondence.

- Skilled in departmental/facility start-up, call center management, process re-engineering, staff mentoring and information technology transfer.

- Experience with international business practices and protocols, particularly in Europe, Africa and the Middle East; familiar with French.

- Knowledge of Total Quality Management, Malcolm Baldridge Quality Standards and Crosby Procedures; familiar with LANs, WANs, mainframes, Windows and numerous software applications, including UNIX, GUI and Oracle.

EMPLOYMENT: <u>Barth Mortgage Company</u>, Nowhere, IL   1998-Present
Chief Information Officer / Executive Vice President
Manage all network services, help desk activity, data center operations, applications development, security, quality control, testing and business analysis for this $20 billion loan originator, ranked #7 in this industry. Provide systems administration and support for 5,000 employees in 300 branches within eight regions on an AS 400 platform, including 500 personnel at this site.

→ Consistently recognized by executives for meeting goals and expanding profitability.
→ Successfully increased network efficiency by 35 and reduced operating costs by 27% and cost per loan by 20%.
→ Coordinated the processing and closing of $3 billion in loans over the last year.
→ Streamlined daily business applications and policies; achieved and maintained Y2K compliance since March.

<u>Computer Sciences Corporation</u>, Champaign, IL   1996-1998
General Manager
Responsible for a wide range of corporate functions, such as Sales, Operations, Customer Service, Software Design and Conversion, Quality Control, Product Management, Finance and Human Resources.

Provided contractual pricing for billing solutions for over three million subscribers with a staff of 450 employees/contractors and an $80 million budget.

→ Introduced a detailed business strategy with projected client growth of $100 million in new revenue for FY 1998.

→ Increased business volume by 46% in 1997 and exceeded profit margins by 21% in the 1st Quarter of FY 1997.

→ Implemented more efficient software design, development and installation processes, resulting in enhanced strategic growth and customer service.

Chase Manhattan Mortgage Corporation, Tampa, FL   1992-1996
Division Senior Vice President   1994-1996
Oversaw dual sites with over 450 employees, billing for 1.6 million customers with $112 billion in assets and a $100 million budget.
Tasked with development and implementation of comprehensive marketing strategies aimed at new business opportunities in the mortgage billing service industry.

→ Ranked #1 in Customer Service in 1996 by the Peer Group Survey in the Mortgage Banking Industry.

→ Led the team that redesigned the Intelligent Work Station with GUI applications, resulting in 13% better enduser performance.

→ Set up the Automated Communications Data (ACD) network handling 2.7 million calls annually at multiple linked sites.

→ Increased overall service levels by 70% while reducing unit cost by 23%.

Vice President   1992-1994
Coordinated new approaches for systems/servicing of new acquisitions totaling $49.9 billion, along with generation of new fee income.

→ Profitably converted $31.4 billion in loan balances and achieved first-year revenues of over $100 million.

→ Efficiently re-engineered strategic planning and servicing operations to enhance performance and improve customer satisfaction by 43%.

Department of Education, Washington, DC   1991-1992
Special Assistant to the Secretary of Education
Recruited to design and develop the Federal Direct Loan Program, and its support Servicing Center, with over $940 million in new originations in the first year.

→ Specially chosen as the Senior Operation Executive for Operations and Systems for this federal department.

→ Also integrated systems for Loan Servicing Billing, Payment Management and Debit Collections.

Sallie Mae Corporation, Tampa, FL   1988-1991
Vice President - Servicing/Originations   1990-1991
Responsible for all contractual pricing and servicing of origination business for the Chase Manhattan Bank account, valued at $750 million.

Managed a professional staff of 600 at dual sites handling Marketing, Billing, Processing, Customer Service, Regulatory Compliance, Documentation and Human Resources.

→ Generated $850 million in new business through an effective marketingstrategy in originations and servicing.
→ Consolidated and reorganized departments into cross-functional work teams, reducing operating costs by 21%.

Director - Loan Servicing Operations   1988-1990
In charge of account acquisition, customer service, collections and financial tracking of one million clients, with supervision of 550 employees and a budget of $67 million.

→ Reduced total servicing costs by 13%, including customer correspondence by 10%.
→ Established links through communication platforms between Collections and Customer Service, resulting in greater productivity.

RELATED EXPERIENCE:

➤ Completed special assignments in senior financial management positions with a variety of business opportunities with staff of up to 123 employees, including accountants and auditors.
➤ Personally reduced operational and administrative costs by 42%; computerized a full range of business functions.

EDUCATION:

Harvard University, Cambridge, MA
Completed the Executive Management School (Finance) program.

Golden Gate University, San Francisco, CA
M.B.A. Degree in Management/Finance

University of Georgia, Athens, GA
M.A. Degree in History

Auburn University, Auburn, AL
B.S. Degree in Physics

ADDITIONAL TRAINING:

* Defense Language Institute, Monterey, CA.
* Mortgage banking functions, such as ARMS, HUD 235 loans and investor requirements.
* Banking regulations, cash management and EFT/ACH.
* Call center management - telecenter support, telemarketing, routing and call attempt management.
* Computer systems and applications - UNIX/AIX, GUI, Oracle, Windows NT, Service Management System (SMS), Computer Output Laser System (COLS) and CIBER Standard.

Recognized as a 'best resume' at a State of IL Dept. of Employment Security seminar.
Sent 50; received 17 interviews and a new job.　　　　　*(See corresponding letter)*

JAMES FLYER

224 Jefferson Lane
Streamwood, IL 60107
Res.: 630/555-1355

OBJECTIVE: *SALES / ACCOUNT MANAGEMENT*
A position where profit-building skills would be utilized. Willing to travel or relocate for the right opportunity.

PROFILE:

➢ Comprehensive experience in sales, marketing, and strategic planning, including responsibility for international projects and multi-million dollar territories.

➢ Conversant in Thai and well-versed in business customs and procedures in Pacific Rim countries, with two years' experience in Southeast Asia.

➢ Plan and conduct market research and analyze competition, products, demographics, and industry trends. Proven ability to build long-term business relationships.

➢ Train and supervise sales teams in lead development, presentations, product lines, post-sale support, and total account management.

EMPLOYMENT: <u>Beach Insurance</u>, Oak Lawn, IL   1997-Present
Sales Manager
Direct retail and wholesale sales efforts, including marketing, client relations, and market research, for this independent broker of all types of insurance coverage.
Manage the marketing strategies for retail business; formulate and execute plans to meet production goals.
Develop market intelligence on various product lines and markets.
Plan and conduct sales seminars and sales management meetings for agents.
Act as the liaison between the firm and 800 field brokers. Actively recruit and contract new brokers.
Build relationships with brokers to increase visibility and sales. Work with brokers to resolve issues such as collections.

◆ Recruited 30 new brokers to the team within the last 1 year.
◆ Participated in bringing agencies in on a new online system that provides more efficiency to operations and client service.

<u>States Insurance</u>, Carol Stream, IL
Division Sales Manager   1987-1996
Responsible for $130 million in insurance sales throughout Northern Illinois and most of Wisconsin.
Provide team leadership for eight employees in target marketing, lead development, and the sale of annuities, life products, property/casualty lines, and asset management services.

Perform long- and short-term strategic marketing to meet corporate objectives.

Work closely with brokers and area managers to expand sales of ASI products, primarily through strong relationships with customers.

Coordinate all budgets, forecasts, and reporting for salaries, expenses, and two offices.

- Sales increased from less than $100 million to $117 million.
- Travel extensively and develop/conduct training modules and special programs for various markets.

Field Sales Manager   1978-1987

Directed 63 independent agents in all aspects of business development, including product and sales training.

Handled all strategic planning, competitive analysis, and target marketing.

- Premiums increased from $8 million to $35 million.
- Recognized for the single largest premium increase in a year.

Field Sales Representative   1976-1978

Promoted and sold all product lines through independent agents, with a premium volume of up to $4 million.

- Negotiated contingent bonus agreements and trained new agents in rating and underwriting.

U.S. Department of State / Defense, Republic of Vietnam   1973-1975

Officer-In-Charge of Construction: Thailand

As Administrative Assistant to the Comptroller/Administration officer, performed a full range of logistical and government functions, including travel and visa arrangements for U.S. military and civilian personnel.

Arranged housing and acted as custodian of all classified documents as *Protocol Officer* for the organization.

As *Director of the Support Department*, supervised 143 local national employees and three managers, including all finance, personnel, and transportation matters.

- Gained extensive experience in communications with senior Thai military and government officials and their aides.
- Prepared itineraries for military and government leaders, working with members of the U.S. Embassy in Thailand and offices of the Secretary of Defense, Secretary of the Navy, and Commander-in-Chief, Pacific.

EDUCATION: Florida A&M University, Tallahassee, FL

B.S. Degree: Political Science

Graduated Cum Laude

- Completed various courses in insurance sales and management.

From out of country with no green card: Sent 40; received four interviews. (See corresponding letter)

GOSHEN D. NANI
Coni 2280
Buenos Aires, Argentina

Cellular Phone: 541/555-3907   Business: 541/555-1001   E-mail: Goshen@hotmail.com

INTERNATIONAL BUSINESS DEVELOPMENT
Strategic Change Management

PROFILE:

➢ Comprehensive experience in senior-level business development in diverse, emerging and high-growth international commercial markets, with full P&L responsibility.

➢ Formulate startup, turnaround and growth strategies to take advantage of shifts in capital investment opportunities, market competitiveness and industry growth.

➢ Advise senior management on global economic and market trends; negotiate cross-border third-party client/vendor licensing/franchising and joint-venture agreements for strong market penetration and client relationships.

➢ Manage and train high-performance teams to meet strategic business goals; skilled in strategic planning, gap analysis, market positioning, capital investment/portfolio mix analysis, product launch and facility site selection/design; M.B.A. degree.

➢ Well-versed in intercultural communication and business practices; travel to client sites in Uruguay, Argentina, Brazil, Chile, Brazil and the United States; work with suppliers in China and Korea; fluent in Spanish and English.

CAREER BACKGROUND:

<u>Sync Investment Group</u>, HQ, Gallup, TX
Operations Director, Sync, Inc.   1/97-Present
Direct all business development operations, including commercial, marketing, administration and distribution services, for this footwear and apparel company, acquired in 1997 for franchiser of Sync, Hard Rock Cafe and Planet Hollywood for Latin America with $1 billion in assets.

➔ Launched Vans in Argentina and Uruguay, after securing $1.5 million in startup funding, and generated $20 million in new revenues within the first six months of operation.

➔ Ranked #1 worldwide in opening sales for apparel, at an unheard of 30% of total sales on launch.

➔ Conceptualized the market expansion project, Vans Brazil investment project, expected to generate $50 million in revenues within the first six months and to gain a 35% market share within the first year of implementation; placed on hold due to the severe downturn in the Brazilian economy.

➔ In charge of project control management of a $30 million tourist complex.

Controller, Hard Rock Cafe and Planet Hollywood, Latin America   6/96-1/97
Responsible for the planning, administration and policies of all financial operations for these two $65 million venture projects at 14 sites in the Caribbean, Uruguay, Argentina, Brazil and Chile.

➔ Specifically developed and managed Planet Hollywood operations in Sao Paulo, Rio De Janeiro, Buenos Aires, Punta del Este and Santiago de Chile.

➔ Analyzed Hard Rock Cafe operations in San Juan (Puerto Rico), St. Thomas and Buenos Aires.

➔ Evaluated market opportunities in Latin America and presented investment recommendations to senior management and the Board of Directors, including a radio station and a major Disney production.

<u>Petroken S.A.</u>, Buenos Aires, Argentina

1990-1996

Economic and Financial Planning Manager

2/92-5/96

Evaluated the financial status of company operations for this $250 million subsidiary of the Royal Dutch Shell Group and recommended market expansion opportunities, acquisitions and new business ventures.

→   Initiated a marginal contribution review of local and export markets, which resulted in the entry into a new $140 million niche market.

→   Introduced the first company quality improvement process and achieved earnings of 5% over sales in cost savings and a reduction to near zero errors within the first six months of implementation.

Controller

10/90-2/92

In charge of all corporate financial administration, with a focus on planning and budget control, with a budget of 60% over sales directly managed by a 15-person staff.

→   Produced and implemented the first corporate accounting and planning systems.

→   Developed and introduced internal control procedures; recommended corrective actions working closely with internal and external auditors.

<u>3M Argentina S.A.</u>, Buenos Aires, Argentina

1988-1990

Manager, Budget Administration

Responsible for corporate budget administration and audit control for this $60 million pharmaceutical and chemical company with three manufacturing plants and 130 employees, including monthly financial reporting, forecasting, sales analysis, currency position evaluation and economic review of capital expenditures.

Prior Employment

1979-1988

Chief Accountant, <u>IECSA S.A.</u>, Argentina: handled all joint venture, capital investment and construction project audits and evaluation.

Senior Auditor, <u>Deloitte & Touche</u>, Argentina: audited Frigorifico Rioplatense, Consignaciones Rurales, Bull Argentina and Argenblue S.A. (licensee of apparel manufacturers including Wrangler and Calvin Klein).

Accounting Analyst, <u>Securities and Exchange Commission</u>, Washington, D.C.

TRAINING: <u>Numerous professional development seminars completed include</u>:
Capital Markets, Enforcement Training Program, SEC, Washington, D.C.
Techniques and Analysis of External Audits, Deloitte & Touche
ISO 9000/14000 Normative and Quality Development in Shell Capsa
Certification: Internal Auditor, Bureau Veritas.

EDUCATION: <u>University of Belgrano</u>, Buenos Aires, Argentina
Master of Business Administration, 1997
Focus: Finance and Marketing

<u>University of Belgrano</u>, Buenos Aires, Argentina
Bachelor of Science Degree: Public Accounting

Used about five with personal contacts; hired for new position.

THOMAS DAILY
112 Strawberry Hill Avenue, No. 6
Stamford, CT 06902   Residence: 203/555-9548   E-mail: daily@compuserve.com

EXECUTIVE MANAGEMENT
C.E.O./President/C.O.O.

PROFILE: ➢ Comprehensive senior management experience in small-to-large service, manufacturing and distribution operations, specializing in business expansion and new product development, with full P&L responsibility, in a variety of U.S.-based and international industries.

➢ Advise CEO/President and Directors on emerging industry trends; proven ability to lead organizations through turnaround, critical startup and growth strategies; effectively spearhead acquisitions and joint ventures; private placement/IPO experience; corporate board member.

➢ Skilled in strategic planning, market positioning, sales and account management, product rollout, process reengineering; contract negotiation, licensing agreements, client/supplier relations, government affairs and recruiting and managing high-performance teams.

➢ Well-versed in intercultural business communication; consistently develop solid business contacts and relationships; in-depth knowledge of multiple-site MIS and electronic commerce.

CAREER BACKGROUND:

Dedicated Pharm Co., Inc., Long Island, NY   1997-Present
C.E.O. / President
Hired to turn around this international manufacturer and distributor of pharmaceutical products, employing 122, with direct P&L responsibility for $10 million in annual revenues.
  ▹ Increased sales by 40% to overcome a five-year deficit.
  ▹ Eliminated 30% of overhead costs in the manufacturing functions and improved productivity by 50%.
  ▹ Re-positioned the Rx and OTC product lines to target three new high-growth market segments.
  ▹ Developed and introduced seven new ANDA's (FDA-approved Rx products).
  ▹ Established licensing and distribution agreements with distributorships in the Ukraine, China, Taiwan, Hong Kong and Nigeria; other countries in process.

Nuthouse Consultants, HQ, New Canaan, CT   1982-1997
Partner and co-founder of this consulting firm, specializing in turnaround and interim management projects.

Chef, Inc., HQ, Dallas, TX   12/96-5/97
Vice President and General Manager
Directed startup operations to expand into the hospitality and institutional feeding markets.
  ▹ Generated sales revenues of $10 million in the first year.
  ▹ Produced a business plan for a joint venture between Cendant and a hotel franchise chain.

Veri Corporation, St. Petersburg, FL   1/96-12/96
Executive Vice President/C.O.O./Director
Developed and implemented a five-year strategic plan, with a focus on export trade for this startup $1.5 million manufacturer of infection control products for institutional, industrial and retail clients.
  ▹ Hired, trained and directed a 114-person sales and telemarketing group in less than two months.

_____
99

<u>Kushi Macrobiotics Corporation</u>, Stamford, CT   5/94-12/95
President/C.E.O./Director
Founded this natural/health foods marketer and manufacturing company in partnership with the internationally acclaimed Michio Kushi.

> ▷ Raised $2 million from a Private Placement Memorandum and $7 million from an IPO Prospectus; lead due diligence presentations to the financial community.
> ▷ Created and rolled out a 33-item premium product line in nine months.

<u>Culinar Sales Corporation</u>, Blandon, PA   9/91-5/94
President/C.O.O.
Hired to turn around operations and improve profits of this U.S. specialty and fancy food manufacturing subsidiary of Culinar, Inc. of Canada; positioned the company for divestiture in 1993.

> ▷ Increased sales by 92% by end 1993 and reduced sales costs by more than 50%.
> ▷ Improved ACV distribution from 15% to more than 70% in less than two years.

<u>Rim Industries, Inc.</u>, Mt. Vernon, NY, **President/C.O.O./Partner**   1985-1991

<u>Savoy Industries, Inc.</u>, New York, NY, **Executive Vice President/C.O.O.**   1984-1985

<u>Hickson Advertising Agency</u> New York, NY, **Senior Vice President/General Manager** 1982-1984

<u>International Telephone & Telegraph Corporation</u>, New York, NY   1974-1982
Group Vice President, Marketing & Development, Food Group   9/75 -12/82
In charge of strategic and daily operations of more than 20 U.S. and European food/pharmaceutical companies with $2 billion in sales, including Continental Baking, Ashe Pharmaceuticals, Wonder Salted Snacks and Gwaltney Meats, with direct P&L responsibility for a $250 million marketing budget.

> ▷ Generated a 25% gain in media sales for same-dollar buys.
> ▷ Spearheaded a business development team which completed three acquisitions.
> ▷ Adjunct Professor of Marketing, University of Connecticut Graduate School of Business, 1980-1982.
> ▷ Promoted from **Group General Manager, Cosmetics & Pharmaceuticals**, 9/74-9/75.

<u>Revlon, Inc.</u>, New York, NY   1970-1974
Director of Marketing
Responsible for the marketing and sales of Moon Drops, Natural Wonder, Ultima and Ehterca product lines.

> ▷ Achieved $400 million in annual sales.
> ▷ Launched six new products with combined revenues of over $75 million.

<u>Almay Cosmetics Company</u>, New York, NY   1966-1970
Director of Marketing & Sales
Managed ophthalmic and dermatological ethical and proprietary product lines.

> ▷ Pioneered today's Almay; repackaged the line from prescription products to fashion cosmetics.
> ▷ Increased sales tenfold, from $1 million to $12 million within one year.
> ▷ Promoted from **Marketing Research Manager**.

EDUCATION: <u>Long Island University</u>, New York, NY
                Coursework in the Master of Business Administration program.

                <u>Ohio State University</u>, Columbus, OH
                Bachelor of Science Degree: Chemistry and Marketing Research

Sent 15; received six interviews.

ANGEL GUARDIAN
119 Ridge Court
Loveland, OH 45140
Residence: 513/555-1731   Business: 513/555-9593   E-mail: angel@ix.netcom.com

CORPORATE INFORMATION SYSTEMS MANAGEMENT

PROFILE:
➤ Comprehensive experience in senior-level management of advanced information system and technology functions, with P&L responsibility for corporate policies, standards and strategies, in rapidly changing, highly competitive growth environments.

➤ Skilled in business development, strategic planning, risk analysis, business process re-engineering, product innovation, contract negotiation and budget administration; well-versed in market research processes, including potential analysis/forecasts of demographic, economic and psychographic data and sales performance interpretation.

➤ Advise senior management on business implications of technologies to achieve financial goals; effectively monitor emerging technologies and alternative IS organizational structures; direct high-performance teams through critical startup and restructuring.

➤ Extensive knowledge of object-oriented design methodologies, multiple-tier client/server, WAN/LAN and virtual system technologies; design and implement efficient consumer response, category product management and commerce-based interactive systems.

TECHNICAL KNOWLEDGE:

■ *Client/Server and Network Systems:* TCP/IP, Internet/ Web site developers, Appdesigner, Enera, PowerBuilder, Visual Basics, OSF DCESNA, Ethernet, Token Ring, Novell WAN/LAN.
■ *Database Languages:* DB2, IDMS, DB2-6000, 4GL.
■ *Operating Systems:* MVS, VMS, UNIX, CICS, DOS.
■ *Hardware:* IBM ES/9000s, IBM AS/400, DEC VAX 3900, RISC 6000 UNIX.

CAREER BACKGROUND:

Eckstein Consulting, Loveland, OH   1996-Present
Provide consulting services and technical assistance in information system and technologies planning, management and operations, specializing in Year 2000 impact analysis and compliance, ECR systems and commerce-based systems, targeting consumer market businesses.

Key Client
Cruncher Company, Chicago, IL: contracted to develop an $800,000 sales and marketing system that will profile targeted demographic/psychographic data for this worldwide magazine publisher to identify new markets, forge retail partnerships and re-engineer distribution logistics.
→ Increased sales by 29% and reduced expenses by 35% on system implementation.

G-Greetings, Inc., HQ, Cincinnati, OH   1990-1996
A $650-million, 8,000-employee, international paper product manufacturer and retailer.
Vice President, Information Systems
In charge of the planning, administration and direction of corporate information systems functions, including the Order Processing Department and Telemarketing/Marketing Research Services, with full P&L responsibility for a budget of $12.8 million.

Managed a staff of 170 at headquarters and provided oversight management of 24 IS employees located at four divisions:

- *Paper Factory*, WI, $165 million sales revenues: installed an Island Pacific Retail P.O.S., AS/400 system connecting 160 stores; involved in due diligence proceedings prior to the purchase of this company in 1992.
- *Cleo Division*, TN, $225 million sales revenues: implemented AS/400 gift wrap manufacturing, inventory and distribution systems.
- *Mexico/United Kingdom Divisions*, $16 million in sales revenues: LAN networks, UNIX, PC and distribution systems; part of senior management team to start up operations from ground zero.

Key Results

→ Initiated and produced the first comprehensive company technology strategic and operational plans, including a Year 2000 impact analysis and software/application replacement recommendations.

→ Achieved labor cost savings of $1.5 million by implementing activity-based costing procedures, automated inventory selection and financial/administrative process improvements.

→ Decreased labor costs by an additional $750,000 on implementation of vendor developed manufacturing and distribution systems for carton marking, shop scheduling and pick-to-light applications.

→ Orchestrated the development and implementation of category management, efficient replenishment and computer-assisted ordering programs, including EDI and geodemographic data, to support a rapid 6%-8% growth in sales volume by $3.8 million.

→ Reduced administrative costs by $2.5 million by implementing an EDI/EFT system between suppliers and retail customers, handling 25,000 electronic invoices monthly.

→ Effected a cost avoidance of $400,000 annually in hardware costs; developed a three-tier client/server network and prepared more than 600 customized PC configurations for field sales access to individual customer sales performance data.

→ Re-negotiated hardware and maintenance contracts, to increase discounts by 10% on an average annual capital expenditure of $10 million.

Caressa, Inc., Fort Lauderdale, FL   1988-1990
Vice President of Information Systems / Partner LBO
One of seven partners to purchase this family-owned, women's brand-name footwear importer-wholesaler, with five divisions and 60 retail stores nationwide.
→ Directed all information systems and voice/data telecommunications functions.

R.G. Barry Corporation, Columbus, OH   1981-1988
Vice President of Information Systems / Divisional Officer   6/83-2/88
Responsible for the planning, administration and supervision of the MIS division for this national manufacturer of shoes and slippers, with a retail division of 110 stores.
Hired, trained and directed 90 professionals in software/systems projects, maintenance of client LAN and database management systems, and post-installation technical support.
Administrated an operating budget of $8 million.
→ Acquired and managed the full Marketing Research Group.
→ Promoted to this position from **MIS Director**, 6/81-6/83.

Ward Foods, Inc., New York, NY   1973-1981
Corporate Director, Information Systems
In charge of the restructuring and operation of MIS, seven data centers and a marketing research team, providing services to multiple divisions of this food manufacturer of candy, snack foods, cookies, pies, seafood and ice cream products.
Managed 105 employees and a $6.8 million operating budget.
→ Created this position, centralized operations and brought marketing research into the MIS function to meet the intensified demand from expanding product lines.
→ Downloaded, compiled and distributed market information from online databases such as American Demographics Magazine, Nielsen strategic mapping and Claritas Area Market Management.
→ Introduced television area market research into the advertising campaign for a new candy product rollout in Ohio, Virginia and the throughout the South.

Singer Sewing Machine Company, HQ, New York, NY   1961-1973
Director
→ Gained a solid foundation in managing corporate information systems through progressive promotions from **Systems Analyst**, **Senior Programmer** and **EDP Auditor**.

RELATED EXPERIENCE:
>**Lecturer/Adjunct Faculty**: Management Issues in Technology   1980-Present
>>Xavier University
>>Ohio State University
>>Franklin University
>>Various national conferences

AFFILIATIONS:
>General Merchandise Apparel Industry Committee (GMAIC)
>■ *Voluntary Interindustry Communication Standards (VICS) Retail Committee, Industry Committee, Charter Member*: developed and implemented EDI standard for industry.
>■ *Efficient Consumer Response (ECR) Industry Committee/Best Practices Operating Committee Co-Chair, EDI Technology Committee*: developed pilot test and implemented Category Product Management, Continuous Replenishment Program and computer-assisted Ordering systems.

EDUCATION:
>Hofstra University, New York, NY
>Financial management and auditing coursework.

>M.I.T. University, Boston, MA
>Cambridge Technologies

>IBM Executive Institute, Poughkeepsie, NY

>Kings Park High School, Long Island, NY

Sent about 30; received six interviews.

WILLIAM E. RINGER

550 Soap Drive
Reston, VA 22091-3717

703/555-6136
E-mail: ring@ix.netcom.com

CHIEF FINANCIAL OFFICER

PROFILE:

➤ Highly successful, executive-level experience in strategic planning, corporate financing, and accounting operations.

➤ Proven ability to build profitable relationships with bankers, venture capitalists, and clients.

➤ Skilled in staff development, motivation, training, and key personnel retention; build strong alliances and teams through professional communications.

➤ Coordinate and direct the efforts of successful IPO issuance; structure the prospectus, gather all relevant financial data, and work with attorneys and underwriters to ensure compliance with SEC regulations.

➤ Proficient in a wide range of applications including Excel, Access, Paradox, MS Word, and WordPerfect, as well as accounting, financial analysis, budgeting, and business valuation software. Conceptualize and direct application development in addition to client/server and LAN installations.

EXPERIENCE:

Boat Lovers, Inc. Alexandria, VA   1995-Present
Chief Financial Officer
Responsible for all finance, treasury, and accounting functions for this specialty retailer of boating accessories with product revenues of $95 million through retail outlets and catalog sales, as well as $35 million in revenues from insurance operations and services for more than 500,000 members.
Overall management of an accounting staff of 50, as well as 15 treasury and 30 facilities personnel.
Utilize financial analysis and forecasting tools to develop and prepare the $130 million annual budget.
Recruit, hire, motivate, and develop top managers.

Work with bank officers to develop all financing and banking arrangements.
→ Successfully increased credit lines from $8 million to $20 million.
→ Headed the committee to create a company Web site. Directed project from start-up to current 100,000 hits per week, generating sales of $10,000 per month.

A. J. Skin & Associates, Inc., Oakton, VA   1993-1995
Chief Financial Officer
Managed the accounting, finance, and human resource departments for this real estate investment company.
Coordinated the activities of tax accountants and auditors in preparing 25 properties for the creation of a real estate investment trust.

→ Directed the installation of a relational database accounting system for 14 commercial shopping centers and 14 residential garden style apartment complexes with eight remote sites and a management company.

→ Developed and implemented streamlined processes and productivity improvements leading to a reduction in accounting staff from 18 to eight.

Sector Technologies, Inc., Alexandria, VA

Chief Executive Officer   1992-1993

Directed the overall operations of this high-tech company engaged in government contract work, as well as development of a proprietary productivity software system for Facility Security Officers.

Effectively handled all aspects of marketing, sales, finance, and operations, including recruiting and developing senior-level managers, strategic planning, and market penetration.

→ Successfully negotiated the sale of the company's assets.

Chief Financial Officer   1987-1992

Responsible for all administrative systems, accounting, and financial activity of the company.

→ Raised combination equity and debt capital for funding a major software development effort.

Arthur Andersen & CO., Washington, DC   1966-1987

Partner

Senior level responsibility with this big eight, international accounting firm. Managed the emerging growth practice; built the division from 10 to 80 personnel.

Responsible for audits and management advisory services to emerging growth companies.

Handled registration with the Securities and Exchange Commission for initial and secondary public offerings as well as obtaining alternate financing sources.

→ Established a microcomputer consulting group that offered systems installation and software support.

→ Planned and conducted seminars in "Effective Presentations," "Effective Selling," and "Successful Negotiations."

EDUCATION: Abilene Christian University
                        Bachelor of Science Degree in Accounting, Minor in English
                        Certified Public Accountant

PROFESSIONAL: Hold various professional memberships including:
                        US CPA Society,
                        American Management Association.

Sent 10; received one interview.

DENNISON BOWERS

1135 Fairview Terrace
Malden, MA   02148

781/555-4759
Dsdy@state.ma.us

MANAGEMENT CONSULTING

ROFILE:

> Comprehensive experience in multiple aspects of business operations, including contract administration, regulatory compliance, staff training, and procedure development/implementation.

> Proven ability to troubleshoot and develop creative, innovative solutions to business challenges; successfully manage change for improved performance and efficiency.

> Demonstrated success at identifying processes and complex systems; work with clients to streamline operations, establish goals, and implement strategies to achieve those goals.

> Skilled in team development and project management; communicate objectives, plan and organize work flow, and conduct individualized training.

> Proficient with Lotus; working knowledge of Excel, Word, WordPerfect for report preparation; experience in Internet research.

EXPERIENCE:

<u>Department of Public Health</u>, San Francisco, CA
Fiscal Administrator   8/94-Present
Responsible for all aspects of fiscal management and contract administration, including budgeting, project management, expense authorization, and training for Justice Resource Institute programs.
Motivate and supervise a staff of seven consultants. Handle all personnel administration for the site, including processing of applicants and arranging benefits.
Approve/code all invoices, authorize employee expenses, reconcile bank statements, and direct petty cash disbursements.

→ Perform research and data collection for development of special reports.
→ Prepare General Ledger Summary reports.

Grands Management Specialist / Consultant   12/93-8/94
Provided comprehensive guidance and administrative support to contract managers and agency staff with 300 contracts throughout the state.
Provided for proper documentation and regulatory compliance of contracts and grants.
Participated in the development of policies and procedures.
Assembled/processed contracts, subcontracts, and grants administered by the AIDS bureau to ensure compliance with state policies.

→ Documented and recommended system improvements to the Director of Administration. Implemented and directed approved policy changes.

→ Trained Contract Managers on management systems, general contract requirements, procedures, and protocols.

→ Acted as a primary liaison, providing technical assistance to MIS and Purchase of Service units for the development of contract policies.

Camp McKee, Cambridge, MA   1/88-9/93
Contracts Administrator
Responsible for various aspects of contract management, including project management, client relations, and budgeting.
Worked with clients to develop and administer special billing requirements; established billing dates according to client payment cycles.
Prepared, issued, and processed client invoices.
Assisted project managers in scheduling, budgeting, and control of projects.

→ Filed contracts and related documentation with contract accounting.

→ Prepared and issued a monthly billing report to senior management.

Senior Accounts Payable Specialist
Trained new associates in accounts payable as well as organizational policies.
Coordinated the input of and payment of vendor invoices and check requests.
Disbursed, maintained, and reconciled petty cash funds.

EDUCATION: Cambridge College, Cambridge, MA
Master of Management
Concentration on Organizational Theory and Behavior. Received registered copyright for thesis on Managing for Workplace Diversity.

→ GPA 3.8/4.0

American International College, Springfield, MA
Bachelor of Science Degree
Major: Human Relations, Minor: Psychology

→ Named to the Scholastic All American Honor Society.

→ Received President's Recognition Award for Scholastic Achievement and Leadership.

University of Massachusetts at Boston
Certificate in Government Auditing

MEMBERSHIPS: Association of Government Accountants

→ Recognized in *Government Financial Management Topics* (Dec. 1997) "The Face of Public Service."

National Association of Female Executives

Sent 40; received seven interviews.

GEORGE A. STOKER

1121 E. Balmoral
Chicago, IL 60656

773/555-6600

ATTORNEY / MANAGER / CONSULTANT

PROFILE:

➢ Comprehensive experience as business manager and attorney, including full responsibility for contract negotiations, staff supervision and new business startups.

➢ Legal background includes litigation and successful resolution of complex matters related to the buying and selling of businesses, contract disputes, family law, arbitration and various real estate transactions, including development of subdivisions.

➢ Business management experience includes procedure planning and budgeting, insurance coordination, purchasing, vendor relations and inventory control.

➢ Familiar with Windows for data entry and retrieval, correspondence and status reporting.

CAREER BACKGROUND:

Law Offices of G. Stoker, Chicago, IL   1984–Present
Attorney & General Manager
In charge of the setup and operation of this law firm, including the hiring, training and supervision of one associate and two support personnel.
Represent individuals in a wide range of legal matters including family law and divorce, probate, incorporations, real property transactions, title searches and examinations.
Perform contract writing and corporate asset purchases; counsel clients and oversee corporate buyouts and sales; prior experience with personal injury and worker's compensation cases.

▹ Supervise all matters of the practice and establish good working relationships with co-counsel and opposing counsel.
▹ Chosen as legal representative of United Insurance Company on various home and mortgage insurance and licensing issues.
▹ Advisory Board Member: Attorney's Title Guaranty Fund; County Approved Arbitrator.

All Star Foods, Schaumburg, IL   1983-1985
Manager / Owner
Responsible for profit/loss and virtually all operations of food distributor and bakery, including budgets and cost-effective purchasing and distribution in Illinois.
Developed and managed all functions, including staff hiring, training, supervision and performance review.

▹ Directed facility maintenance and repairs for an 8,000-square-foot building.

EDUCATION:

John Marshall Law School, Chicago, IL
Juris Doctor Degree   1983
▹ Licensed to practice in the State of Illinois.

Loyola University, Chicago, IL
Bachelor of Arts Degree   1979
Major: Political Science; Minor: English

Sent eight resumes; received five interviews.

MARKUS RISER
468 Prairie Avenue
Glendale Heights, IL 60139
630/555-4251

BANKING / MARKETING

PROFILE:

➢ Comprehensive experience in sales, marketing and new business development in the banking industry, including competitive analysis, market/demographic research and strategic planning.

➢ Skilled in advertising and creative promotions; handle sales presentations and communications in a professional manner; fluent in English and French; semi-fluent in Greek and Arabic.

➢ Effectively train and supervise staff in all banking procedures, with a sharp eye on personal customer service; strong background in loan origination, processing and closing.

➢ Familiar with Windows 98 and Premier II for the setup and maintenance of client accounts.

EXPERIENCE: <u>South Urban Bank</u>, Carol, IL

Branch Manager 1997-Present
In charge of all branch operations, including the hiring, training, scheduling and supervision of up to nine employees in sales, customer service and new accounts.
Responsible for all outside sales, bank promotions, advertising and daily operations.
Handle creative development for print advertisements.
Designed and implemented a customer profile sheet to track client mortgages, deposits and financial status for cross selling and financial planning.

→ Assets have grown from $1 million to $30 million over the last two years.

→ Promoted to this position from:

Assistant Manager 1996
Involved in the setup and operation of the Wheaton location, including all purchase requisitions, staff recruitment, training and quality control.
Worked closely with the Federal Reserve.

→ Selected as one of four in the company to assist in the opening of this bank.

Personal Banker 1995-1996
Established new accounts and determined/met specific customer needs with a strong knowledge of all bank services.

Trainer   1994-1995
Conducted extensive staff training for six banks in all operations,
including teller procedures and troubleshooting.

Teller   1993-1994

Petrie Stores Corporation, Bloomingdale, IL   10/90-9/93
Store Manager
Effectively hired, trained and supervised a team of 16 in all sales and
customer service activities.
Coordinated the sales floor, including planning and implementing creative
promotions and display setup.
Handled customer returns, quality control and problem situations with
tact and a personal, yet professional approach.

→   Gained excellent experience in communications, sales and customer
    service.
→   Promoted to this position from:

Cashier

EDUCATION: Sorbonne University, Paris, France
                 B.A. Degree in French   1989

                 Lewis University, Joliet, IL
                 Trained in Interior Design   1992

LICENSE: Licensed Interior Designer.

Sent about 70; received eight interviews.

CARL F. WALKER

221 South Windham Lane
Bloomingdale, IL 60108
Residence: 630/555-9067   Business: 630/555-4103   E-mail: 4657@kwom.com

---

CORPORATE SALES AND MARKETING
Willing to Relocate

PROFILE:
▸ Comprehensive experience in senior-level management of marketing and sales functions of consumer and industrial products, with P&L responsibility for business development in U.S./international markets.

▸ Skilled in account acquisition and management, including market research, competitor analysis, lead generation, product introduction, demand forecasting and contract negotiation; effectively identify market opportunities and formulate penetration strategies.

▸ Well-versed in direct/sell-through sales organizations, manufacturing processes and EDI/JIT distribution systems; monitor industry trends and market conditions; utilize Macintosh Excel, MS Word, MapLinks, PowerPoint and the Internet.

▸ Effectively recruit, train and supervise direct and independent sales representatives to meet business and financial goals; orchestrate new business relationships in Europe, Australia, Japan, Central/South America, Mexico and Canada.

CAREER BACKGROUND:

<u>Flawless, Inc.,</u> (formerly Vera, Inc.), Chicago, IL   1990-Present
An international subsidiary of the publicly traded, $950 million Gee Enterprises firm, manufacturing glass and mat board product for the picture framing and fine arts industry.

Director of International Sales and Marketing   7/97-Present
Promoted to this position to direct the global business expansion objectives of the company.
Handle all aspects of strategic planning for international market development, including creation of marketing plans.
Identify, contact, recruit and contract new distributors.
Arrange for the translation of all marketing materials.
 → Opened six new distributors on three continents in the first 90 days.

Director of Sales   6/95-7/97
Responsible for a direct and sell-through sales organization nationally and internationally, working closely with a manufacturing/distribution center in Chicago and distribution centers located on the East Coast and in Paris, France.
 → Reduced the cost of sales by 9% incrementally over three years in a mature market and doubled revenues to $28.5 million in five years.
 → Provided oversight management of a 300-dealer distribution network; refocused field staff on distributor account maintenance and process improvement to resolve channel problems.
 → Consolidated customer service and the direct/independent sales operations into three regional territories and proposed implementation of an operations manufacturing computer system.
 → Launched five new products, three in 1996, including an anti-reflective glass and mirrors packaged for the custom picture framer.

Director of Sales and Marketing   12/90-6/95

In charge of the planning, administration and direction of worldwide sales and marketing functions, including marketing and customer service, with responsibility for an operating budget of $2.8 million. Supervised three regional sales managers, eight direct sales staff and 21 independent representatives. Directed advertising agency jobs through the creative process and directed prototype testing; contracted key agencies such as Murphy Sutton, RPM Graphics and Spindler Claps Associates.

→ Increased sales revenues from $14 million to $24 million.

→ Key player in acquisition due diligence activities of Miller Cardboard Company in 1994, including merger plan and pro forma development.

→ Conducted annual status report presentations to the Board of Directors and at company national sales meetings attended by the Chairman, Group VP and Division Manager.

→ Proposed and implemented the first national industry information exchange forums, *Conservation Framing Forum* and *TruVue Forum on Framing Technology*.

→ Negotiated and secured distributor contracts with firms in Europe, Central/South Americas, Asia/Pacific Rim and North America.

Castle Rock Manufacturing Company, Minneapolis, MN   4/89-12/89

Vice President, Sales and Marketing

Developed the initial marketing plan to pre-sell major capital equipment to the photo processing industry; pre-sold 10 units at $1 million at startup.

Clark Moulding Company, Garland, TX   1987-1989

National Sales Manager   9/88-4/89

Managed 32 independent sales and direct representatives in product development, marketing and promotion activities, with a budget of $1.9 million, for this manufacturer of extruded aluminum picture framing moldings, sold to the picture frame industry through a national distributor wholesale system.

→ Member, Corporate Review and Planning Committee.

→ Devised the first comprehensive sales/marketing strategic plan, generating $10 million in sales.

→ Promoted from **Eastern Sales Manager**, 3/87-9/88: restructured 14 territories for operations.

Viracon, Inc., Chicago, IL   1979-1987

Director of Consumer and Industrial Products Division   9/83-3/87

Responsible for all national sales, marketing and customer service activities, including new product development coordination, product design and marketing strategies for this division manufacturing flat glass products for the appliance, automotive, display and picture framing industries.

→ Took sales to $12 million in a highly competitive market.

→ Developed a customer profile system to improve sales forecasting, inventory control and distributor sales response to product inquiries.

Sales Manager, O.E.M. Products Division   5/82-9/83

Directed the product/marketing support for 15 company sales representatives and supervised customer service; personally handled all national account contracts.

→ Revised quoting/pricing procedures and devised cost factors.

→ Increased sales by 20% over 1992 sales, to $4 million.

Territory Salesman   3/81-5/82

EDUCATION: St. Cloud State University, St. Cloud, MN
                Bachelor of Science Degree in Recreation Business   Minor: Marketing

Was seeking to relocate: sent about 60 overseas; received two interview offers.

RANDY PROFICIENT

234 Juncal

345 Ciudad de Buenos Aires

Argentina

E-mail: ano@perel.org

Residence: 54.11.4825.5477

CORPORATE EXECUTIVE MANAGEMENT
CEO, President or Senior Vice President

PROFILE:

➢ Entrepreneurial and Fortune 500 corporate senior-level management experience in international business development, specializing in breakthrough joint ventures and global partnerships, with P&L responsibility, in rapidly changing, highly competitive environments.

➢ Advise CEO, Directors and senior managers on policy issues and emerging industry trends; formulate growth-oriented capital investment strategies to maximize ROI and market share; lead organizations through turnarounds, startups, mergers/acquisitions.

➢ Recruit and mobilize multi-functional high-performance teams; skilled in client needs assessment, opportunity identification, market positioning; country risk analysis; product/service introduction, communications logistics and advanced technologies; well-versed in capital market financing and investor relations; CPA; MBA.

➢ Well-versed in intercultural business practices and communication; interact with government agencies, investment/merchant banks and corporations to forge cross-border public/private trade alliances and networks; fluent in English and Spanish.

CAREER BACKGROUND:

<u>Huron Consulting</u>, Buenos Aires, Argentina   1972- Present

Independent Contractor

Provide management consulting services in organizational leadership, strategic planning, venture financing, mergers and acquisitions, and marketing/communications, for private and public sector organizations.

➜ Fortune 500 clients include Visa, COMSAT, Bell Atlantic, Fiat and Alcatel.

Major Projects

- *TEL (SWW)*: produced and implemented a business plan to develop this company's call center operations throughout Latin America; assessed country risks and market entry strategies for Mexico and Central/South American countries.

- *COMSAT:* chief architect, in the creation of a financial and telecommunication consortium, for a strategic partner, to launch COMSATArgentina; Consortium won the bid to privatize the basic telephone system.

- *Applied Energy Systems*: participated in the privatization of government utilities in Argentina and Brazil.

- *Alcatel:* sold the Argentine subsidiary of this telecommunications firm for a profit of $35 million.

- *Centro de Computos:* pioneered the introduction of state-of-the-art computer systems in Argentina.

<u>Goodrich Capital International</u>, HQ, New York, NY   1997-Present

President, Argentina

In charge of this investment bank's South American cross-border M & A operations, located in 12 countries.

➜ Completed the Wharton School of Business program *Strategic Thinking and Management for Competitive Advantage*, at the University of Pennsylvania, PA.

<u>Banco Mercurio</u>, Buenos Aires, Argentina   1993-1996
C.E.O. / Board Member
Recruited by the owner of a privately held venture group, to start up this cross-border retail bank with full-service, technology-based operations.

→ Set up and implemented a Private Banking Division.
→ Achieved a profit of $25 million for this division, despite the continuing economic downturn due to the 1994 Mexican financial markets crisis.
→ Restructured banking and brokerage affiliate operations in Argentina, Uruguay and the Bahamas.
→ Drove up profits to a $60 million profit base from startup, despite the faltering economy.

<u>Banco Del Buen Ayre</u>, Buenos Aires, Argentina   1983-1993
Member, Board of Directors / Executive Committee
Elected to the Board of Directors to stem a loss of $63 million in profits and transform operations into an advanced technology-based, customer-oriented financial services business.

→ Introduced the first customer self-service 24-hour banking units into the Argentina retail banking market, including home banking and ATM networks.
→ Generated a net worth of $225 million and profits of more than $50 million annually, which facilitated the sale of this bank to Banco Itau of Brazil.

<u>Spicer and Oppenheim</u>, HQ, New York, NY   1975-1983
Partner in Charge, Latin America
Directed all aspects of business operations in Latin America for this accounting firm, ranked first among Wall Street firms and 12th worldwide.

Other Positions   1964-1984
- *Associate Professor, MIS,* <u>University of Buenos Aires</u>, Argentina.
- *Editor/Columnist,* <u>Ambito Financiero</u>: a daily financial journal similar to *The Wall Street Journal.*
- *Chairman of the Board/Founder,* <u>Centro de Computos, S.A.</u>: a service bureau offering computer services.
- *Board Chairman/Founder,* <u>CAESCO</u>: the first trade organization for the computer industry in Argentina.
- *Associate Producer/Correspondent,* <u>CBS TV News</u>, Special Events Unit, New York, NY.

DIRECTORSHIPS: <u>Served on numerous boards of directors including:</u>

Motorola	Bell Atlantic
Telefunken	Visa
Comsat	Fedders
Alcatel	Fiat Group Companies
Cia. Financiera DO-AI	Cia. Financiera Del Plata

EDUCATION: <u>University of Buenos Aires</u>, Argentina
Master of Business Administration
Certified Public Accountant

Sent about 50; received four interviews.

JANICE T. STAMPER

3456 Ava Road   eck@mediaone.net
Reading, MA 01867   781/555-6913

SENIOR VICE PRESIDENT / CEO

OBJECTIVE: A position utilizing the ability to adapt, capitalize, and thrive in rapidly changing business environments.

PROFILE:

➤ Comprehensive, executive experience in new business development, including full P&L responsibility for strategic planning and high-tech product lines.

➤ Effectively set up and manage highly profitable business units, from budgeting to effective team training, management, and motivation.

➤ Proven ability to expand profits through creative planning and coordination of all essential functions, from initial concept to coalition building, PR, and market establishment to vendor sourcing and quality control.

➤ Oversee market research, creative promotions, and top-level contract negotiation; analyze competitors and design/meet financial models; experience with Internet-based software and systems.

➤ Holder of several successful patents; skilled in the commercialization of new technology, including direct interface with customers, market analysis, and high-level strategic planning; oversee product pricing, costing, and market segmentation.

EXPERIENCE: <u>JCN Corporation</u>, Rochester, NY and Burlington, MA

Document Service Group   1995-Present

Vice President, Business Development

Responsible for all P&L functions related to the commercialization of JCN technologies and integrated systems solutions.

Handle extensive primary and secondary market research and the writing of business plans, as well as industry segmentation, competitive analysis, and benchmarking.

Directly involved in developing and marketing incubator systems to sell to the publishing industry, with the potential to expand JCN into billion-dollar markets.

Manage designers, architects, and coders in the development of such products as high-speed, turnkey book production systems for copying, cover printing, cutting, and binding.

Establish goals and controls; monitor results to consistently increase profit margins, enhance market position, reduce operating costs, and meet strategic objectives.

→ Create and implement accurate financial models to maximize market penetration at the lowest cost.

→ Recognized by the publishing industry for the "Book In Time" program, generating more than 500 senior management leads in the publishing industry in nine months. This is now the subject of a Harvard Business School case.

→ Developed and managed the highly regarded "Pony Express" program, an Internet printing method tied to major overnight delivery carriers.

→ Primary Architect for Xerox's professional service organization (XPDS), providing systems integration focused on document management.

→ Performed competitive benchmarking work on Hewlett Packard, resulting in total restructuring of the Channels organization (SOHO products).

Electronic Data Systems (EDS), Cambridge, MA   6/94–4/95
Partner
As Partner with the management consulting group, hired and directed a strategic planning team to work with SBUs and sell additional, non-outsourcing services. This group was eventually combined with another EDS acquisition, A.T. Kearney.

Braxton Associates, Strategy group of Deloitte and Touche, Boston, MA
Director / Partner   1985-1994
Full P&L responsibility for marketing and personal sales of more than $1 million annually.
Developed successful corporate and business unit strategies for a wide range of domestic and international companies.
Created new and revised strategic plans.
A sampling of companies and projects includes:

Central Regional Bell Operating Company: Researched and assessed the market for delivery of interactive and passive broadband services to homes and small businesses.

Eastern Regional Bell Operating Company: Directed a competitive benchmarking and financial analysis of regional bell operating company ownership of cable services.

Pennsylvania Telecom Commission: Directed 20 focus groups across the state to gauge public receptivity to video-on-demand services.

A fiber optic manufacturer: Performed acquisition screening for potential candidates in the fiber optic industry. Spun-off a multi-layer capacitor manufacturing operation to a major competitor.

A major cable TV electronics supplier: Determined customer needs for this major manufacturer of TV cable boxes. Assessed manufacturing options for a new diode manufacturing facility in Europe.

The largest electrical products supplier: Responsible for channel strategies, including pricing, competitive analysis, distribution streamlining, direct sales, and working with manufacturers' reps. for industrial products.

An office products supplier: Developed strategic plans to transition from old to new technologies.

A major publisher: Determined manufacturing equipment needs, plant locations, and consolidation efforts.

The largest photographic supplier: Determined market acceptance criteria for a CD-ROM based product.

The Government of Taiwan: Assessed social and economic effects of acquiring the multi-billion dollar McDonnell Douglas commercial airplane manufacturing operation.

A major materials company: Performed innovative market segmentation and growth projections for separation technology in water purification.

A major home builder: Developed strategies for penetration of new housing segments.

* A wide range of projects – not listed – were related to printed circuit boards, photographic plates, automotive/scientific instrumentation, and A/E design services.

Chomerics Corporation, Woburn, MA   1984–1985
Director of Marketing
Successfully marketed and sold computer peripherals to OEM accounts.
Note: This company was acquired by AMP, which relocated to Ohio.

Prior Experience:

Polaroid Corporation, Cambridge, MA
Engineering Manager
Directed engineering teams in the design of integrated circuits and advanced imaging technologies.

* Holder of seven patents used in millions of consumer and industrial camera systems including analog, digital, and microprocessor designs.

EDUCATION: Massachusetts Institute of Technology, Cambridge, MA
Bachelor of Science in Electrical Engineering
GPA: 4.2/5.0

Boston University, Graduate School of Business, Boston, MA
Master of Business Administration with Honors

Harvard Business School Executive Marketing Course

Sent 35; received nine interviews: four from headhunters and five from companies.

RALPH S. OLOG
237 Heather Lane
Bartlett, IL 60103
630/555-9676

CFO / CONTROLLER

PROFILE:

> Comprehensive experience in the direction and setup of accounting, finance, and information systems, with full responsibility for procedures, mergers, acquisitions and special projects.

> Skilled in risk management and capital equipment selection and justification, including cost-effective contract negotiations with vendors and suppliers.

> Utilize Platinum, Ross Renaissance systems, WAN setups, Windows, DOS, Lotus and Excel for spreadsheets and status reporting; familiar with WinView and WinFrame, Novell, UNIX and Windows NT, as well as MRP, ADP, Ceridian and Simplex systems.

> Analyze and streamline all key systems for multiple locations, including accounts payable/receivable, payroll, credit, collections, and benefit plans, including 401K and profit sharing.

EMPLOYMENT:

<u>Millenium Pizza Products LP</u>, Version, IL
Formerly part of <u>Century Management, Inc.</u> (below)
CFO / Controller   1995-Present
In charge of all finance, accounting, and MIS operations for this multi-site manufacturing company, with sales of $80 million.
Handle extensive budgeting and project reviews.
Effectively manage all treasury functions, including extensive contact with banks, insurance brokers and the evaluation of alternative financing.
Train and supervise a team of 12 in all accounting and computer services.
Oversee financial statement preparation, AP/AR, billing, and payroll functions.
* Acted as lead person for the installation of a Ross MRP system, using a Novell network and a UNIX base; currently switching to NT.
* Consolidated two manufacturing companies and added a third company; merged them into one entity.
* Selected and installed a Simplex time card system.
* Secured financing for a $24 million expansion of the Schaumburg location, as well as the previous $16 million buildout, utilizing operating leases and other standard types of financing.

<u>Century Management, Inc.</u>, Chicago, IL
CFO / Controller   1990-1995
Responsible for all accounting and finance operations for this $30 million general partner, managing multiple partnerships, including two manufacturing facilities, three separate restaurants, three holding companies, and a real estate partnership.
In charge of training and supervising up to six in all financial statement preparation, AP/AR, billing and payroll functions, and MIS procedures.
* Established all financial reporting systems.
* Treasury functions included the evaluation of alternative financing and working with banks and insurance brokers.
* Sold 50% of ownership in the manufacturing entities in 1995, working extensively with buyers and attorneys and forming Millenium Pizza Products LP.

The Havi Group, L.P., Westmont, IL   12/88-9/90
Manager: Financial Analysis
Developed and supervised all essential corporate accounting, risk management and financial analysis functions for this $1.5 billion foodservice distribution and purchasing services company.
* Projects included the analysis of acquisition candidates, strategic planning, and annual budgeting.
* Directly involved in developing and implementing all corporate finance policies and procedures.

Staley Continental, Inc., Rolling Meadows, IL   3/87-7/89
Senior Internal Auditor
Conducted detailed financial, operational, capital expense, and special project audits of food and manufacturing facilities.
Supervised two staff auditors in the execution of all audit processes, including planning, fieldwork, and the preparation of audit reports.
* Directed the setup of standard accounting systems and procedures for a newly acquired company.

Anchor Hocking Corporation, Lancaster OH   2/85-2/87
Staff Auditor
Performed operational and financial audits for this $750 million manufacturer of tableware, hardware, and packaging products.
Conducted plant and divisional audits of inventory, standard costs, accounts payable/receivable, insurance, and payroll functions.
Reviewed and evaluated the adequacy of internal controls surrounding these functions.
* Worked closely with senior management and produced formal reports and presentations for audit findings and recommendations for system improvements.

Wasson and Company, CPAs, Newport, KY   12/83-11/84
Staff Accountant
Provided all major accounting services to businesses in Cincinnati and Kentucky, including the preparation of tax returns, audits, reviews, and statements.

EDUCATION: University of Cincinnati, Cincinnati, OH
                    B.B.A. Degree: Accounting   1983
                    Accounting GPA: 3.69/4.0
                    * **Cooperative Education Program:** Gained practical accounting experience with two companies: Alexander Grant and Hydra Systems.

                    Certified Public Accountant: State of Ohio

STEVEN B. TIRED
3451 Gain Street
Westborough, MA 01581
Jirn@aol.com

Res: 508/555-5125

Fax: 508/555-1853

MANAGEMENT / CONSULTING

PROFILE:

➢ Successful executive experience in new business development and business system analysis, including full P&L responsibility for creative sales, marketing, and project management.

➢ Skilled in long- and short-term strategic planning and organizing, co-ordinate startup operations, and quickly capitalize on rapidly changing market trends.

➢ Effectively hire, train, supervise, and motivate staff and management teams in all operations, from initial product development to promotions, distribution, and networking.

➢ Conduct in-depth analyses of entire business systems and communicate with technical staff and managers to improve operations, ranging from sales to accounting and internal functions.

➢ Handle multi-million-dollar contract negotiations, as well as written and oral presentations in a personal, yet professional manner.

EXPERIENCE:

<u>Stephanie's, Inc.</u>, Westborough, MA   1/97-Present
Executive Consultant
Established, and currently manage, this executive management consulting business, including extensive business analysis, system development, and project execution.

Key accounts include:
June 1998-Present: **VP: Marketing/Business Development** for Interactive Stuff, Inc. Developed, produced, and marketed high-quality Internet, online, and PC CD-ROM games. This company owns iMagic Online, a pay-for-play online service with customers from more than 70 countries; titles are sold through 15,000 outlets worldwide.

Sept. 1997-Sept. 1998: **Interim Chief Executive** for Itchu, Int'l.
Established a new entertainment division, "The Print Club" (a $2 billion business in Japan), to produce and place photo sticker kiosks; coordinated partners in Japan.
In charge of all procedures, staffing, and the development of detailed business plans.
Initial shipments began in December, 1997, with initial orders exceeding $1 million; projected 1998 sales are $20 million.

* Itochu is one of the largest trading companies in the world, with gross sales exceeding $160 billion.

Jan.-Sept., 1997: **Vice President of Sales and Marketing** for Virtual Music Entertainment, Inc.

Responsible for creative planning and new business development, including sales and marketing, the writing of business plans, coordinating corporate partners, finding new partners such as Creative Labs, and managing international relationships.

* VMS develops software with proprietary technology to add interactivity to any CD-ROM; artists include Aerosmith, The Who, and the estates of Janis Joplin, Jimi Hendrix, The Grateful Dead, and Stevie Ray Vaughn.

<u>Virtual Entertainment, Inc.</u>, Needham, MA   2/96-12/96
Senior Vice President: Sales and Marketing
Directed sales and marketing for this emerging publisher of entertainment software products.
Creatively managed direct mail, retail, and direct consumer response to home users.
Additional responsibility for OEM bundling and the professional market.
A full range of business development efforts included creative packaging, advertising, radio & TV promotions, and various public relations events.

* Successfully doubled sales volume from under $600,000 to more than $1.2 million in nine months.
* Personally managed the largest sales rep. firm for software: SMP.
* Worked closely with graphic designers to develop a "look" for product lines.
* Established corporate direct mail programs that improved cash flow, expanded the market, and allowed this company to improve gross margins.

<u>LG Electronics, Inc.</u>, formerly GoldStar, Englewood Cliffs, NJ 10/94-2/96
Vice President / General Manager
Established a new division including all fiscal matters, team hiring, procedures, and operations for this subsidiary of LG Group, a $60 billion conglomerate manufacturing products for GoldStar and Zenith, based in Seoul, Korea.
Acted as corporate spokesperson for the 3DO hardware business.
Directed a complete packaging design and makeover.
Developed and negotiated all contracts with software developers.
Member of the executive committee, involved in all U.S. operations.

* Created a comprehensive marketing campaign and successfully coordinated efforts of 3DO partners, including Panasonic, Electronic Arts, and the 3DO company.

* Successfully launched an innovative marketing campaign and three software titles; improved market share in the 3DO category from less than 15% during the first few months to more than 65%.
* Established a new division and expanded sales volume by more than $20 million in the first year.

Sega of America, Inc., Redwood City, CA   1992-1994
Group Director: Sales / Marketing
Most recently in charge of sales and marketing for the eastern U.S.; responsible for a team of six and sales exceeding $500 million.
Responsible for customer negotiations and developing partnership programs. Oversaw budgeting, planning, and allocation for all product categories in the region.

* Directed the launch of a new toy division as National Director of Sales and Marketing for the entire country. This highly successful project expanded distribution and built first-year revenues to almost $100 million; helped establish Sega as one of the top 10 toy companies in its first year.
* Personally developed very strong relations with major corporations, while greatly improving customer relations.
* Gained computer experience in the development of sales and inventory models.

Child World, Inc., Boston, MA   1985-1992
Vice President, Merchandising
Directed a team of 12 buyers and all corporate negotiations, product selections, overseas product development, and all financial planning.

* Responsible for more than $500 million in annual sales volume in such categories as electronics, video games, juvenile products, bicycles, seasonal products, and preschool items.

Gold Circle Stores, Inc., Columbus, OH   1979-1985
Senior Buyer

EDUCATION: Ohio State University, Columbus, OH   1979
                   B.A. Degree: Economics

Sent only one to a headhunter; received three interviews and a new job.

Noel Church, CPIM, CIRM

1123 Water Park #19
Van Nuys, CA 91401

310/555-8433   lac@ey.com   Eves: 818/555-8062

SENIOR CONSULTANT / PARTNER

PROFILE:

➤ Comprehensive experience in complete project management, including the setup and streamlining of ERP and Oracle applications for highly profitable manufacturing and distribution.

➤ Skilled in the detailed analysis of legacy systems; perform cross functional IT and logistics management; familiar with ISO 9001, FDA and GMP requirements.

➤ Experience in complete supply chain management with certification in CPIM and CIRM through APICS; analyze and streamline supply chain requirements regardless of software.

➤ Skilled in writing training materials, documentation and conducting training programs on real-time system use by staff and management.

➤ Strong technical background in a wide range of computer systems and networks, including state-of-the-art databases, RF terminals, bar codes and data access tools for in-depth analysis and prompt data entry/retrieval.

EXPERIENCE:

Superb Controls, Chat, CA   7/93-Present

ERP Implementation Manager

Responsible for the setup and implementation of supply chain, inventory and operations planning functions using Oracle ERP applications software for six manufacturing and seven distribution centers in the U.S. and Canada for this $270 million company.

Directly supervise a team of 5 in MRP, including the writing - and teaching from - training materials.

Perform ERP (enterprise resource planning) with a two-year project budget exceeding $17 million.

Handle all budget planning for financial, order entry and technical systems.

Active member of the SAM (software for agile manufacturing) team; identified and purchased enterprise-wide software for running the company.

Coordinate full system implementation, including operational analysis, solution design and identification of business needs to build pilot environments, test software and meet changing business requirements.

This company manufactures and distributes disposable supplies for hospitals and operating rooms.

* Perform detailed incorporation of: domestic and international forecasting, DRP, safety stock levels (specific to product volume demand history), sourcing rules, MDS and MPS options and loads, as well as MRP and min/max planning.

* Utilized an Oracle memory-based planning engine for planning runs of minutes rather than hours.

* Designed a supply-chain process to allow production and distribution to function in a demand flow environment.

* The first plant went live on time and under budget, using Oracle NCA version 10.7 for full manufacturing, encompassing inventory, BOM, costing, WIP, supply chain and full implementation of HR.
* Involved in preparing RFI and RFQ documents.

MRP II Manager

Managed systems to coordinate manufacturing resources and planning, especially related to order processing, purchasing, inventory control and shipping of $80 million in annual sales volume in the division.

Coordinated the entire operations budget while standardizing units of measure. Redesigned production assembly areas.

* Designed, implemented and installed an RF (Radio Frequency) terminal network for real-time transaction processing.
* Implemented a bar code marking program.
* Substantially contributed to improving inventory accuracy to 99%.
* Established procedures for change processes that complied with FDA, BMP and ISO 9001 requirements, yet reduced lead times for quick change implementation.
* Assembled an Executive Information System (EIS) to summarize mainframe data in graphical format for daily management review of business status.
* Computerized shop finite scheduling on the shop floor for optimal allocation of machines and tooling.

Materials Management Solutions, Van Nuys, CA   3/91-6/93

Consultant

Developed and implemented materials management projects related to cost-effective purchasing, receiving, shipping, warehousing, bar coding, MRP II and computer systems.

Retained primarily by clients in both manufacturing and service industries.

Baxter Healthcare Corporation, Glendale, CA   3/81-2/91

Most recent positions first:

Project Manager

Directed special projects as well as purchasing, vendor relations, contract negotiations and inventory control for 15 Baxter Plasma Collection Centers.

Supervised one purchasing coordinator and an inventory control coordinator.

Gained experience with EDI specifications and field layouts.

Directed the fast track, final validation of the Baxter Screening Lab computer system.

* Oversaw $1.2 million in capital projects for lab redesign and equipment.
* Negotiated a successful agreement with a major supplier, resulting in a 15% savings on production supply parts.
* Designed and implemented a bar code system for electronic ordering, receiving and inventory control for Plasma Centers.
* Tripled sales volume of plasma preparations to Baxter and Puerto Rico.

Noel Church

Senior Project Engineer

Directed various projects at all levels of manufacturing with numerous production departments.

Played an integral role in the future planning and direction of production areas, with an emphasis on materials management.

Gained experience on multiple computer platforms.

* Completed a $400,000 redesign of the Packaging Department.
* Projects resulted in cost savings and productivity improvements.

Package Engineer

Installed numerous, beneficial updates and revisions in product packaging configurations and design.

Directed the installation of process equipment.

* Projects included the design of bulk-shipping configuration to Japan, resulting in annual savings of $500,000.
* Invented and patented a plastic bottle hanger.

EDUCATION:

APICS Certified in Integrated Resource Management (CIRM), including logistics, customers and products, manufacturing processes, support functions and integrated enterprise management; 6/92-11/93.

APICS Certified in Production and Inventory Management (CPIM), including Material Requirements Planning, Just-In-Time, Capacity Requirements Planning, Master Planning, Production Activity and Control; 7/90-3/91.

Hebrew University, Jerusalem, Israel
Completed two-thirds of requirements toward MBA degree specializing in Marketing. Successful completion of courses including accounting, finance, operations research, pricing and customer behavior; 10/78-7/80.

Bar Ilan University, Ramat Gan, Israel
B.A. Degree: Psychology; 1974

PERSONAL:

Member: American Society of Healthcare Material Management, American Production and Inventory Control Society.

Member: Advisory Board Member for the School of Management Science at California State University, Northridge.

* U.S. Patent #4,413,741 for plastic IV bottle hanger.
* Honorable Mention, Pharmaceutical category, SPHE Packaging Competition, 1988.

This aspiring executive sent 40 and received 18 interviews.

SUSAN TRIER

5687 Brook Lane
Bartlett, IL 60103

duffa@msn.com   630/555-1658

SALES REPRESENTATIVE

PROFILE:

➢ Comprehensive experience in sales and new business development, including full responsibility for account management, upselling, and personal client relations.

➢ Familiar with market research, strategic planning, and target marketing; handle competitive analysis, forecasting, status reporting, and top-level sales presentations.

➢ Skilled in pricing and creative promotions and programs; determine specific customer needs and product pricing; negotiate contracts, write/ implement bids, and provide ongoing sales support.

➢ Assist in hiring, training, and supervising staff in sales procedures, product lines, and contract administration.

➢ Knowledge of ISO 9002 and computer systems including Windows 95 and MS Office: Word, Publisher and Excel; basic knowledge of PowerPoint.

EXPERIENCE:

Stacey & Co., Inc., Hoffman Estates, IL, (sold to Ringo Corp. in 1996)
Senior Contract Administrator   1986-1998
Responsible for lead development and the sale/administration of corporate service contracts for medical equipment.
Developed leads from warranty information; quoted prices, and negotiated prices via phone and in-person presentations.
Analyzed and submitted government bids for contractual agreements.
Reviewed/resolved credit disputes; conducted sales forecasts, and coordinated ISO 9002 services.
Provided personal client communications and follow-up while tracking and analyzing medical business trends related to service contracts and customer needs.

Trained four contract administrators in all procedures.

→ Personally closed and processed more than $10.5 million in service contracts.

→ Initiated a telemarketing program – adopted nationwide – which improved the contract renewal rate by 25%.

→ Achieved a warranty to contract conversion rate of 92%.

→ Acted as liaison between the contract department and senior management for initializing two new computer systems.

→ Worked closely with the contract department and senior management to create a policies-and-procedures manual for ISO 9002.

→ Earned numerous awards for commitment to excellence.

SUSAN TRIER   **Page Two**

→   Promoted to this position from:

Senior Service Assistant   1982–1986
Handled extensive sales forecasting and personnel issues.
Communicated with customers to ensure quality of installations and service
calls and develop new policies as required.

→   Established a critical account list for prompt follow-up.

→   Created a database to track parts usage.

→   Earned numerous Outstanding Service Awards.

Senior Marketing Assistant   1978–1982
Supported the Regional Sales Manager in all aspects of sales forecasting and
personnel.
Coordinated shipments of instruments to new customers through
manufacturers, installers, and service representatives.

→   Created a national account contact schedule for sales representatives.

→   Researched competitors' products and developed competitive profiles.

EDUCATION: Trained extensively in:
Partnership Selling, 1996

Hallmark Service Sales Professional Development and Contract Selling, 1995

The Glomark Institute, Columbus, OH: Sales and Marketing Program for
High-Tech Service Sales, 1994

Strategic Selling, 1993

Negotiation Dynamics, Far Hills, NJ, 1992

W.R. Harper College, Palatine, IL
Completed various business and marketing courses, 1989

PERSONAL: Board Member of Single Parents, Inc.
Sunday School teacher, Fox Valley Unity.

ALBERT ROBINSON, CPA

2348 Saple Street
Fairfield, IA 52556

515/555-5401
allioop@aol.com

EXECUTIVE MANAGEMENT

PROFILE:

➢ Comprehensive experience as Director, COO and CFO, including full P&L responsibility for new business development, business analysis, financial matters and system streamlining.

➢ Skilled in building business through equity expansion, procedure planning, cost reduction, expense control and accounting oversight for nationwide operations.

➢ Research and write detailed, concise business plans and prepare financial forecasts; plan and conduct presentations to potential investors.

➢ Proficient in hiring, training and supervising technical and support staff at all levels; encourage new ideas and cultivate a creative team atmosphere to attract and retain quality people.

EXPERIENCE:

<u>New Frontiers</u>, Fairfield, IA   3/93-Present

Director, Executive Vice President and CFO

In charge of four department managers and virtually all operations for this company, with 3,200 shipping locations nationwide.

Responsible for all financial matters, including building equity through investor relations, budgeting, forecasting, treasury administration and financial reporting.

Perform market research and strategic planning.

Full oversight of operational audits, data services, MIS, administrative departments and accounting.

Analyze call loads vs. total customer service satisfaction and overhead.

Effectively coordinate MIS in determining information requirements, prioritizing requests and managing the development process.

Handle extensive staff and management hiring, training, supervision and motivation in a strong, creative team environment.

→ Constantly develop and communicate new marketing and program strategies to middle managers, resulting in a doubling of revenue and shipping locations.

→ Developed accurate internal systems to track customer shipments, activity, cash transactions and overall customer demographics.

→ Saved more than $100,000 by renegotiating equipment warranty agreements.

→ Reduced costs by 20% by negotiating the company's communications contract.

ALBERT ROBINSON, CPA   **Page Two**

→   Constantly recognize opportunities in functional areas to exceed customer expectations, benefit the total company culture and improve financial results.

→   In charge of selecting an investment banking organization and raising $5 million of permanent equity; prepared investment memorandums, monitored investment contacts and coordinated/ participated in investor presentations and negotiations.

→   Negotiated/procured an $800,000 revolving credit facility for this early-stage enterprise.

→   Developed and negotiated a corporate lease agreement that doubled the Company's office space for less than $3 per square foot and enabled the consolidation of two warehouse locations.

<u>Chicago Holdings, Inc.</u>, Pittsburgh, PA   4/90-3/93
Vice President
As a private equity investor, identified and evaluated investment opportunities in consumer finance companies for this venture organization. Worked with other investors and negotiated investment valuations and amounts, while providing post-investment management services.

→   This company was a major investor in The Finance Company, below:

<u>The Finance Company</u>, Manassas, VA 4/89-4/90
Chief Financial Officer
Developed and directed investor relationships and all operational accounting, financial reporting and treasury functions for the corporate holding company and two remote regional operation sites.

→   This company underwrote consumer finance loans.

<u>Marine Midland Capital Markets Corporation</u>, New York, NY 4/85-4/89
Director, Chief Financial and Operations Officer
Managed the securities operations, regulatory reporting and compliance function for Marine Midland Bank's Public Security Division.

<u>Emanuel and Company</u>, New York, NY   4/83-4/85
Controller
In charge of broker dealer security operations and regulatory/financial reporting for the investment subsidiaries of this investment banking operation.

<u>PRIOR EXPERIENCE</u> with <u>Touche Ross & Co.</u> as **Audit Manager**

EDUCATION: <u>West Virginia University</u>, Morgantown, WV
Bachelor of Science, Business Administration
*Graduated Cum Laude

Sent about 50; receeived eight interviews and two job offers.

FRANK JEFFERSON

2325 Ban Court
Bartlett, IL 60103

E-mail: far@ibm.net   630/555-2380

ELECTRICAL ENGINEERING/MANAGEMENT

PROFILE:

➢ Extensive background in all aspects of technical support and the service/repair of high-tech equipment including client relations, project management, staffing, financial analysis, programming and technology management.

➢ Work extensively with client base to provide high-level support, obtain feedback, build business relationships and understand the needs of the customer; effectively research and identify market needs.

➢ Proven ability to manage multi-site operations; provide technical training, organizational skills and motivation. Handle budgeting, P&L and financial analysis/reporting.

➢ Experienced in network installation, including layout design, groupings, set-ups, application installation and upgrades.

➢ Comprehensive project management skills include team development, organization, scheduling and budgeting. Design and develop software applications; skilled in C, C++, Pascal, Visual Basic, Access, Novell 4.x, NT, Windows 95 and Novell Workstations.

EXPERIENCE: <u>Totally Keen Surveys</u>, Itasca, IL   1985-Present

Regional Service / IT Manager   1995-Present

Direct all aspects of service and information management for this innovative, high-tech company. The Sweden-based company manufactures various surveying equipment using global positioning satellites.

Supervise all operations for nine workshops throughout the Americas providing for the repair of equipment.

Manage all aspects of technical support and provide high-level support for clients.

Prepare and administer an aftermarket operating budget of $1.5 million.

Perform financial analysis, with responsibility for profits.

Work extensively with clients to gain feedback on new products and learn the particular needs of each client.

Maintain regular contact with regional offices and manage the workflow.

Prepare and submit reports on service statistics.

Analyze trends and provide feedback to headquarters.

Perform quality audits to ensure compliance with ISO 9000 requirements.

Develop various applications in C and C++.

FRANK JEFFERSON
Page Two

→ Handled all aspects of installing a network for 50 users: contracted service for wiring, set-up user profiles and installed software.

→ Developed and maintain database for service offices. Implement various technology to make information more accessible to satellite offices.

→ Boosted division profitability by 28% over two years.

→ Travel to the various shops to provide training in the technical aspects of service and new product development, and to exchange information.

Service Manager   1992-1995
Responsible for managing two service offices.
Trained and directed a team of six associates.

→ Handled all client relations and technical support.

→ Determined pricing for spare parts.

Service Engineer   1991-1992
Performed equipment service and maintenance as well as technical support.

→ Reassigned to the U.S. from Sweden.

Service Engineer, Stockholm, Sweden   1988-1991
Serviced equipment brought in from sites around the world and provided technical support to satellite offices.
Set-up special tools for service.

Test Engineer, Stockholm, Sweden   1985-1988
Utilized test equipment to run functional analyses of circuit boards and sub units for spare parts inventory.

EDUCATION: Kingston University, London, England
Bachelor of Science Degree in Electrical Engineering:
Concentration in Communications and Control with CAD / Computing.

LANGUAGES: Written and oral fluency in English and Swedish.

Used only one resume; received one interview and was offered the job.

Wallace Rodgers

236 North Court
Des Plaines, IL 60016

W998@aol.com   847/555-7893

MANAGEMENT / MARKETING

PROFILE:

- ➤ Comprehensive experience in the heavy equipment industry, including forecasting, competitive analysis, and the negotiation of sales and leasing agreements.

- ➤ Familiar with market research, strategic planning, and new business development, including distributor networking and contract negotiations.

- ➤ Skilled in finance and budget administration, forecasting, and long- and short-term planning.

- ➤ Handle cash requirement forecasting and statement analysis, as well as loan agreements, P&L statements, and balance sheets.

- ➤ Plan and conduct seminars and various written and oral presentations in a professional manner.

EXPERIENCE:

The Construction Solutions Company, Addison, IL   2/80-Present
Vice President: Risk Management and Corporate Secretary
Responsible for developing and presenting a strong corporate image in the heavy equipment industry, with direct involvement in marketing, sales, and profit expansion.
Negotiate sales and lease agreements while keeping a sharp eye on competitors' rates and product lines.
Network closely with distributors and promote product lines; constantly analyze risks associated with contracts, purchase agreements, vendors, suppliers, and proceedings.
Directly involved in staff training and development in company procedures and product lines.
Constantly analyze and reduce risks associated with sales contracts, purchase orders, litigation proceedings, and employee personnel matters. Maintain the quality of vendor and purchasing relationships and act as company representative in sensitive matters.

Responsible for a wide range of functional areas including:
Credit Management: Work closely with sales representatives to expand sales through credit procedures. Designed and implemented all credit department functions, including establishing and managing new accounts. Negotiate settlements and disputes while supervising two support staff.

Manager of Human Resources, Manager of Casualty Insurance and **Employee Benefits Manager**: Researched and purchased/designed all employee benefit packages, including savings and profit-sharing plans. Administer all business insurance including sourcing, cost-effective purchasing, and implementation. Maintain aggressive, positive programs.

Forms Manager: Establish and maintain inventory levels of forms; oversee design, purchasing, and updating of business cards and all printed matter. Analyze and control costs and reduce waste.

Safety Director: Responsible for the design, implementation, and review of safety procedures and policies for adherence to OSHA and government guidelines. Train workers on safety issues and maintain vendors' material safety data sheets.

Member: Corporate Board of Directors: (1993-Present) Directly involved in long- and short-term planning and all major business decisions of this company.

Harris Group, Arlington Heights, IL   11/78-2/80
General Manager / Part Owner
In charge of sales development through marketing, promotions, and advertising for two successful restaurants.
Effectively hired, trained, and supervised up to 80 in all operations, including direct customer service and upselling.
Purchased and managed all food, beverages, capital equipment, and supplies.
→   Performed cost analyses, payroll processing, and overall business management.

PRIOR EXPERIENCE:

American Bakeries Company, HQ, Chicago, IL
General Credit Manager
Oversaw sales and credit activities for this $500 million operation, including sales expansion through more effective customer service.
Hired, trained, and supervised a staff of nine and a national staff of 75.
Negotiated directly with customers, banks, and attorneys regarding credit and sales contracts.
→   Established provisions for bad debts, departmental budgeting, and expenses; forecast credit losses.

Swift and Company, Subsidiary of Esmark, Chicago, IL
Regional Credit Manager

EDUCATION:

College of Great Falls, Great Falls, MT
B.S.B.A., Accounting

Attended Northwestern University in Evanston, IL, for two years.

DePaul University, Chicago, IL
Law Program; enrolled 1984-1985

MEMBERSHIPS:

U.S.A. National Credit Union, Homewood, IL
Member: Board of Directors

MILITARY:

U.S. Air Force, **Sergeant**
Four Years

Some would say Merril is "overqualified"; he was very selective and was seeking a very unique position. He sent about 200; received six interviews and a job offer.

Merril Chase

99961 Snake Road
Luken, CA 92630
Res: 949/555-6465   Chase@anet.net   Office and Fax: 949/555-4700

EXECUTIVE MANAGEMENT

A position utilizing the ability to adapt, capitalize and thrive in rapidly changing business environments.

PROFILE:

➜ Comprehensive executive experience in domestic and international business development, including full P&L responsibility for entire companies and complex, high-tech projects with top executives and government agencies.

➜ Proven ability to expand profits through creative strategic planning and coordination of all essential functions, from initial concept to coalition building, PR, and market establishment to lease and financing packages, vendor sourcing, computer systems, and quality control.

➜ Establish and manage entire leasing programs and related financing, including the design and implementation of operations for banks, independent lessors, and major corporations.

➜ Skilled in capital development and the sourcing of venture funds for multi-million dollar projects.

➜ Spearhead global distribution networking and international sales, including market research, creative promotions, and top-level contract negotiation; analyze foreign competition and improve relations with overseas governments and partners; bilingual in Greek.

➜ Effectively hire, train, and motivate technical staff and management teams; establish goals and controls; monitor results to consistently increase profit margins, enhance market position, reduce operating costs, and meet strategic objectives.

EXPERIENCE: Ross Funding Corporation, Luken, CA   1981-1998
President
Concurrent management and consulting roles with:
D.A.T. Holdings Ltd., UK (**Chairman**); D.A.T., AB Sweden, (a D.A.T. subsidiary); Clean Air North America, Inc., Luken (**Chairman & CEO**), and Syntec, Ltd. UK (**Chairman**).
Commercial Consultant to the City of Luken (Dept. of Water and Power), 1988-1991 and Southern California Edison, 1989-1991.

OVERVIEW:
Director: Electric Vehicle Initiative
Under an EPA mandate and a resolution by the City of Luken for cleaner air and commercial development, directed a highly successful, multi-billion dollar international R&D program to establish the primary electric vehicle (EV) initiative, from initial strategic planning and infrastructure to financing, production, and coalition building on a worldwide basis.
Performed or directed all strategic planning, contract management, lease financing, and government and regulatory affairs, as well as all sales and marketing initiatives.

Diplomacy

Developed strong diplomatic and business relationships with auto industry leaders worldwide and government agencies throughout Europe and Asia, especially China, for a complete EVehicle program.
Founded the Luken EV Commercial Advisory Board, composed of high ranking, Fortune 500 level executives.
Co-founder of a Washington, DC, lobbying agency, The Electric Transportation Coalition, which acquired national visibility through key state and federal legislators and regulators. Established acceptance by key governments and automakers through effective lobbying.
Worked closely with a top U.S. General and foreign officials on a multi-billion dollar electric transportation program for the People's Republic of China.

Communications and Coalition-Building

Worked closely with Fortune 500 firms and top officials at U.S. and foreign governments.
Promoted electric transportation to national fleet and leasing associations.
Conducted numerous speeches and presented the program worldwide to foreign governments and all major car manufacturers with excellent response.

⇨ Wrote and distributed a highly successful request for proposal for 10,000 vehicles.
⇨ Major automakers produced at least prototype EVs as a result of this initiative.

Finance

Created financial and regulatory plans to assist automakers in market penetration.
Conducted external audits of leasing and financial portfolios for several California banks.

Infrastructure and Logistics

Addressed the entire infrastructure issue, including insurance and finance matters, with fleet companies and auto manufacturers.

Technology

Acquired and managed the latest commercial technology and manufacturing techniques with a sharp eye on diplomacy and cultural matters.
Facilitated technology transfer and defined all parts, products, systems, and procedures.
Provided a catalyst for R&D efforts of the big three automakers, overseas automakers, and various utility services.

⇨ Oversaw production of two prototype vehicles, demonstrated at auto shows in Frankfurt, Tokyo, Sweden, Hong Kong, and Luken.
⇨ Earned "Best of What's New in Technology" from *Popular Science* magazine, 1991.
⇨ As Member of the Board of Directors of Syntech, Ltd. UK, directed R&D and infrastructure for the developing utility load leveling storage systems and fuel cells for electric transportation.

Marketing

Established profit potential and the ability to preserve and expand market share in the U.S. and abroad (including Asia and Europe), to spur major economies and companies to substantially invest, adapt the program, and integrate their auto manufacturers' efforts.
Created commercial incentives for manufacturers and promoted a worldwide effort to manufacture and market electric vehicles.

Specific achievements include:

⇨ Designed and implemented a plan for Denning Mobile Robotics to commercialize the only truly autonomous robot at the time. This led to an increase in bottom line profits of 2% on $200 million in new business.

⇨ Established a $225 million line of credit for a national car rental corporation. In addition, created a used car leasing program for vehicles removed from the rental fleet; projected annual income from leased vehicles was estimated at $750 million.

⇨ Working extensively with top GM executives, who announced its introduction of the Impact Vehicle in Luken.

⇨ GM's vehicle launch triggered announcements of EV programs from all major auto manufacturers around the world.

Details of Hands-on Management

Personally managed companies selected by the city of LA: C.A.T. Holdings, Ltd., UK and C.A.T. AB Sweden, Clean Air North America, and a majority interest in Syntec, Ltd., a fuel cell development company.

As part of the EV initiative, developed and implemented a detailed plan to manufacture and market electric vehicles through C.A.T.'s Swedish subsidiary, C.A.T. AB, and Clean Air North America.

⇨ Through strategic alliances, acquired $20 million in contingency capital.

⇨ Directing development of a $55 million hybrid electric vehicle program and raised $20 million in capital from a strategic partner.

⇨ Reduced overhead by $500,000 annually.

<u>Compulease, Inc.</u>, Downey, CA   1975-1981
Founder and President
Directed systems development and integration operations, including the design and implementation of lease financing packages for newly released IBM equipment.
Performed detailed consulting for leasing companies and banks.
Directed marketing and business development.

**PRIOR
EXPERIENCE:**   <u>Medical Data Systems, Inc.</u>
                             Director: Data Processing

                             <u>Applied Data Systems</u>
                             Manager: Computer Operations

                             <u>Borg-Warner Corporation</u>
                             General Data Processing Supervisor

AFFILIATIONS: Founder: Luken Electric Vehicle Commercial Advisory Board.
                             Co-Founder: Electric Transportation Coalition, Washington, DC.
                             Member: SAF Executive Committee, Scripps College, Claremont, CA.
                             Member: Executive Committee, Hellenic Heritage Foundation, Luken, CA.

PERSONAL: Married; enjoy travel and antique car restoration.

Mailed several and posted on the Internet; received eight interviews and four e-mail inquiries.

Kirk Shipman
233 Creek Drive
Tyler, TX 75707
Shipper@gte.net

Home: 903/555-0133   Cell: 903/555-7731

EXECUTIVE MANAGEMENT: SOFTWARE

PROFILE:

- Successful experience in multi-million dollar turnarounds, including P&L responsibility for national and international business development, successful product rollouts and distribution, with experience in North America, Europe and the Middle East.

- Executive management experience in application software, distribution, databases, operating systems, logistics, computer hardware, client/server networks, and consulting; familiar with major manufacturers including Microsoft, Oracle, and Novell; manage the design and development of Internet applications and Web-based products.

- Effectively hire, train, and supervise staff and managers in all aspects of marketing, financials, account acquisition, and management, as well as technical products.

- Skilled in creative project management, strategic planning, and "out-of-box" thinking, resulting in dramatic improvements in bottom line profits.

- Effectively managed both large and small organizations, regional, national, and international; coordinate financials, inventory management, customer service, help desk, warehouse management, logistics, municipal government relations, and utilities.

CAREER BACKGROUND:

Gray Matter, Inc., Buehler, TX   1996-1998
President
Directly involved in all aspects of business turnaround, with full P&L responsibility for corporate identity, product evolution, marketing, and sales. This is the software division of a $14 billion international corporation focused on software applications for governments, municipalities, and privately held utilities.
Responsible for the hiring, training, and supervision of 46 employees; directly supervised a team of five.
Effectively managed all phases of market research, product design, multi-media, Internet promotions, print, public relations, and life cycle management.

- Instrumental in expanding this company from $2 million to $7 million.
- Increased recurring revenues by over 300%
- Increased average transaction from $6,000 to over $200,000.
- Led the company from a loss of 43% of revenue to profitability in six quarters.
- Anticipated and recognized technology and market shifts and responded quickly to these changes. Successfully aligned distribution channels with current and future product strategies, while identifying and targeting optimum vertical markets for the company's products.
- Responsible for product development and project related to software applications for financial applications, customer service, distribution, utility, municipal government, and logistics.

- Determined product priorities based upon customer needs versus development resource requirements.
- Gained experience in Web-based, mission critical projects, client/server knowledge, databases, and operating systems.
- Developed strategic plans, including the vision for a new client/server Windows product to replace legacy DOS products; obtained funding, completed projects under budget and in less than 12 months when industry estimates called for 30 months.
- Converted a staff with no Windows experience to one capable of outperforming the consultants we hired and retained 100% of staff at completion of projects.

The Thomas Group, Inc., Dallas, TX   1995-1996
Senior Consultant
This is a $75 million international publicly held consulting firm.
Managed consulting engagements and determined and met specific client needs.
Performed task definition, options evaluation, project management, and systems application experience.
Specialized in process improvement for product development, customer support, and sales management. (Recruited to join Sensus SofTech as President.)

- Worked with Fortune 500 companies in industries such as software development and distribution.
- Accomplished reductions in sales cycle times of up to 60%, while increasing successful close ratio from 24% of opportunities to over 60% success.
- Assisted a $110 million software company in developing strategic plans for a new, Internet-based product to replace legacy product in the real estate industry.
- Performed process improvement for software development, customer service, help desk, evaluating acquisition opportunities, and sales cycle management.

UDS, Inc., Dallas, TX   1987-1995
President and CEO
Promoted due to results achieved for this distribution software application company.
Spearheaded a successful turnaround and ignited a stagnant, declining operation.
Directed this software application company from previous five-year record of losses to profits of 16% on revenues in five quarters.
Oversaw 92 employees and six direct reports.

- Expanded sales from $5 million to $25 million during this period.
- Recognized for quality service and products and developing loyal customers, resulting in impressive sales. (Left due to hostile takeover by a major competitor.)

Executive Vice President Product Development & Marketing
Rapidly promoted and immediately successful in streamlining operations, finding more productive methods to achieve top performance, eliminate waste, and reduce unnecessary expenses.

Vice-President, Sales and Marketing

Doubled revenues in two years and increased margins 40% for this leading provider of hardgoods distribution software applications and computer hardware and services. Established market share dominance domestically and in Canada.

- Earned Chairman's Award from parent company for performance in top 1% of over 750 employees worldwide.
- Generated positive cash flows of 18% of revenues, the first positive cash flow performance in company history.
- Reduced operating expenses by 55% in 12 months while revenues increased substantially.
- Improved Customer Satisfaction Survey ratings from base of 1.6 (on a scale of 1 to 5) to 4.27; achieved similar results on Employee Satisfaction surveys.
- Decreased Bad Debt expense from almost 10% of revenue to under 1/2 of 1% of revenue.
- Redesigned support and services fee structures, doubling monthly recurring revenues.
- Restructured the consulting services department; increased revenues six-fold while reducing staff size and operating expenses.
- As VP of Sales and Marketing, doubled sales in two years.
- Rewrote contracts, resulting in dramatically reduced sales cycles.
- Implemented new pricing and commission structures, which increased gross margins by 35%
- As Western Regional Manager, expanded a territory with six salespeople from $1.2 million to over $6 million in 10 months.
- Closed the largest transaction in company history within six weeks of beginning employment.

<u>The Gladstein Company Inc.</u>, Shawnee, OK   1975-1987

Senior Vice President

Achieved strongest volume growth in the history of this hardgoods distribution company. Directed all phases of operation, including logistics, sales, marketing, branch operations, purchasing, and MIS. Four locations and 52 employees.

- Sales grew from $2 million to $15 million during this period.

EDUCATION:

<u>University of Tulsa</u>, Tulsa, OK

B.S. Degree: Accounting

- MBA Graduate Studies; Minor: Marketing

Active in a fraternity, holding offices of President, Treasurer, Rush Chairman, and Social Chairman, as well as Chapter Advisor during graduate school.

Mailed about 60; received 20 interviews and a job offer; promoted at current job and stayed there!

MILES CLOSER, CFA

234 Setts Ave. #245
Cambridge, MA 02139-3174
Res: 617/555-1462 Ofc: 617/555-2747 MER@tfn.com

SALES MANAGEMENT / MARKETING

PROFILE:

- Comprehensive experience in management and new business development, including full profit/loss responsibility for creative product development, management, and international marketing and distribution.

- Chartered Financial Analyst with successful experience in financial planning and mergers and acquisitions; perform detailed analysis of budgets, assets, and competitors.

- Coordinate marketing communications, including the design of creative pieces for advertising, direct mail, and PR; oversee production for technical product lines and establish and implement quality and financial controls.

- Experience in the setup of new operations, with full responsibility for staff and management hiring, training, and supervision in sales and product lines.

- Act as spokesperson to the press and speak on industry topics at a wide range of trade shows, forums, and seminars.

EXPERIENCE:

Erin Financial Services, Boston, MA

General Manager 1994–Present

In charge of profit/loss and the development, support, and marketing of the PERAscope software application for performance measurement, used by top institutional money managers.

The system is offered on in-house, outsourced, and online bases and ranges in price from $20,000 to $250,000 annually; it is used by many large trust banks, money managers, companies and consultants for detailed performance measurement, attribution, and risk analysis.

Directed the turnaround of this group, including the selection and integration of new technology, products, and personnel.

Hired, trained, and currently supervise a team of 42 people, including four direct reports and managers in two states.

Full oversight of product quality, integrity of sales teams, and 10 different products.

- Reorganized and streamlined the organizational structure and greatly improved customer response and quality.
- **Technology:** Converted from aging, non-Y2K-compliant technologies and made tough decisions on product terminations.
- Launched beta and live versions of PERAscope; achieved growth from 1995 introduction to more than $1 million annually in recurring revenue, and a compound growth rate of 135%.
- Currently directing the research of, and expansion into, international markets.

Thomson Investment Software: PORTIA

Positions of increasing responsibility include:

Vice President of Sales, Marketing, and Product Management 1993-1994

Successfully directed a product design group consisting of a marketing manager, sales manager, and two market managers.

Complete oversight for all marketing strategies, including advertising, public relations, collateral, promotions, market research, and product design for the Americas.

Designed and introduced a new advertising campaign and completed/executed a major market research survey with more than 500 respondents.

Member of Massachusetts' state-sponsored trade mission to Mexico.

- Sales increased 20% over 1993.
- Achieved 95% of the *new business* plan and 110% of the overall revenue plan.
- Implemented the division's first advisory panel, consisting of major investment management firms.
- Researched, wrote and developed Thomson's first comprehensive sales manual.

Director of Sales   1992-1993

Initiated market analysis of Central and South America, while directing the division's first Latin America sale to the Central Bank of Venezuela.

Earned management responsibility for London and Hong Kong offices, based on strong domestic sales and sales management success.

- Spearheaded the sales team to 125% of *new business* goal (34 clients) and 124% of overall sales plan in 1992; promoted based on record-breaking sales: 1992 and 1993.
- Increased sales to 185% of *new business* goal ($4.87 vs. $2.65 million plan) and 130% of add-on sales goal in 1993, a 40% increase over 1992 and 64% over plan.

North American Sales Manager   1990-1992

Promoted to Sales Manager, in addition to responsibility for a full sales territory and $600,000 personal quota.

- Effectively organized, coached, and directed a sales team of seven to achieve a $3.2 million goal.
- Achieved 125% of plan; reached 123% of personal sales quota.

Senior Account Executive, promoted from **Account Executive**   1987-1990

Trained/mentored a new sales representative while developing sales in a growing territory.

Chosen as one of the first two people to sell PORTIA. Completed self-study in a Harvard graduate investment class.

- Ranked #1 in sales of seven representatives in 1989.
- Achieved 165% of quota in 1989, with an average sales size of $60,000.

Chase Access Services Corp., Dallas, TX

Senior Sales Representative, promoted from **Sales Representative**   1984-1987

Developed strong sales in a 25-state region.

- Increased annual sales revenue by 91% and number of client banks by 166%.
- Achieved quota performance by 267% in 1985 and 206% in 1986.
- Sales Representative of the Year for 1985.

RepublicBank Corporation, Dallas, TX   1981-1984

EDUCATION:

Columbia Graduate School of Business, Dallas, TX
Graduate: Executive Development Program
Specially nominated by Thomson

The University of Houston, Houston, TX
MBA Degree: Finance

The University of Delaware, Newark, DE
BA Degree: Economics and Political Science

Posted on several Internet databases; received 35 interviews.

SAMUEL JACKSON
233 S. Main Street
New Spring, NY 10516
914/555-7895   fghjm@hardstone.com

EXECUTIVE MANAGEMENT

PROFILE:
➢ Entrepreneurial experience in marketing and new business development, including finance, startup operations, successful turnarounds and initial public offerings (IPOs) in fast-paced industries.

➢ Creative, innovative talents in corporate development, e-commerce, capital raising, the Internet and managing all key business issues and operations.

➢ Highly skilled in business networking for new startups, with extensive Wall Street and venture capital contacts; utilize outsourcing and a wide range of professional services; leverage the latest computer technologies to increase profits and customer satisfaction.

➢ Coordinate product development, distribution and vendor relations; negotiate contracts and handle written and oral presentations in a professional manner.

➢ Profit-building experience with domestic and foreign markets, cultures and practices; handle a diversity of tasks simultaneously, with a sharp eye for detail and the bottom line.

HIGHLIGHTS:
* *Involved in writing the first Energy Futures Contract for the New York Mercantile Exchange. Established Merrill Lynch's first institutional desk to transact institutional trades. Founded the Institutional Energy Group at Drexel Burnham Lambert and opened offices in New York, London, and Singapore.*

EXPERIENCE:
Jackson Steller & Co., Inc., Lotsmore, MD   1997-Present
Managing Director
Investment banker to early-stage companies, including several Internet, e-commerce and other merging growth companies.
Initiate and negotiate private equity financings and M&A advisory assignments.
Focusing on information technology, telecommunications, specialty retail, healthcare and transportation businesses.
→ Negotiated the sale of an Internet data center/e-commerce company.
→ Raised first-round financing for a startup ISP.
→ Successful merger and acquisition assignments include the sale of a telecommunications services company.
→ Sold a healthcare services company.
→ Directed early-stage financing for a leading-edge memory technology company.

Spencer Trask Securities, Inc., New York, NY   1995-1997
Managing Director - Corporate Finance
Investment Banker. Sourced, negotiated, structured and placed private equity financing for emerging growth companies.
→ Raised $6.7 million in equity for a transaction processing company.
→ Successfully financed a turnaround investment in specialized manufacturing company.
→ Acquired a private company that offers unique financial services to municipal governments.

→ Provided valuable input on M&A strategy for an employer-provided health care company.

→ Advised an Internet access company on a private placement offering.

<u>Alex, Brown & Sons, Inc.</u>, Baltimore, MD   1994

Manager

Highly effective in developing private placement financing opportunities while cultivating a high net worth and institutional investor base for these early-stage investments.

→ Attended numerous industry conferences and up-to-date training on market trends and procedures from this top-notch investment banking firm.

<u>McKiernan & Company, Inc.</u>, New York, NY

President / CEO   1991-1994 and 1986-1988

Established this company to advise private companies on financings, M&A and strategic alliances, with a focus on telecommunications, information technology and the petroleum industry.

Performed international consulting with Fortune 500 firms on expanding trade.

Conducted feasibility studies, including one for a refinery expansion in Poland.

A summary of successful transactions includes:

→ Raising $15 million of equity capital in the Persian Gulf for a U.S. company with exclusive rights to a patented process.

→ Advised a major New York investment banking firm on issues related to the privatization of telecommunications, oil and other industries in Ecuador.

→ Researching and negotiating a marketing alliance between Dow Jones and a Saudi Arabian client to develop and distribute petroleum data and global financial information services in that country.

→ Selling and constructing a complex civilian radio transmitter for the government of the Sharawi Republic in western Africa.

→ Negotiated the purchase of an international communications network for the new Arab investors in United Press International (UPI).

→ Advised on strategic alliances for investors and the Miami International Airport on proposed construction of a foods auction market.

President / CEO during 1986-1988: Specialized in the brokering and trading of energy derivatives and options for institutional accounts.

Cleared trades with Broadcourt Capital, Prudential Bache and Elders.

<u>Intex Holdings, (Bermuda) Ltd.</u>, New York, NY   1987-1991

President / CEO

Retained by this company to turn around a pioneering effort to create an electronic exchange to allow for electronic trading of commodity and financial futures transactions.

Successfully negotiated a joint marketing, development and distribution agreement with Telerate, Inc. to combine a proprietary Intex software with Telerate's global, installed subscriber base and give exchanges a better alternative to Reuters/CME Globex.

→ Successfully beta tested an order routing system with the Chicago Board of Trade/CBOT and the London International Financial Futures Exchange (LIFFE).

<u>Drexel Burnham Lambert</u>, New York, NY   1982-1986
First Vice President
Established Drexel's Institutional Energy Group, servicing numerous domestic and international trading firms, airlines, refiners, petroleum distributors and other accounts.

→ Managed trading desks in New York, London and Singapore, with combined production in excess of $5 million.

<u>Merrill Lynch & Company</u>, New York, NY   1977-1982
Vice President / Manager
Established this company's first institutional energy futures trading desk in the commodity division headquarters.
Hired, trained and directed a team of 15 broker/traders.

→ Ranked as the largest producer in the Commodity Division in 1981, with gross production in excess of $5 million.

PRIOR EXPERIENCE: **Vice President and Division Manager**: J.R. Sousa & Sons / ARCO Refining and Marketing.
Purchased an existing business and established this company's New York state operations. Acquired and upgraded a marine oil terminal and directed all phases of the company's wholesale and retail gasoline and fuel oil marketing, distribution and trading.

ADDITIONAL: **Frequent speaker and lecturer** at petroleum trade association conventions and NYMEX and International Petroleum Exchange (IPE) seminars. Wrote and presented papers at conferences sponsored by the International Association of Energy Economists (IAEE) at the University of Toronto and at Cambridge University.

Publicly Delivered papers and publications include *"Using Futures to Stabilize Energy Costs and Profits"* and *"Spot and Futures Markets."* Quoted in the *Oil & Gas Journal, Institutional Investor, Barron's, Intermarket, The Wall Street Journal, Trading Systems Technology* and other media.

LICENSES: Series 7 & 63, NASD Licensed and Registered.

AFFILIATIONS: Member: Marist College Board of Trustees, 1981-Present.
Formerly: Digital Express Group, Inc., (DIGEX) Board of Directors.
Formerly: New York Mercantile Exchange (NYMEX), Board of Governors.
Formerly: J-Vee Co., Inc. Instructor

EDUCATION: <u>Marist College</u>, Poughkeepsie, NY
Bachelor of Arts Degree - History

Sent about 60 through mail and email; received five interviews.

CARY EVANS

213 Mar Heights Court #129
San Diego, CA 92130

Cgas@aol.com   619/555-9760

EXECUTIVE MANAGEMENT

PROFILE:

➢ Comprehensive experience in new business development, including P&L responsibility for marketing, intellectual property, R&D, and operations management in technology industries from start-up through acquisition.

➢ Skilled in entrepreneurial-driven functions ranging from product development, staffing, and procedures to long- and short-term strategic planning, media relations, and the establishment of synergistic alliances.

➢ Effectively manage budgets and financial matters; negotiate contracts and coordinate vendors, suppliers, and distribution channels for effective product pull-through.

➢ Perform all aspects of sales, including account closing, with excellent presentation skills for selling technical products and services in both domestic and international markets.

➢ Proficient in applied technologies, software, and systems integration.

EXPERIENCE: <u>Super-Link Systems, Inc.</u>, Waterslide, CA   1991-Present

Founder and CEO
Responsible for the design and development of embedded firmware control systems (central server with an online service) and data communications used to optimize water use for residences, businesses, and government accounts.
Plan and implement all marketing strategies, including media relations, market research, creative promotions, and advertising.
Effectively hire, train, and supervise staff and management teams in product lines and all marketing and sales techniques.
Develop long- and short-term plans, as well as financial projections and private placement to raise capital.
This business integrates weather data, communications over cable systems, and utility cost savings to the customer.

➔ Oversee circuit design, high-level software programming, and all engineering functions with programmers and technical staff.
➔ Successfully negotiated cable trials and beta testing with Time Warner Cable, Cox Communications, Jones Intercable, and alliances with water utilities.
➔ Negotiated license agreements with strategic business partners.
➔ Personally secured fully issued patents with broad claims and obtained registered trademarks.

CARY EVANS
Page Two

SAFE-Time Emergency Systems, Inc., Westlake Village, CA   1980–1990

Co-Founder and President
Eventually negotiated the sale of this business to DuPont (at 16 times initial investment).
Developed business with numerous multi-national Fortune 100 companies.
Personally established distribution and sales to Europe, Asia, the Middle East, Canada, and Mexico, and in the East Coast and Gulf Coast of the U.S.
Directed 30 to 40 staff and managers with an annual multi-million dollar run rate.
This company developed and sold scientific software, bundled with advanced systems, interactive graphics, and instrumentation to the chemical and petrochemical industry for monitoring and tracking hazardous chemical leaks.

→ Established this company as the #1 supplier through high-visibility media, such as *The Wall Street Journal, The New York Times, Business Week, Chemical Week, CNN, and other TV stations.*

→ This company grew 50% annually with high profit margins during my tenure.

→ Negotiated for up-front customer deposits, which greatly improved cash flow and reduced working capital.

→ Hired, trained, and motivated a high quality, efficient team of technical and support staff and managers in engineering, sales, production, and quick response customer service.

EDUCATION: Pepperdine University, Malibu, CA
M.B.A. (Partial fulfillment, Presidential Key Executive Program) 1990.

Colorado State University, Fort Collins, CO
M.S. Degree: Environmental Resources

University of Colorado, Boulder, CO
B.S. Degree: Aerospace Engineering

**COMPUTER
SKILLS:**   Proficient in spreadsheets, graphics, word processing, e-mail, Internet, and all major Windows applications.

PERSONAL: Married with one child; enjoy skiing, hiking, boating, and travel.

Sent about 22; received two interviews.

DAVID BARNICLE

239 Mercury Drive
Schaumburg, IL 60193-5185

847/555-3911
barn@gateway.net

HEALTHCARE ADMINISTRATION

PROFILE:

➤ Comprehensive experience in healthcare and operations management, including responsibility for new startups, special projects, procedures and communications.

➤ Research and write policies, procedures and training materials; design and implement budgets and forecasts; strong knowledge of insurance codes and medical terminologies.

➤ Skilled in team training, supervision and motivation; coordinate systems and procedures in fast-paced situations.

➤ Experience in cost-effective purchasing and vendor relations, as well as overhead reduction and computerized status reporting; utilize Windows 95 and 98, MS Word 97 and Excel for correspondence and spreadsheets.

➤ Plan and conduct written/oral presentations and meetings for staff, management and the public in a professional manner.

EXPERIENCE:

Marion Medical Clinic, Ellyn, IL   1995-Present
Practice Manager
In charge of an entire OB/Gyn Department and the training and supervision of 15 employees supporting seven physicians.

Reimbursement Specialist
Constantly analyze, update and implement clinic fee schedules, including all insurance procedure codes supporting 160 physicians in 20 departments. Create and implement office policies, procedures, business forms and monthly financial reports to meet constantly changing demands.

→ Act as liaison between clinical staff, including doctors and RNs and the billing office to maximize insurance reimbursements.
→ Effectively train and develop clerical and clinic staff.
→ Control the department budget and work directly with physicians.

Vesicare, Inc., Torrance, CA
Office Administrator   1994-1995
Created a more effective reporting system and trained numerous employees in its use.
In charge of daily profitability and operations of a regional office.

DAVID BARNICLE

Handled extensive telephone and in-person communications with all types of patients.

Verified insurance benefits, oriented beneficiaries on coverage and produced medical reports for locations in Illinois and Colorado.

Vein Clinics of America, Schaumburg, IL   1989-1993

Quality Assurance & Training Manager

Computer Systems Coordinator, promoted from:

Patient Relations Coordinator / Sales Representative

Personally directed the setup, implementation and support of 17 healthcare facilities nationwide.

Utilized Gant charts to open locations within strict timelines.

→ Worked closely with computer programmers to create new menu items and perform beta testing on a proprietary system; effectively trained end-users in all system operations.

→ Trained and developed Regional Managers, Office Managers and PRCs in front-office operations.

→ Created and implemented front-office policies and procedures, as well as monthly financial reports.

→ Supervised up to six employees, including scheduling performance reviews and terminations.

Obstetricians - Gyn, P.C., Omaha, NE   1979-1988

Clinical Supervisor - LPN

Effectively hired, trained, scheduled and evaluated up to seven nurses supporting 10 physicians.

Updated the policy and procedure manual and maintained optimal patient flow.

Oversaw OB-Gyn diagnostic procedures and interfaced with physicians, an administrator and other medical staff at all levels.

→ Conducted/facilitated Continuing Education Units (CEUs) for clinical staff.

EDUCATION: College of DuPage, Glen Ellyn, IL   1998-Present

Communications

Metro Tech Community College, Omaha, NE   1984

Completed courses in **Management / Supervision**

Southeast Community College, Fairbury, NE   1973-1974

Licensed Practical Nurse (LPN)

Sent 20; received two interviews

BETH PLUSH

2398 Willow Lane
Bloomingdale, IL 60108

Res.: 630/555-7665
Ofc.: 312/555-2160

HUMAN RESOURCES / BENEFITS ADMINISTRATION

PROFILE:

➢ Comprehensive experience in human resource procedures and operations, including full responsibility for staff orientation and benefits administration.

➢ Skilled in the management of department systems and procedures for claims processing, benefit payouts, payroll, billing, and full COBRA processing.

➢ Effectively recruit, hire, and train staff and management for multiple locations.

➢ Work closely with managers regarding hiring decisions and procedures related to worker discipline, terminations, and various state and federal regulations.

EXPERIENCE:

Zachary's, Inc., Chicago, IL   12/81-Present
Employment / Benefits Manager
Responsible for virtually all benefit and employee matters in support of more than 800 employees at numerous locations nationwide.
Directly supervise two employees in all HR functions, including benefits and payroll.
Update and maintain personnel and benefit files for all workers nationwide.
Instrumental in consolidating benefit packages for all employees.
Handle extensive recruiting and advertising; write job descriptions and handle resume screening, initial interviews and communications with hiring managers.
Personally counsel employees as required regarding job performance; conduct exit interviews as required.
Oversee the processing of all company unemployment claims and represent the company in unemployment hearings.

→ Work closely with managers and advise them on hiring decisions, discipline, terminations and correct HR procedures.
→ Processed wage assignments, garnishments and IRS levies.
→ Coordinated with managers to evaluate jobs and create job descriptions in a special wage and salary project.
→ Administer all benefit programs for life, health, dental, insurance and 401 (K) profit sharing plans.
→ Formerly in charge of all COBRA functions.

BETH PLUSH

→ Oversee all leaves of absence in accordance with FMLA standards.
→ Updated the performance and salary review procedure.
→ Directed the conversion to a new health insurance provider for more than 500 employees.
→ Managed the conversion to new 401(K) profit-sharing plans.
→ Planned and conducted orientation sessions with staff and managers to explain new benefit programs.
→ Formerly responsible for processing worker's compensation claims.
→ Promoted to this position from:

Assistant Training Director   5/83-10/86
Conducted group and individual training in sales at many Chicagoland locations.
Researched, wrote and developed a company newsletter, including photography and story writing about company events and exceptional staff.

→ Personally trained first-line retail supervisors.
→ Promoted from:

Personnel Secretary   12/81-5/83
Gained experience in HR procedures, including employee tracking, file updating and status reporting.

COMPUTER SKILLS: Familiar with Windows and MS Office, including MS Word and Excel.

EDUCATION: Southern Illinois University, Carbondale, IL
B.S. Degree

PERSONAL: Chairman: the American Cancer Society Bike-A-Thon, 1983-1987.

Coordinator for the Crusade of Mercy.

Sent 10; received 10 interviews.

Lana Norris

22567 Welland Court
Roselle, IL 60172
630/555-7330

OPERATIONS / MANAGEMENT

PROFILE:

> Comprehensive experience in new business development, staffing and total project management, including cost analysis and reduction for successful operations.

> Skilled in the management of multiple locations, including the setup and improvement of departments, systems and procedures.

> Effectively hire, train and supervise staff and managers in personal customer service, sales presentations, product lines and company policies.

> Plan and implement budgets and forecasts to increase profits, reduce payroll and improve customer satisfaction.

> Utilize in-house databases and computer systems including Windows, Amisys, Access, Accel, MS Word and Internet resources for spreadsheets, status reports and correspondence.

EMPLOYMENT:

<u>Health Plans of Illinois</u>, Chicago, IL   2/96-Present
Director: Claims and Enrollment
Effectively manage claims and enrollment departments, including organizing and delegating jobs and hiring, training and monitoring a front-line and processing staff of 11.
Determine and meet specific department goals; conduct regular staff evaluations and motivate all team members for high-quality work and prompt turnaround.
Instrumental in planning and implementing virtually all department and company policies and procedures with the company president, CEO and CFO.
Perform detailed analysis of statistics and trends for improved quality and excellent cost control.
Coordinate third party liability and re-insurance reimbursements.

→ Increased membership from zero to 30,000 through effective staff training, precise documentation and attention to detail.
→ As Operational Interface: work closely with IS department staff to evaluate and maintain the mainframe computer and update configurations as needed.
→ Assisted in configuring the Amisys database and computer system; worked closely with programmers and trained staff in effective use.
→ Earned regular bonuses for reaching financial goals.

<u>New City Life</u>, currently owned by Aetna, Oak Brook, IL   9/94-9/95
Account Service Representative
Provided total support to ten service staff in customer enrollment and claim submissions for multi-product and multi-site clients.

151

Handled extensive communications with providers.
Worked closely with clients to resolve service issues, including claims
utilization and the reporting of medical care activity.
Gained an excellent knowledge of claims, insurance codes and procedures.
Performed proofreading and correcting of certificates of coverage.
→   Effective in servicing more than 3500 lives.

<u>Euclid Managers, Inc.</u>, Elmhurst, IL   9/94-9/95
Marketing Representative
Responsible for the marketing and sale of group health products, primarily to
brokers.
Developed sales leads and conducted presentations for lines including United
Healthcare, Blue Cross/Blue Shield and Delta Dental.
Negotiated rates with brokers; conducted enrollment meetings and provided
creative ideas for marketing and advertising.
→   Chairperson: Continuing Education for the DuPage Chapter of the
      National Association of Health Underwriters.

<u>Share Health Plan of Illinois</u>, Itasca, IL   7/87-9/94
and United Health Care of Illinois
PPO Coordinator   1991-1994
Established the PPO Customer Service Department, including the training and
supervision of all customer service staff.
Created and implemented all department policies and procedures.
Provided extensive training and support of groups and individuals.
→   Member of a breakout group that streamlined ER claim processing
      procedures; greatly improved accuracy and processing efficiency.
→   Analyzed and improved claim processing procedures as member of the
      Continuous Quality Improvement Committee.

Claims Liaison   1989-1991
Acted as liaison between claims and customer service departments.
Provided research and resolution of claim issues.
Developed and streamlined procedures to implement claim tracking and
processing efficiency.

Customer Service Representative   1987-1989
Answered incoming HMO calls and educated customers on benefits and
procedures.

<u>Sony Corporation of America</u>, Itasca, IL   5/85-7/87
Accounts Receivable / Adjustments

Mailed 100 over two months; received 12 interviews and accepted a new job. He checked/used Yahoo to find cost of living differences in various states: http://verticals.yahoo.com/cities/results/compare.html

MARCUS SELLER
21167 Garry #108
Bloomingdale, IL 60108
630/555-7524

INTERNATIONAL SALES / MARKETING

PROFILE:

➢ Proven abilities in sales and product development, including profitable domestic and international experience, market penetration, and total account management.

➢ Skilled in complete sales program planning, as well as account acquisition and competitive analysis, especially for industrial and technical product lines.

➢ Plan and conduct sales presentations for senior-level clients; design sales proposals and price quotes; perform new product introduction and personal client development.

➢ Extensive contacts worldwide with vendors, suppliers, major manufacturers, and distributor networks; lived in several European and Asian countries; familiar with French and Japanese.

➢ Skilled in AS/400, Netscape Navigator, Microsoft Outlook, and Corel WordPerfect for account tracking and updating, spreadsheet analysis, and sales forecasting.

EXPERIENCE:

The Hester Group, Chicago, IL   1996-Present
Account Executive - International Sales
Responsible for the promotion and sale of exhibit space around the world, primarily to major U.S. and Canadian industrial firms.
Handle relationship sales and business development with a focus on more than 400 manufacturers.
Utilize a solid background in construction and other industrial equipment, markets, and business trends.
Exhibitions are held in Europe, Singapore, China, Mexico, and Argentina.
→ Set sales records for the World of Concrete in Asia, 1997.
→ Constantly update and maintain account information for timely, accurate account follow-up.

Illini Products, Chicago, IL   1994-1996
Sales Representative
Effectively marketed and sold a variety of construction equipment and power plants, including gas and diesel engines and generator sets.
Implemented promotions and performed all aspects of lead development and account management, including needs analysis for numerous accounts throughout Illinois and Indiana.
Created and implemented custom sales proposals, pricing, and contracts to expand clients' profitability.

Key accounts included: United Airlines, American Airlines, and numerous OEMs.

Sold product lines from: Kohler, Deutz, Ford, Lister Petter, and Gillette.

Travel Agents International, St. Louis, MO   1986-1994
President / Owner
Directed the setup and operation of this full-service company, including all staffing, procedures, and operations.
Oversaw sales and customer service functions on a daily basis.
Hired, trained, and supervised a team of 25 in sales, order processing, and troubleshooting with tact and a personal approach.
Gained experience with a wide range of cruises, tours, hotels, rental cars, and corporate travel.
→   Ranked in the top 15% of 350 agencies every year.
→   Established the first of 6 agencies in the St. Louis area.
→   Introduced a unique cost-savings program to St. Louis.

Caterpillar, Inc., Peoria, IL   1962-1985
Management: Sales, Marketing, and Advertising
Responsible for a wide range of duties in various positions, including business expansion through effective promotions, advertising, and media relations.
Sold all major products, including construction equipment, diesel engines, transmissions, and generator sets.
Markets included construction, mining, industrial, logging, power generation, and marine.
Trained and motivated sales staff in field sales, forecasting, account tracking, and product introduction.
Lived and worked in Switzerland, Singapore, the Philippines, and Japan.
Gained an excellent knowledge of Caterpillar distributors.
→   Introduced several new products, including one that captured more than 50% of the U.S. market.
→   Lowered costs by $1 million by eliminating unnecessary attachments.
→   Managed a highly successful national sales motivation program, resulting in sales exceeding budget by 30% and $30 million.

EDUCATION: Rensselaer Polytechnic Institute, Troy, NY
B.S. Degree: Management Engineering
Minor: Civil Engineering

St. Lawrence University, Canton, NY
B.S. Degree: Liberal Arts

E-mailed (only) to about 200 companies; received 12 interviews.
I mentioned he should also do regular research and mailings!

MELVIN BOWERS

777 West Lake Street
Plainfield, IL 60544

Res: 815/555-7021   chai.com@world.att.net   Cell: 312/555-6148

INTERNATIONAL BUSINESS / OPERATIONS

PROFILE:

➢ Comprehensive experience in new business development, startup operations, and project management, including full P&L responsibility for marketing, staffing, and procedures.

➢ Skilled in hiring, training, and motivating sales teams in technical product lines; perform market research, strategic planning, creative product development, and key account management.

➢ International experience in joint venture administration, market development, contract negotiations, and financial analysis; fluent in English, Arabic, and French.

➢ Well-versed in import/export procedures and foreign business practices and customs.

➢ Proficient in cost reduction and business analysis to reduce fraud and theft; oversee security procedures with a knowledge of government and product regulations.

EXPERIENCE:

Fraizer Board of Investigators, New York, NY   5/93-Present
Specialist
Conducted corporate investigations and analyzed/reduced theft and fraud; reported findings, and made recommendations to top management to quickly solve security problems.
Performed risk management and conducted investigations of a wide range of business transactions.
Supervised a team of five and answered internal inquiries, managed risk and protected valuable assets.
Organized investigations with various law enforcement agencies and reviewed/improved workflow and procedures.

→ Analyzed and evaluated technical intelligence for the FBI, including threats and hostile acts affecting national security.
→ Reduced a backlog of various cases to zero.
→ Was granted Top Secret security clearance and utilized state-of-the-art, sensitive equipment and information.
→ Certified by the Department of Justice in Arabic (Fluent in all Arabic dialects).

International Management Information Services, Paris, France   3/87-4/93
International Marketing Manager
Personally established the entire sales function, including staff hiring, training, and supervision for software sales.
Conducted market research and top-level sales presentations.

MELVIN BOWERS

Performed extensive research and test-marketed, packaged, and sold OCTIMIS, an eight-module software package.
→ Successfully negotiated joint ventures with corporate America and greatly expanded markets in the Middle East.
→ Personally acquired key accounts such as Timex and IBM.
→ Successfully increased revenues by 45%.
→ Assigned as the exclusive representative for the U.S. headquarters in Langley, VA.

Banque de Participation et de Placement (BPP), Paris, France   5/86-3/87
International Business Consultant
Conducted extensive research and determined potential for overseas expansion for this international bank.
Performed research and compiled/wrote detailed analyses of 15 countries, with an emphasis on real estate, tourism, and import/export potential.
→ Personally identified markets and potential office sites.
→ Directed the opening of a BPP branch in Libreville, Gabon.
→ Determined profitable investment alternatives in Europe and the U.S.

International Business Consultant, Langley, VA   6/84-4/86
On an independent basis, researched and wrote credit reports on four African and Middle Eastern nations using World Bank and International Monetary Fund (IMF) criteria, resulting in the grant or denial of aid or loans.
Coordinated and directed major international media events with local media and public relations firms.
→ Planned and supervised international conferences in the U.S., including the INTERPOL conference in Washington, DC in 1985.
→ Conducted international teleconferences in Arabic, French, and English on key business issues involving European, African, and Middle Eastern nations.
→ Conference work was supervised by the CACI and local PR firms.

**PRIOR
EXPERIENCE:**   Radio-Television Morocco / RTM, Morocco
Associate TV Director / Editor-in-Chief
Interviewed numerous government officials and VIPs for nationwide broadcast.
Covered local, national, and UN events.

EDUCATION: University of Hartford, CT
MBA Degree   1982
Granted a USAID scholarship to the U.S.
Computer systems: familiar with Windows 98, 95, and 3.1, as well as MS Word 97; knowledge of Web page design and various word processing software.
Completed various software consulting courses covering SAP and Lawson.

Didn't mail any: e-mailed about 250; received 20 interviews.

MICHAEL Z. STEVENSON
776 White Court
San Ramon, IL 64583

Stevie@bell.net   925/555-4250

DOMESTIC / INTERNATIONAL FACILITIES MANAGEMENT

PROFILE:

➤ Skilled in total project management, including plant design, facilities specifications, new construction, and vendor/contractor relations; negotiate contracts and manage multi-million dollar budgets for complex projects.

➤ Creatively manage the implementation of energy conservation systems for central energy center. Reduction of chillers' online hours and cost of operations. Improved cooling efficiency of all A/C systems. Produced savings in energy for reheat boiler operation.

➤ Managed large campus facilities, as well as multiple country sites and real estate leases for sales offices. Directed millions of s.f. of T.I. changes, upgrades, and conversions.

➤ Comprehensive experience in manufacturing operations, including full responsibility for new startups of products and facilities, staffing, and cost control for high-tech product lines.

FACILITIES MANAGEMENT EXPERIENCE:

<u>O'Dell International</u>, Poedunk, IL   1990-1992
Project Manager: Facilities Design and Construction
Reported to the President of this $1 billion international computer manufacturing company.
Effectively controlled costs for two construction sites through close scrutiny of contractors, architects, and design engineers, as well as vendor relations and quality oversight.

* Reduced construction costs by 40% at a site in Germany by conducting a total redesign of factory floor layouts and functional areas of a 150,000 ft² plan.
* Full responsibility for a $26 million design and construction budget.
* Analyzed facilities and managed all construction for a 100,000 ft² project in the Philippines.
* Defined requirements for electrical, mechanical, and architectural layouts.
* Selected and managed installation of diesel generators for back-up power.

<u>Memorex / Sys Corp.</u>, Santa Clara, CA   1985-1987
Director of Facilities
In charge of all facilities for this $5 billion manufacturer of mainframe computer disk drives.
Responsible for 2.5 million ft² of facilities (18 buildings).
Managed a $6.5 million capital budget and an annual operating budget of $22.4 million.
Directed daily plant maintenance, including grounds, janitorial, electrical, HVAC, clean rooms, DI water, solid waste, fire sprinkler, central energy plant, and emergency power/UPS systems.
Researched/performed all space planning, layouts, and the remodeling of buildings.

* Coordinated all facility engineering for factories in Mexico, Canada, and Singapore.
* Selected sites for regional sales offices, including design and lease-hold improvements.
* Directed site selection and the setup of a 150,000 ft² facility in Singapore.

Corus System, Inc., San Jose, CA   1982–1985
Director of Corporate Facilities and Security
Initially designed and managed the construction of a 30,000 ft² factory for disk-drive assembly in Oregon. Executed total project responsibility for contractor selection and procurement of capital equipment. Managed daily plant safety and security, plus facility engineering and maintenance.
* Managed the installation and qualified all manufacturing process equipment.
* Promoted in one year and relocated to San Jose.
* Directed the layout of a new 225,000 ft² facility in San Jose.
* Provided floor plans to architects, defined HVAC and electrical loads to contractors for a "build-to-suit" complex. As Construction Project Manager, maintained daily on-site inspections to monitor all "build-to-suit" tenant requirements.
* Assisted in relocating more than 500 people from six buildings.

MANUFACTURING MANAGEMENT EXPERIENCE:

Infant Advantage, Inc., San Ramon, CA   1997–1999
Director of Operations
Directed a new start-up product into volume manufacturing, from product re-design to prototyping and high-volume production.
Personally hired, trained, developed, and managed a technical and support team.
Directed the installation and configuration/establishment of a full MPR-order fulfillment system.
Managed all functions in various departments, including Design Engineering, Materials, Contract Manufacturing, Document Control, and Quality Control.
* Directed the total redesign of the product, greatly improving robustness and quality; reduced RMA's by 75%.
* Researched and selected an offshore manufacturing vendor and directed the prototyping and preparations of documentation and tooling for the transfer of manufacturing to China.

Read-Rite Corporation, Milpitas, CA   1992–1997
Director of Manufacturing
Specifically chosen to create a new group for the manufacturing of Thin Film MR tape recording heads at this $800 million disk drive recording head company.
Recruited and hired a team of designers and engineers to move a product from R&D labs into production.
Successfully transferred all processes to a China contract manufacturer for high volume.
* Conducted all planning and execution for rapid-process development and tool designs.
* Managed staff and procedures in various departments, including Engineering Tool Design and Drafting, Manufacturing, Manufacturing Engineers, Quality Control, Material Control, and Document Control.
* Performed fast-track tooling and directed prototype acceptance.
* Provided full process documentation for tools and all assembly processes.

Applied Magnetics Corporation, Goleta, CA   1988–1990
Director of Operations
Recruited to join this $600 million magnetic recording head manufacturer.
In charge of manufacturing configuration, scheduling, and quality for ferrite recording heads.
* Developed cost-effective processes for manufacturing operations in Korean factories.
* Completed extensive training and performed detailed documentation and process transfers.
* Developed and improved yields through cost-effective process changes.

<u>Seagate Technology</u>, Campbell, CA   1987-1988
Director of Operations
Created a new division to develop and prototype mini-composite recording heads; successfully transferred all operations to Thailand.
Personally recruited, hired all technical/support staff and management.
Designed and built a laboratory facility, including equipment selection, tooling, jig setup, and development of manufacturing processes.
Effectively managed the daily operations of Engineering, Administration, Facilities, Materials, and Manufacturing departments.

* Conducted competitive analysis and handled extensive vendor research and selection/ negotiations.
* Gained full product qualification and acceptance for profitable production.
* Provided full documentation and tool design, while controlling the start-up budget.

PRIOR
EXPERIENCE:
    Project Engineer: 3M: Minnesota Mining and Manufacturing
    Manufacturing Manager: National Semiconductor

EDUCATION:
    <u>California Polytechnic University</u>, San Luis Obispo, CA
    Bachelor of Science, Industrial Engineering
    Minor in Electrical and Electronics

TRAINING &
CERTIFICATION:
    <u>University of California</u> at Santa Barbara
    Hazardous Materials Management Certificate, currently half complete.

    SPC Certificate and Gage Capability; TQM; JIT training;
    LTP: Licensed Tax Preparer (H&R Block), 1990
    Federal and California State Personal Tax Preparation
    Memberships: ASTME; AIIE; SPIE; SQE
    Skilled in computer systems including MS Windows, Excel, Word, PowerPoint, and Project.

DISTINCTIONS:
    Highest achievement of "Programs for Profit" (two years) Commendation for "Outstanding Performance."

Sent 10; received two interviews in first two weeks.

SAMUEL REDHEAD
925 Fox Court
Gaithersburg, MD 20882
Residence: 301/555-8621   Business: 202/555-8197   E-mail: samhed@nas.com

_____

INVESTOR RELATIONS
Director or Vice President

PROFILE: Comprehensive senior-level experience in investor and media relations management, specializing in global capital markets, stock market structures, and trade policies, in fast-paced, rapidly changing environments.

➢ Advise CEOs, CFOs, directors, senior management, and clients on industry issues and emerging trends; formulate strategies for best ROI on institutional and individual client investments in the Nasdaq-Amex stock markets.

➢ Partner with top management on consulting services to European, Eastern European, African, and Asian government agencies for solid investments in U.S. markets; skilled in client needs assessment, risk management, media/public relations, and financial services.

➢ Recruit and mobilize cross-functional high performance teams; effectively explain technical, complex matters in understandable terms at all levels; company spokesperson featured in the national press, global trade journals, and newspapers.

➢ Utilize Bloomberg, Nasdaq NWII, FactSet, dBase/Foxpro, MS Access, Lotus, MS Excel, MS Word, WordPerfect, ISQL, and various graphics packages; well-versed in Internet technologies and implications.

CAREER BACKGROUND:

The Investment Group, HQ, Washington, DC   **1992-Present**
Manager and Spokesperson, Media Relations   4/97-Present
In charge of all aspects of media relations, including investment relations programs, for the largest stock market worldwide, specializing in policy and technical issues, with P&L responsibility for public information.
⇨ Media spokesperson on policy and market issues.
⇨ Formulate responses to inquiries on such matters as the market making system, trading rules and systems, and the economics of markets.
⇨ Compile and provide financial, statistical, and trend analyses to internal and external constituents.
⇨ Prepare press releases on market, firm, and technology issues; hold media and company briefings.
⇨ Meet regularly with international dignitaries to discuss salient features of an efficient capital market, capital formation, and trading systems during the process of restructuring domestic capital market infrastructures.
⇨ *Current Special Assignment*: Interim Director, The Amex Stock Exchange New York office.

Market Analyst, Nasdaq International, London, United Kingdom   7/95-10/96
Recruited to restructure and develop the infrastructure and personnel of this international headquarters.
⇨ Trained marketing staff on stock market functions, theories, and practices.
⇨ Consulted prospective new issuers on requirements and options for raising capital on U.S. markets.
⇨ Liaison to investment banks and consultants; coordinated "road shows" and director visits.

⇨ Prepared and edited marketing material for non-U.S. marketing initiatives.

⇨ Wrote and presented reports to current and prospective equity investors; produced country economic reports.

⇨ Handled international journalist inquiries relating to all aspects of capital markets.

⇨ *Contributing and economics editor:* Nasdaq International Magazine, read by over 2,000 institutional investors, CEOs, and CFOs.

Research Analyst, Economic Research and Strategic Planning, Washington, DC   8/93-6/95

Conducted research to improve market quality, such as spreads and volatility.

⇨ Monitored market information for Securities and Exchange Commission filings.

⇨ Served as Nasdaq contact for the FIBV, JASDAQ, and Tokyo Stock Exchange.

⇨ Responded to data requests and information inquiries from the Media Relations Department.

⇨ Represented Nasdaq at numerous academic conferences, including the *Journal of Finance* conference.

Research Associate   9/92-8/93

Researched and analyzed studies related to the securities markets.

⇨ *Team Leader:* produced a monthly Nasdaq statistics manual for executive management.

TRT/FTC Communications, Washington, DC   1990-1992

Financial/Revenue Analyst   4/90-9/92

Analyzed and modified proposed customer agreements with investments up to $50,000 per contract for this $400 million telecommunications firm.

⇨ Negotiated customer agreement discount structures and investments with regional managers.

⇨ Processed commission discounts for each account and salesperson on a quarterly basis.

⇨ Hired as **Financial Analyst**, 8/90-4/91.

The Aries Corporation, Arlington, VA   1990

Research Assistant

Assisted this management consulting firm and the Big 8 accounting firms with proposal preparation for World Bank, Asian Development Bank, and Agency for International Development projects.

EDUCATION:

    George Washington University, Washington, DC

    Master of Business Administration

    Concentration: International Finance

    University of Maryland, College Park, MD

    Bachelor of Arts Degree: Finance

Used one resume as requested for an interview through headhunter; declined the job offer.

James T. Wannamaker
77732 Club Court
Plymouth, MI 48170
734/555-9355

EXECUTIVE MANAGEMENT: MARKETING - SALES - TECHNOLOGY

PROFILE:
- Comprehensive corporate management experience. Focus efforts toward marketing and sales development, organizational/infrastructure development, financial planning, and developing staff and managers.

- Skilled in market development through effective business plan development, "selling" the product, market share acquisition, and profitability.

- Demonstrated practice of "Challenging the paradigms of normalcy." Today's electronic market still has explosive growth potential. Market leadership requires aggressive and extraordinary strategies, commitment to longevity, results-oriented management teams, and unequaled customer relations.

- Strong background in "taking the product to market" by developing product exposure and recognition, distribution and sales channel development, product/company image, and product flow logistics. Also experienced in Japanese and Matrix management methods.

- Prior experience in product design, development, and manufacturing processes.

ACHIEVEMENT SUMMARY:

<u>Optrex LCD Corporation, U.S. Operations:</u> Successful and fortunate in taking this company from sales of $29 million to $252 million in seven years. Created infrastructure from the ground up and increased market share from 7% to 22%, and profitability from negative to a robust condition, 1991-1999. Motivated management team to create "family" culture internally and philosophy of "relationship" selling towards customer.

<u>Hitachi LCD/CRT Division:</u> Joined this division in 1988 with mission of penetrating the computer industry leaders. Created a special task force to improve harmony and create a competitive spirit. Increased sales from $17 million to $27 million by 1991.

<u>Hitachi Semiconductor Division:</u> Core objective was to grow "Micro-Computer Sales" while developing national application engineering infrastructure, customer strategy, and a team-oriented culture.

EXPERIENCE:

<u>Elia America, Inc.,</u> Division of Ali Glass, the world's largest LCD manufacturer.

Director: Sales/Marketing Operations   1992-Present

Directly responsible for all sales and marketing activity in North and South America, MIS, Purchasing, and material operations. Excellent management team of 5 senior managers.

* Team achieved a six-year period of 50% annual growth.
* Increased market penetration from 7% to 22%.
* Implemented a "culture" of relationship-selling.
* Bridged a strong understanding/relation between American and Japanese staff; virtually eliminated culture barriers and created a single team.
* Implemented an MBO structure and bonus reward system in a results-oriented management team.

---

* Developed a U.S. based, value-added production operation to:
  1. Reduce dependency on financial support from the parent company.
  2. Establish an unmatched market advantage.
  3. Set up a U.S. based "Design Center."

Hitachi America, Chicago, IL   1988-1992
Division Engineering Manager - Electronic Display Division
Managed up to 17 sales/technical staff and managers, as well as all aspects of technical marketing
and application engineering.
Created a special task force and regained this division's market position.
Realigned market focus, narrowed the customer base and focused on major OEMs.
* Achieved 60% budget growth for this division over three years.
* Planned and implemented current U.S. sales and engineering structures.
* Supervised a design center and QC laboratory.
* Implemented a more effective distribution program in conjunction with sister divisions.
* Created a QC tracking and early warning system.
* Developed a technical service center for this division.
* Initiated the use of satellites for a worldwide design center communications program.

Hitachi Semiconductor Division responsibilities:
National Application Engineering Manager - San Jose, CA   1986-1988
Directed tactical field activity for this division's strategic account base.
Acted as liaison to a Japan-based design center.
Involved in LSI Architectural development for a four- and eight-bit product family.
* Indirectly responsible for custom/semi-custom LSI sales budget of $8 million/month.
* Developed a national engineering program and centralized management functions.
* Created a technical training program and MBO career development programs.
* Developed a strategic business plan for a new 16-bit microfamily through beta level.
Regional Engineering Manager - Dearborn, MI   1985-1986
Responsible for all aspects of regional sales engineering, including objectives, budgets, personnel
planning, bonus structures, and territory assignments.
* Established strategies for a custom LSI growth plan and achieved budget expansion from
  $2.5 million to $3.5 million/month.
Application Engineering Specialist - Dearborn, MI   1984-1985
Designated microprocessor application specialist to GM, Ford, and Chrysler corporations.

Ford Motor Company, Electronics Division, Dearborn, MI
Product Design Engineer - Electronic Instrumentation   1981-1984
Senior Test Engineer - Electronic Systems Engineering   1978-1981
Product Development Engineer   1976-1978
Product Design Engineer   1974-1976

EDUCATION: Oklahoma State University, Stillwater, OK
                        B.S. Degree: Electronic Engineering   1972

ARNOLD JABBER

5467 Whiteside Drive
Hanover Park, IL 60103

630/555-5456
lord@world.net

MATERIALS MANAGEMENT

PROFILE:

➢ Comprehensive experience in logistics and materials planning, including full P&L responsibility for special projects and Distribution Requirements Planning (DRP) in manufacturing environments.

➢ Coordinate new product introductions and design/implement custom MRP, inventory and forecasting systems.

➢ Effectively hire, train and supervise staff and management in freight routing, distribution, inventory control, and warehouse operations.

EXPERIENCE:

<u>Apex Photo Film USA, Inc.</u>, Snapper, IL

Materials Planning and Logistics   1992-Present

Manage more than 8,000 SKUs and virtually all MRP and logistics, including sales forecasting and DRP with production staff.
In charge of multiple complex projects; negotiate contracts with vendors and suppliers, including all major freight carriers.
Perform cost-effective purchasing of OEM products, packing materials and capital equipment.
Coordinate new product introductions with manufacturing managers.
Conduct group and individual training of staff and supervisors in logistics and company procedures.
Authorize purchase agreements with numerous vendors.
Utilize Windows applications including MS Word, Excel, PowerPoint and a custom inventory system.

→ Increased inventory turns by 400% and reduced months-on-hand from 2.7 to 1.5.
→ Reduced monthly inventory from $30 million/month to $20 million, while sales grew 22%.
→ Instrumental in developing and implementing a custom MRP and forecasting system.

Inventory Control Manager for Distribution   1988-1991

Trained and supervised staff in a warehouse management system, including physical inventories and freight claim processing.

Distribution Supervisor   1986-1988

Supervised a team of four and wrote/expedited freight bills.
Gained excellent experience in distribution operations.

EDUCATION:

<u>W.R. Harper College</u>, Palatine, IL

A.A. Degree in Business

Certificate in Materials Management

MEMBERSHIP:

APICS: Association of Production and Inventory Control Society
since 1992.

Sent 30; received four interviews and a new job.

SINATRA FRANCIS

5634 Passer Drive
San Pedro, CA 90732

710/555-5303
Swinger@alumedu.net

OBJECTIVE:

Management Consulting - Business/Technology
An entry-level position utilizing analytical and quantitative abilities in team building, communications, organization, and strategic planning.

PROFILE:

- Highly skilled in project supervision, multimedia presentations, information technology, report generation, technical research, and team participation.
- Coordinate a wide variety of team projects, including database management and the formulation of quantitative/analytical engineering models for applications in the medical, space, and aircraft design industries.
- Effectively plan and conduct technical presentations in a professional manner for executive audiences; research and produce articles and reports for publication.
- Consistently recognized by executive management and colleagues for cross-discipline talents in needs analysis, troubleshooting, and problem resolution in high-pressure technical environments.

TECHNICAL BACKGROUND:

➢ Knowledge of Windows 98/NT, UNIX, DOS, BASIC, Pascal, HTML, MS Office, FrameMaker, and Internet applications.
➢ Familiar with AutoCAD, Pro/ENGINEER, I-DEAS, Maple, Mathematica, and programming with MATLAB (SIMULINK, Nonlinear Identification Toolkit, Image Processing Toolbox).
➢ Currently hold an Engineer-in-Training license #XE093436 through the California Department of Consumer Affairs since 1994.

EMPLOYMENT:

Bolton Hospital, Boston, MA   1996-1998
Bioengineering Research Assistant
Responsible for project consulting with an interdisciplinary team tasked with studying applications between mechanical engineering and cardiopulmonary physiology.
Worked closely with doctoral biomedical engineers, medical staff, and physicists in data collection, analysis, and solution generation.

→ Team-led the development of new methodologies for analyses of a variety of medical data per Positron Emission Tomography (PET) applications.
→ Personally drove a project to develop a mathematical model to analyze PET data; quantitatively tracked gas exchange in lungs using PET medical images.
→ Efficiently partnered with team members in over 72 full-day PET experiments, along with generation of collaboratory protocols and procedures.
→ Key participant in 10 major bioengineering projects, as well as author of two papers presented during conferences of the American Thoracic Society and Biomedical Engineering Society from 1997-1999.
→ Also submitted original research for publication in four different biomedical engineering and medical journals.

Rockwell Space Systems Division, Downey, CA   1995-1996
Technical Assistant

Key participant with senior engineers in the dynamic/structural analyses of current/advanced versions of Space Shuttle payloads during on-orbit flight phases.

Served as a co-author for many detailed in-house reports for tracking and monitoring project activity.

→ Revised and updated spreadsheet programs for quantifying and summarizing on-orbit loads for U.S. shuttle missions with the Russian Space Station, "Mir."

C&D Interiors, Inc., Huntington Beach, CA   1994-1995
Intern

Tasked with a case study involving the testing of miniature honeycomb panel sandwich structures for mechanical strength and flammability properties for aircraft applications.

→ Recommended numerous modifications to select better materials, meet specifications, and enhance redesign efforts.

→ Created and updated a searchable database to collate and analyze test results.

EDUCATION:

Massachusetts Institute of Technology, Cambridge, MA   1998
M.S. Degree in Mechanical Engineering; GPA: 4.2/5.0.

→ Researched and wrote a thesis in bioengineering titled, "Quantification of Regional Perfusion, Shunt Fraction and Ventilation Using Positron Emission Tomography: A Nonlinear Tracer Kinetics Model."

→ Vice President of Young Alumni with the MIT Club of Southern California.

Loyola Marymount University, Los Angeles, CA   1995
B.S. Degree in Mechanical Engineering; Cum Laude, GPA: 3.7/4.0; Dean's List five of eight semesters.

→ Completed several engineering projects involving mechanical and automotive applications.

→ Recognized as 1995 LMU Outstanding Graduate in Mechanical Engineering; 1995 LMU Senior Mechanical Engineering Student of the Year; and 1994 LMU Junior Mechanical Engineering Student of the Year.

→ Member of several key honorary societies, such as Tau Beta Pi, and listed in *Who's Who Among Students in American Universities and Colleges.*

ASSOCIATIONS:

American Society of Mechanical Engineers.

Society of Automotive Engineers.

Sent 200 through e-mail only; received 10 interviews and a new job.

Mohammed Fighter
23899 Blue Ocean
Columbia, MD 21045

ali@hotmail.com   *443/555-5267*

PRODUCTION OPERATIONS / MANAGEMENT

PROFILE:

➢ Comprehensive experience in production operations, including full responsibility for production line setup and streamlining, quality control, staffing, and budgets.

➢ Strong knowledge of ISO 9002, MRP, JIT, TQM, planning and logistics; coordinate job schedules, vendor relations, and handle cost-effective purchasing and inventory control.

➢ Utilize Excel for spreadsheet development, graphs, charts, and data diagrams; coordinate budgets and forecasts, and compile/present status reports for senior-level personnel.

➢ Effectively hire, train, and supervise technical staff and production teams, including job scheduling, performance reviews, and motivation.

EMPLOYMENT: Sumner Computer Corporation, Inc., Baltimore, MD   1998-Present
Production / Technical Manager
Responsible for the setup and operation of complete, turnkey production lines for the manufacture of high-end personal computer systems sold by major national accounts.
Utilize state-of-the-art systems and procedures for product assembly, testing, and packaging.
In charge of ISO-9002 certification for all activities.
Effectively manage all production activities for the cost-effective assembly of more than 250 PCs per day, ranging from simple desktop systems to complex servers.
Manage various production supervisors, engineers, technicians, and line teams.
Supervise in-house development and training programs for all categories of production staff.
Plan and prepare concise, detailed production schedules.
Develop master schedules to establish sequence and lead times for each operation and meet strict shipping dates, according to sales forecasts and customer orders.
Establish sequence of assembly, installation, and other manufacturing operations to guide production teams.
Expedite operations to cut delays and constantly update schedules to meet unforeseen conditions.

→ Daily production turnover has increased from $50,000 to $300,000.

→ This is the largest national manufacturer of whitebox computers for major national accounts, such as Lockheed Martin.

→ Constantly analyze production specifications and plant capacity data to determine manufacturing processes, tools, and human resource requirements.

→ Plan and schedule workflow for various divisions according to established manufacturing and lead times.

→ Prepare budgets and production/accounting reports.

→ Maintain excellent quality and quantity of products at minimal cost.

→ Effectively led the production team to meet initiatives in quality and cycle time.

<u>Ace Computer Systems Limited</u>, Kaduna, Nigeria   1995-1998
Technical / Plant Manager
Planned and established a complete, state-of-the-art production line for manufacturing personal computers.
Managed all assembly processes for more than 50 PCs per day.
Trained and supervised a successful team of technicians and assemblers.

→ Managed technical staff providing support in the Customer Service department.

→ Improved productivity by 100% over a period of 6 months through more effective management.

<u>Construction +Engineering Contract, AG</u>, Wiesbaden, Germany
Hardware Engineer   1994-1995
Updated and maintained all the computer hardware for the company's subsidiary: Dentate & Sawoe Construction company in Nigeria.
Diagnosed and repaired all types of hardware and software related problems for over 800 PCs.

→ Trained numerous technicians in preventive maintenance processes.

<u>Lilleker Brothers Limited</u>, Belfast, Northern Ireland
Electrical Engineer   1993-1994
Supervised electrical and telecommunication installation works in various projects executed by Lilleker Brothers Limited in Nigeria.

EDUCATION: <u>Ahmadu Bello University</u>, Zaria, Nigeria
Bachelor of Engineering   1994
Major: Electrical Engineering
Specialization: Electronics and Communication

<u>University Of London</u>, London, England
General Certificate of Education   1988

Extensive training in:
Network Cabling Systems, NT administration, Advanced PC Maintenance, C-programming, Visual Basic Programming, and MS Office.

Sent about 200 via mail and e-mail: received 20 interviews.

Lester E. Square

7771 Ashfield Court
Bloomingdale, IL 60108

mer@aol.com

Res: 630/555-0279
Cell: 630/555-0724

CONSULTING / MANUFACTURING

PROFILE:

> Comprehensive experience in high-tech manufacturing and turnaround operations, including full P&L responsibility for product development from concept to international marketing.

> Perform detailed business analysis for acquisitions and high-tech system streamlining; utilize TQM, ISO 9000, and Six Sigma concepts.

> Skilled in long- and short-term strategic planning, budgeting, forecasting and product sourcing, and pricing with extensive contacts worldwide, especially Thailand; knowledge of the Thai language and Asian business customs.

> Effectively hire, train, and supervise technical staff and management in product design, retooling, production, quality control, marketing, and sales.

> Conduct top-level presentations and negotiate contracts in a professional manner.

EXPERIENCE:

Top Die Casting, Ltd., Bangkok, Thailand   1998-Present
Director of Engineering
Responsible for the turnaround of this company, a major supplier to Seagate Technology, with $40 million in sales.
Conduct in-depth research to locate and transfer technologies used by 2300 employees, producing die castings, including actuators and base plates.
Directly supervise a team of 80.
Utilize a solid background in procedures, including precision machining, composite insert molding, and metallurgy.
Work closely with design engineers in the development of prototypes.
Directed and improved all sales and marketing efforts as the number one advisor to the company principal.

* Expanded the key client base from one to four through research and sales efforts, thus saving this company.

* Utilized an extensive knowledge of Seagate Technology products and business techniques developed with that company, 1990-1994.

* Directed all retooling and production line setup, from vendor sourcing and cost-effective purchasing of parts and machinery to staff and management training.

* Refocused efforts from micro-management to highly successful teamwork, motivation, and job ownership-from line workers to management.

Lester **E. S**quare   **Page Two**

Concise Industries, Elk Grove Village, IL   1995-1998
Director of R&D/Sales and **Operations Manager**
In charge of research and development of cellular manufacturing in support of
a turnkey program for Caterpillar.
Directed total manufacturing operations for sheet metal assemblies and climate
controlled enclosures for the telecommunications industry.
*   Managed a wide range of business interests for the company owner, in-
       cluding cash transactions and contract negotiations.
*   This was a privately owned company with several business interests.

Seagate Technology, Scotts Valley, CA   1990-1995
Senior Materials Manager / Vendor Quality
Conducted extensive research of vendors and suppliers, including their prices,
operations, and capacity.
Worked directly with design engineers to ensure profitable, large-scale production.
Trained suppliers in effective communications to meet Seagate requirements and
improve speed and profitability.
*   Established systems to better respond to critical supply issues worldwide.

MDA Thailand, Ltd., Bangkok, Thailand   Contract: 3/90-12/90
Managing Director
In charge of the Thailand facility of a U.S.-based company, producing machined
castings and fine-blanked components for the disk drive industry.
Directed a team of five managers, while creating and implementing training for
150 production personnel.
Trained office staff in communications with foreign suppliers.
*   Analyzed and improved procurement procedures.
*   Greatly reduced monetary waste while leveling spending to match sales
       volume.

Precision Founders, Inc., San Leandro, CA   1982-1990
International Market and Finished Parts Manager
Managed an entire offshore program for this manufacturer of aerospace equip-
ment, computer peripherals, and high-tech investment castings with gross an-
nual sales of $32 million.
*   Increased output of international sector from $2.8 million to $10 million
       in 18 months.

PRIOR
EXPERIENCE: 1973-1982:
                       Sales Representative: Sold high-tech equipment and tools to various industries.
                       Tool and Patternmaker: Created wood and metal patterns from drawings.

EDUCATION: Indiana University, Purdue University at Indianapolis, Indianapolis, IN
                       Completed 12 hours in Effective Business courses.

                       Metals Engineering Institute, Indianapolis, IN
                       Completed 30 hours in Metallurgy.

Sent 40 and received 10 interviews.

SALLY M. BOND
2266 Metto Court
Naperville, IL 60540

007@gte.net   630/555-4880

MARKETING / PRODUCT DEVELOPMENT AND MANAGEMENT

PROFILE:

- Effectively manage product marketing to commercial customers with P&L responsibility; plan annual marketing strategies and implement programs, including advertising and sales promotion components; build distributor and end-user sales.

- Conduct primary market research and surveys, perform data analysis and assess customer specifications and requirements. Prepare sales proposals and presentations for clients and staff.

- Create sales materials and coordinate trade shows. Work effectively with advertising agencies and develop direct mail programs targeting end-user markets.

- Manage communications with the sales force and act as marketing liaison between field sales and corporate staff. Assist with formal sales training.

- Knowledge of various PC and Apple systems, including MS Works, MS Word, ACT!, Lotus 1-2-3, Freelance, WordStar and WordPerfect.

EMPLOYMENT:

Breamer Marketing, Oakbrook Terrace, IL   1/93–Present
Account Executive
Responsible for promoting the *Target Trak* and *Volume Trak* market reporting service to foodservice manufacturers through direct sales.
Provide support in client service and verify foodservice distributor cost data and product information.
→ Developed a strong knowledge of competing food and non-food products, used in creating new sales and marketing strategies.

Elmhurst Management Service, Elmhurst, IL   1/92-1/93
Contract Associate
As Independent Market Consultant, performed in-depth professional interviews, data analysis and primary research for organizations marketing to industrial/ commercial customers, including assessing client customer product quality requirements.

Kellogg Sales Company, Franklin Park, IL   4/90-11/91
Foodservice Division Product Manager
Managed the marketing of Kellogg's Eggo Waffles and Mrs. Smith's Pies to commercial customers with P&L responsibility. Planned annual marketing strategy. Implemented marketing programs including advertising and sales promotion components. Built incremental distributor and end-user sales. Researched and developed tactical and strategic market plans and conducted sales training.

Managed market communications and acted as liaison between field sales and corporate staff regarding marketing programs, sales issues and customer service.

Piggybacked on successful retail Special-K Waffle market and targeted the school/healthcare commercial/institutional market segments where low fat content is significant. Worked with the American Dietetic Association to get professional approval of the low-fat designation. Developed a consumer preference brochure to market consumer category Eggos to institutional and commercial foodservice operators. Designed direct mail campaigns targeted towards healthcare and commercial/institutional market segments.

→ Developed the *Eggo School Backpack* promotion for school foodservice.

→ Achieved 20% sales growth through targeted promotions; secured improved awareness in brand target markets.

→ Responsible for winning a state-awarded bid for 24,000 cases.

Orval Kent Food Company, Wheeling, IL
Marketing Manager, New Products   11/88-4/90
Assistant Marketing Manager   7/87-11/88
Productively managed, planned and implemented new product introductions of refrigerated prepared salads and entrees. Facilitated new product development and influenced decisions on pricing, packaging and logistics. Effected in-house media buying, planning and expenditure tracking; coordinated packaging graphics development and administered a multi-account budget. Implemented packaging changes for company's 100+ product line, including branded, private-label and distributor-label products, marketed to commercial end-users and consumers.

Alyn Darnay Productions,Inc., Chicago, IL   7/86-7/87
Marketing Consultant
Developed strategic marketing plans through compilation and analysis of primary and secondary research data. Researched consumer groups.

Mandabach & Simms, Inc., Chicago, IL   8/84-8/85
Assistant Media Planner
Implemented media buying and planning for 13 national marketing organizations at this advertising and public relations firm. Supervised media cost estimating staff.

EDUCATION: Northwestern University, Evanston, IL   Graduated 1986
Master of Science in Advertising

University of Illinois, Urbana, IL
Bachelor of Science in Advertising   Graduated 1984
Earned 51 hours toward undeclared second major in **Modern German Studies.**

In only the first week: sent 20 to recruiting firms; received one interview and compliments on the resume.

Darlene D. Mitchell

997 Stratford #27

Bloomingdale, IL 60108

Yeow@aol.com   630/555-1216

MANAGEMENT / OPERATIONS

PROFILE:

> Comprehensive experience in new business development and team leadership, including P&L responsibility for new startups, procedures, and operations.

> Skilled in the direction of creative marketing, advertising, and sales; handle product sourcing, vendor relations, and competitive analysis to meet rapidly changing trends in U.S. and Canadian markets.

> Highly proficient in change management, including staff and management hiring, training, and supervision in sales, direct customer service, and product lines; strong knowledge of HR procedures and regulations.

> Proven ability to greatly increase sales through team motivation and leadership at multiple locations; oversee budgets, forecasts, purchasing, and inventories.

> Plan and conduct written and oral presentations for senior-level staff and management on topics including Franklin Time Management and new sales/customer service techniques.

CAREER BACKGROUND:

Zachary Studio, Inc., U.S. and Canadian locations

District Manager - Chicago, IL   1997-Present

Responsible for five middle managers and all aspects of market expansion, staffing, procedures, and operations streamlining.

Current project includes site selection/acquisition and a major venture with Venture Corporation.

Closely analyze profit potential of new locations, including sales figures of previous vendors.

Utilize a knowledge of Canadian and U.S. laws related to new startups, taxes and licensing, and human resources issues.

Manage 20 portrait studios throughout Illinois, Wisconsin, and Iowa, including hiring and indirectly supervising a team of 100.

Coordinate creative functions and distribution for promotions and advertising, including direct mail.

Constantly analyze and control operating costs through vendor negotiations and effective purchasing.

◆ Effectively train and develop managers in sales, photographic, and acquisition departments.

◆ Handle a wide range of public relations issues.

◆ Managed the opening of a new division: "Pix Venture Portrait Studios." Opened 28 new portrait studios in Venture stores; performed detailed market and demographic research to ensure high profitability.

- Responsible for successfully "selling" the idea of a price increase for portrait services to senior executives.
- Instrumental in eliminating non-profitable telemarketing operations, resulting in major cost-savings.

Area Manager, Burlington, Ontario, Canada   1995-1997
Supervised two managers and the entire Canadian division of this company, including 24 studios in Ontario.
Indirectly managed six to eight employees at each location, including interpretation of HR regulations and issues.
- Directed all aspects of business development for photographic sales and marketing departments at the studio level.

Regional Sales Director - Special Project   1996-1997
Implemented a new portrait product, including profitable pricing structures.
Developed sales techniques and trained floor staff in them through professional meetings and presentations in Canada, New England, Pittsburgh, and the Midwest.

District Marketing Supervisor, Burlington, Canada   1994-1995
Performed general management, including staff hiring and training in all telemarketing procedures.
Researched and implemented a new telemarketing system in marketing units in Canada and New York State, including scripts, dialing procedures, and personal communications with potential customers.

Area Marketing Supervisor, Chatham and Burton, Canada   1991-1994
Managed 14-20 telephone sales rooms, including all staff training and development in sales and supervision.
- Met or exceeded quotas on a regular basis.
- Achieved a 54% increase in Club Plan sales in 1991 over 1990, and reduced the cost per unit sold by $4.93.

Area Appointment Supervisor, Chatham, Canada   1990-1991
In charge of training, developing, and supervising outbound appointment and customer service offices in 20 stores throughout Ontario.

Photographer and Photographic Trainer, Chatham, Ontario   1988-1990
Promoted from Studio Photographer to Photographic Trainer.
- Became a Certified Photographic Trainer in the first year.

Certified to conduct 12 management sessions through the Zenger-Miller program.

Sent about 95; received 12 interviews.

CRAIG G. BUEHLER

2116 Lawson Drive
Horsham, PA 19044

215/555-8829
Craig@aol.com

MANAGEMENT / MARKETING

PROFILE:

▶ Comprehensive experience in new business development, including creative strategic planning, marketing, and effective product management.

▶ Direct competitive analysis activities, niche marketing, and research; develop product pricing strategies and mix to quickly respond to market trends and expand profitability.

▶ Coordinate budget planning and sales forecasting; familiar with tools including MS Office word processing, Excel for spreadsheets, PowerPoint presentation software, and Access database software.

▶ Plan and conduct detailed presentations for sales and marketing staff; oversee RFPs, sales promotions, product development, packaging, and delivery.

▶ Oversee the hiring, training, and supervision of staff and management; supervise the writing and development of training programs and manuals, as well as technical documentation.

CAREER BACKGROUND:

BT&T, Various locations.
District Manager, Marketing Services - Bridgewater, NJ   1995-1998
Effectively hired, trained, and supervised a team of nine analysts in the design and execution of product pricing strategies.
Directed extensive research of competitor's products, services and prices to improve BT&T's position, market receptiveness, revenue growth, and profits.
Constantly analyzed and updated the product mix to remain competitive in both wholesale and retail voice and data services.
Identified and developed markets by customer size, then introduced new services to effectively compete.
Utilized decision support data to determine revenue and sales impacts of potential actions, providing marketing and sales with clear alternatives by which to achieve objectives.

▷ Increased revenues 7% and conversation minutes by 11%, thereby exceeding all 1996 and 1997 financial objectives.
▷ Successful in lowering costs by eliminating outdated service offers.
▷ Greatly increased productivity by implementing simplified rate structures; exceeded initial sales forecasts by 300%.
▷ Personally developed winning strategies for customer-specific contract tariff pricing, with a win rate 20% higher than BT&T's market share.
▷ Created strategies that increased revenues by initiating rate revisions on imbedded services, while expanding the growth of lead service offers.

CRAIG G. BUEHLER   Page Two

Product Manager – Westminster, NJ   1993-1995
Responsible for P&L and all functions of initial inbound/outbound service offers (the UniPlan).
Trained and supervised a team of three in all procedures.
Established a front-end process for feedback on sales performance; balanced real-time feedback to quickly augment features, price, and sales proposals.
Designed and implemented new service concepts, including all aspects of prompt development and delivery.
Established a service lifecycle management model, ensuring constant strengthening of new service offers and the elimination of mature services.

> Improved customer segment market share by 10%; developed flexible point-of-sale pricing and contract terms, along with enhanced ordering systems.
> Exceeded P&L targets by delivering the UniPlan service offer in half the expected time, while providing clear direction to the sales channel.

Staff Manager, Wholesale Market Strategy - Basking Ridge, NJ   1990-1993
Conducted extensive research of wholesale markets, products, and prices.
Effectively developed and ensured the implementation of BT&T's wholesale market strategy.
Performed detailed writing and communications for the sales force, outlining sales techniques related to the reselling of minutes and reacting effectively to wholesalers' proposals.

> Revamped credit policies and reduced wholesales market-aged receivables balance by 23 days and bad debt to 17%.
> Restructured the indirect sales agent program to align better with business unit objectives.

Region Director, Region Sales Staff - Morristown, NJ   1987-1990
Directed a full range of staff functions to correctly respond to complex network and equipment RFPs; won $225 million in annual revenue.
Personally managed customer user group relations and the development, packaging, delivery, and execution of national equipment and network sales promotions.

Staff Manager, Technical Marketing - Denver, CO   1983-1987
Researched and wrote technical sales documents on the operation and use of Bell Labs-designed PBXs, voice mail systems, and central office switches. This greatly expanded GT&T's technical marketing knowledge on these topics.

Bell Atlantic, Charleston, WV, and Washington, DC   1970-1983
Promoted from Account Executive to Sales Recruiter and Technical Consultant
Chosen as the #1 Bell System Technical Marketing Consultant in the Country.

EDUCATION: West Virginia State College
                      B.S. Degree: Administration / Marketing

Sent 10; received two interviews.

Samuel D. Sosa

8236 Sleepy Hollow Road
Roscoe, IL 61073
Homer@aol.com   815/555-8109

VICE PRESIDENT: SALES / MARKETING

PROFILE:

> ➤ Executive experience in sales, production, operations, and administration in the baking industry, including P&L responsibility for new startups and business development.

> ➤ Profit-building skills in account penetration, market introduction, and product R&D; manage and/or perform market research, strategic planning, and product pull-through with key corporate clients.

> ➤ Effective leadership skills in hiring, training, supervising, and motivating staff and management teams in lead development, target marketing, account acquisition, and top-level sales presentations.

> ➤ Coordinate systems, procedures, and product lines for maximum profitability, even in slow-growth industries; handle cost-effective purchasing and contract negotiations.

> ➤ Manage budgets, forecasting, and production; utilize Windows, MS Word, PowerPoint and Excel for spreadsheets, correspondence, and financial reporting.

EXPERIENCE:

Banner Ingredients, Inc., Beloit, WI
Director of Sales: Bakery Division - Hillsdale, MI   1/96-Present
As key corporate representative, responsible for new business development through effective market research, strategic planning, product introductions, and promotions.
Train and supervise a team of eight account managers in territories nationwide, focusing on increasing volume and driving the business with an emphasis on wholesale and in-store sales of bakery products, such as mixes, bases, and concentrates.
Directly involved in product R&D and coordinating plant operations to match customer demands.
→ Profit before tax has increased more than 10% in each of the last three years, in a traditionally slow-growth industry.
→ Expanded baking mix sales from 160 million pounds in 1997 to 200 million pounds in 1999.
→ Key accounts have included Best Foods (Entar's), Sammy Lee, Mets, Powers Industries, and Internal Bakeries Corporation (IBC).

Account Manager - DCA Bakery Division   8/94-1/96
Directed the creative promotion, marketing, and sale of bakery mixes, bases, concentrates, fillings, icings, toppings, and equipment to wholesale, retail, and in-store bakeries in the Mid-Atlantic region.

Samuel D. Sosa

Maintained, established, and expanded numerous large accounts for this custom blending company.

→ Increased sales in an under-performing region 50%.

→ Established higher-margin business and a solid account base.

→ Worked directly with product R&D teams to quickly and accurately meet changing customer needs.

Colonial Rich Foods, Inc., Doylestown, PA

Director: Fund-raising Sales 1993-1994

Personally created and established all infrastructure for a new division of this food distributor.

Created and developed sales and marketing concepts.

→ Established a highly profitable growth division.

→ Directly responsible for bottom-line profits and all sales and marketing functions.

CWV, Inc., t/a Rilling's Bakery, Philadelphia, PA

Chief Executive Officer 1989-1993

In charge of re-directing the company focus to wholesale markets, developing an 80/20 wholesale/retail sales mix.

Developed sales teams and successful relationships with supermarket chains, wholesale clubs, major airlines, prisons, and institutions, as well as wholesale bakeries (private label) and contract manufacturing.

→ Managed all sales, marketing, and customer relations for all major accounts.

President 1986-1989

Directed company growth from $1 million to $4 million.

→ Expanded units to nine locations.

→ Retail and wholesale business was added, to account for 30% of sales.

Controller 1984-1985

Supervised general accounting, including AP and AR, for this multi-unit bakery. Planned and directed construction of a 20,000 s.f. baking facility.

→ Managed financial activities, including bank financing and state/city industrial financing.

EDUCATION:

The American Institute of Baking, Manhattan, KS

Certificate: Baking Science and Technology 1982

Resident Course, Class #121

* Graduated #8 of 70.

The Pennsylvania State University, State College, PA

B.S. Degree: Science and Marketing

PERSONAL:

As an avid golfer, thoroughly enjoy business golf and customer interaction. Assistant Coach: baseball and soccer. Assistant Scout Master, Troop 620, BSA.

Sent 185; received 12 interviews.

ELMER FERGUSON
9907 Eagle's Landing
San Antonio, TX 89732-4027

fergie@onr.com

Res: 210/555-5568

OBJECTIVE: A management position where strengths in leading and motivating people, developing promotional programs and strategic plans, and accomplishing company objectives may be utilized.

PROFILE:

➤ Extensive experience in the consumer products industry, managing and motivating personnel to accomplish sales and marketing objectives. Develop and manage budgets and forecasts, identify market opportunities, analyze activities, formulate corrective action, and generally manage organizations. Skilled in developing and implementing sales and promotional plans adapted to the needs of varying markets. Additional skills in staffing, training, and supervising brokers, field staff, and managers in market development.

EXPERIENCE:

Caroline's, Fairfield, IA — 1995-Present
Vice President: Sales & Marketing
National sales responsibility for Kiosk and Internet programs, working with mid-level and executive management of manufacturers and retailers.

* Grew retailer participation to 1400+ stores in 13 months.
* Plan, develop, and implement sales presentations for in-store kiosks.
* Negotiate with retailers to implement meal planning programs.

National C-Net, San Antonio, TX — 1986-1995
President
Total responsibility for forming, staffing, planning, and implementing activities of the organization on a national basis.

* Obtained representation responsibility to the C-store industry nationwide for Heinz, Sunshine, Lever Brothers, and McCormick, plus several smaller firms.
* Grew sales to $30 million over a five-year period, taking the organization from regional to national activities.
* Formed, directed and trained a dedicated C-store sales team from 62 broker offices and branches.
* Effectively increased Heinz distribution by 640+ items in three years, and Sunshine by 1300+ in four years.
* Successfully introduced a new beverage line that generated $5 million in sales during the first year.

ELMER FERGUSON
Page Two

Beatrice Prepared Foods Division, Chicago, IL   1981-1986
National Sales Manager
Complete responsibility for Gebhart, Rosarita, and La Choy brands. Marketing responsibility for Mexican category to all trade classes. Private label development in special cases. Managed a team of three Division Managers and 12 Regional Managers.
* Consolidated, with no loss in volume, three separate divisions, thus cutting expenses and improving overall coverage.
* Increased sales of total firm by 18% in the last three years.
* Designed and implemented a new sales forecasting system to ensure product availability for major promotions.

Vlasic Foods, Inc., Detroit, MI   1975-1981
Division Manager
Total responsibility for Midwest and mid-central market sales development, managing a team of six regional managers and 37 brokers.
* Increased division sales from $16 million to $85 million in four years.
* Developed the first broker evaluation system for the company, resulting in more effective broker motivation.
* Designed and implemented a new promotional planning procedure and effectively managed inventory and marketing funds.

PRIOR EXPERIENCE:

Gillette Toiletries Company, Boston, MA
Assistant to Regional Manager
Recruited and trained all new sales personnel for the Eastern Region, and worked with District Managers to continue developing veteran sales personnel.
* Promoted from Territory Representative after two years in the field in Texas and Michigan territories.
* Generated a 46% increase in Texas in six months.
* Grew the Detroit territory by 23% in less than two years.

EDUCATION: Northwestern University, Evanston, IL
Attended the Beatrice Executive MBA Program, implemented for Senior Managers and Executives. Participated in three annual workshops.

Texas Tech University, Lubbock, TX
Bachelor's Degree: History Major, English Minor

Sir George Williams College, Montreal, P.Q.
Completed one year with courses in Business, History, and English.

Dale Carnegie Sales Course, Professional Selling Skills.

Used only one resume; received interview and accepted a new position.

Morris G. Father

3302 Keys Road
Elgin, IL 60120
630/555-0061

MORTGAGE BANKING

PROFILE:

◈ Comprehensive experience in new business development, including responsibility for special promotions, marketing, and strategic planning.

◈ Skilled in diversification and the development of broker and/or correspondence relationships in multiple states, with a proven ability to increase volume and profits.

◈ Effectively hire, train, and supervise staff in account acquisition, primarily through networking and personal relationships.

◈ Determine systems, controls, and credit criteria, while ensuring compliance; coordinate underwriting and reporting procedures.

CAREER BACKGROUND:

<u>Just Stuff, Division of Western Bank</u>, Irvine, CA
Regional Sales Manager - Elgin, IL   2/98-Present
In charge of hiring and supervising up to 22 account executives, primarily acquiring broker-originated B&C product.
Personally train and coordinate sales staff in multiple states in accordance with business plans and volume goals.
Constantly analyze competitors' rates, products, services, and marketing techniques.
Maintain a high degree of speed, accuracy, and service between brokers and underwriting personnel.
Provide recommendations to update our programs to expand profits while minimizing risk.
Involved in all phases of program development and reporting on market status, including competitors' rates and services.
Coordinate underwriting and reporting procedures, as well as broker selection.

- Currently on target to meet staffing and volume goals by end of the first quarter.
- Developing an extensive network of correspondent flow product.

<u>Access Financial Corporation</u>, St. Louis Park, MN
National Sales Manager   5/97-1/98
Trained and supervised sales teams and planned and implemented strategies to diversify in broker and retail products.

- Promoted to this position from:

Account Executive   5/94-5/97
Fully responsible for business development in the midwest region, as this company's first Account Executive.
Constantly exceeded all goals for monthly volume and new account acquisition.
Developed loans from correspondent sources, comprised of forward commitments, bulks, and flow product.

- Developed in excess of $450 million in 1997.

Morris G. Father

Household Bank, Prospect Heights, IL
Vice President: Consumer Division 1989-1992
Successfully developed a national home improvement financing program for contractors.

Involved in all phases of implementing the home improvement financing program, ensured compliance and established underwriting criteria, forms, and contractor selection criteria.

Responsible for hiring, training, scheduling, and directing all sales personnel in account prospecting, sales presentations, and customer service.

Designed and implemented a national financing program for mortgage brokers.

Involved in all phases of program development, including the analysis and reporting on market status, competitor's rates, products, services, and marketing strategies.

Maintain a high degree of speed, accuracy, and service between brokers and underwriting personnel.

Provide recommendations to update our programs to expand profits while minimizing risk.

- Programs were initiated in Illinois and eventually expanded nationwide.
- Responsible for originating the purchase of mini bulks up to $25 million.
- Programs were implemented in less than 10 months, and well under budget.
- Volume goals were exceeded in the first year and this division turned profitable in the first eight months.
- Personally earned the maximum bonuses available in the first year: 80 percent of base salary.

Dartmouth Plan, Garden City, NY
Vice President: Secondary Marketing 1984-1989
Effectively developed and maintained strong working relationships with financial institutions seeking to purchase bulk portfolios of home improvement or home equity loans.

- Developed new sources, who committed between $1 million and $15 million in monthly fundings.

Insured Credit Services, Division of Republic Insurance Company, Chicago, IL
Senior Vice President and Director of Underwriting 1971-1984
In charge of all underwriting and business development, including supervision of up to 20 Underwriters.

This company specialized in providing credit loss insurance to financial institutions.

EDUCATION: Southern Illinois University and
Elmhurst College: Various business courses.

American Banker's Association: Completed various courses in banking.
Member of the National Home Equity Mortgage Association and numerous State Mortgage Broker/Banker Associations. Member: National Remodeler's Association.

Sent four; received two interviews.

Irving Texan
444 W 844 Temple Drive
Medinah, TX 60157

gbbs@ameritech.net   Res.: 630/555-4041   Message and Fax: 630/555-9312

NETWORK ENGINEERING

PROFILE:

➜ Comprehensive experience in network design, installation and troubleshooting, including full responsibility for special projects and team supervision.

➜ **Certified Netware Engineer;** manage research and development for customized systems; coordinate vendors and suppliers, negotiate contracts and oversee cost-effective hardware and software purchasing.

➜ Skilled in Y2K troubleshooting; experience with data acquisition equipment, sales automation, national surveys, infrastructure, remote access and customized e-mail systems.

➜ Perform detailed needs analysis and establish and implement hardware, software and platform standards. Experience in a wide range of systems listed on page two, along with prior positions.

EXPERIENCE: <u>Capers Manufacturing, Inc.</u>, Chicago, IL   10/95-Present
Director of Desktop Technologies
Responsible for full project management and all Network duties for a 700-node, 45-server LAN environment, including full system research, configuration and installation.
Train and supervise a team of four, while overseeing network operations in 10 countries.
Install and configure all OEM and specialty software packages.
Supervise the group responsible for research and determine desktop hardware and software standards for the global enterprise network, including but not limited to: laptop and desktop computers, palm top computers, printers, plotters, scanners, digitizers, LCD monitors, LCD projectors, faxes and combination technologies.
Perform network backups and maintain NDS tree design and a bindery database.
Supply third level technical support for the help desk and Papers' product support centers.

⇨ Developed and implemented a Sales Automation system using laptop computers, including infrastructure design and remote access; this was a highly successful $250,000 project, *outlined below.*

⇨ Act as Project Manager for various enterprise-wide software and hardware upgrades.

⇨ Effectively research, set up and maintain industry specific hardware and software for data acquisition processes.

⇨ Supervise teams in Desktop Technology, R&D and Papers customer technical support, as well as the entire R&D center.

⇨ Promoted to this position from Help Desk Technician.

Irving Texan
Page Two

Sales Automation Project: Laptop Infrastructure
Upgraded the entire laptop infrastructure, including extensive research, analysis and purchasing of systems used worldwide.
Increased systems from 55 to 200; connectivity now includes remote e-mail, full network and remote access to all application software.
Developed a network of support for end-users and supervised two employees. Conducted extensive research of numerous brands and established all procedures for ordering, repairing, upgrading and refurbishing laptops. Personally developed the standard base software package and hardware specifications. The standard now includes full remote access to network resources, including printing, files, e-mail and shared directory services.

⇨ With a budget of $250,000, this project was completed on time at a cost of only $220,000, spread through several different departments and general ledgers.

⇨ Expanded global coverage of the Capers sales force by more than 50%.

⇨ Stabilized and standardized the system in place to order, maintain, support and expand the laptop base owned byCPapers.

⇨ Developed a strong committed vendor/customer relationship between Fujitsu and Capers; became a full global business partner with Fujitsu, placed on a PO system for all service, sales and support, resulting in a direct, yet global support structure.

P.C. Products and Services, Inc., Roselle, IL   9/91-10/95
Senior Supervising Technician promoted from **Bench Technician**
Bench technician repairing and troubleshooting printers, monitors and PCs. Software troubleshooting and technical support both via telephone and in person. Order and maintain general and specialty supply inventory, product analysis, product usage decisions, personnel scheduling and training for six technicians, warranty paper work for IBM, Compaq, Panasonic, Okidata, Citizen and Star.

Radio Shack, Tandy Corporation, Inc., Elgin, IL   7/88-8/91
Assistant Manager promoted from **Sale Associate**
District resource person for general electronics technical support, general sales, order, inventory and P&L refinement.

MEMBERSHIPS: MCP, CNE, CNA, ICSA, NUI (Novell Users International), Membership IBM Warranty repair certified for laptops and PCs through the Aptiva line Compaq Warranty repair certified A+ Certified Windows 95 certified Full CNE track course attended.

Irving Texan
Page Three

Hardware setup and maintenance experience:
Exabyte Tape robot.
Hewlett Packard Netservers E, Net pro, LC3, LH and LX series servers.
HP Jet Direct cards and boxes.
HP DeskJets all model series.
HP LaserJet 2 through 4L, 4000, 6000, 5si and 5 Color; Hewlett Packard
Design Jet all series plotters.
Motorola bit surfer ISDN modems.
NEC, Fujitsu, Toshiba, IBM, Compaq laptops.
Compaq; Dell; IBM; Gateway 2000; and Clone PCs.
Nematron Data acquisition modules, General Electric Data acquisition
modules.

Network topologies and hardware:
Ethernet, 10baset UTP, 10 and 100 Megabit Hubs, Intelligent Hubs, Switches:
NICS from 3COM, Intel, Xircom, Linksys, Madge, Boca and D-Link.

Operating Systems:
Microsoft DOS 2.0 through 6.22; MS Windows 2.0 through 3.11; Windows
for Workgroups 3.1, 3.11; Windows 95 OSR1, 95 OSR2 and 98; Windows NT
Workstation: 3.1, 3.5, 3.51, 4.0; OS2 2.0 and 2.1.

NOS:
Novell Netware 3.12, 4.11 and Intranetware 4.11 - Install and Configure
Microsoft Networking Microsoft Windows NT Server 3.51, 4.0 - Basic
knowledge only Lantastic NOS.

Network and Groupware:
Exchange client; MS mail client; Castell Faxpress hardware and software; IBM
5250 emulation software using Rumba; WRQ Terminal Emulator Reflection 1,
Versions 4, 5, 5.1 and 5.21; Symantec antivirus for Netware and Windows NT;
Support Magic Enterprise edition V.4.00.0; Seagate Software Winstall;
Bitshare modem pool software; Arcserve V.6.0; Softrack Software tracking;
Adaptecs Smart CD writer; Hewlett Packard's Sure Stor CD writer.

OEM and Specialty Applications
Stairs Financial tracking and reporting system.
Dun & Bradstreet financial tracking and reporting system.
Shot Scope data acquisition software.
Mattek data acquisition software.
Production Process and OPM data acquisition software.
Demand Solutions for DOS and Windows.
Data Streams MP2 Maintenance tracking software Enterprise edition and
Access edition.

Sent about 50; received seven interviews.

LANSING D. CIRCUIT
2281 Papa Court
Carol Stream, IL 60188

kessel@flash.net   630/555-9432

NETWORK ADMINISTRATION

PROFILE:

➢ Skilled in full system design, network administration and operations, including successful installation, troubleshooting and management.

➢ Effectively configure, install and maintain LANS and Windows NT systems, including full documentation; skilled in building, installing and troubleshooting PCs and peripherals, including printers, as well as cabling and routing.

➢ Train and supervise technical and service staff; handle customer relations and written/oral presentations in a professional manner.

➢ Well-versed in TCP/IP; utilize Windows 3.1, 95, 98, NT, DOS, LANtastic, ISDN, TokenRing NICs; WordPerfect, MS Word 97, Excel 97; familiar with Novell 3.12. LANS: TCP, SPX and NetWare.

EMPLOYMENT: Toptronic, Inc., Chicago, IL   8/97-Present
Field Service Technician - Midwest
Determine specific client needs and install, repair and maintain re-flow ovens and automated re-work stations for printed circuit boards.
Interface with representatives from key accounts such as Motorola, 3Com and Visteon.
Conduct group and individual training for internal staff and end-users.
Involved in escalation from Tier-1 support; work closely with managers, field engineers and application engineers regarding customer issues.
Responsible for a wide range of technical functions, including the setup of Windows 95 as a Peer to Peer NOS; perform software upgrades and install and configure operating systems, including Windows 95/98 and Windows NT.
Effectively design, develop and maintain test platforms, including building test networks and evaluating test procedures and equipment.

→ Offered a Service Manager's position after only one year.
→ Specially selected for trade show presentations and to maintain all software and control systems for Visteon's new prototype oven.
→ Document system installation, configuration and optimization.
→ Determine reliability of single-level piece parts, including testing, verifying, approving and determining which vendors to utilize.

Medical Equipment & Imaging Services, Carol Stream, IL   2/95-Present (PT)
and:
Computer Hardware Engineering, West Chicago, IL   2/93-8/95
Consultant / Technician
Responsible for the setup and operation of these consulting companies, including all procedures, marketing and personal client relations.

Handle component-level troubleshooting of systems ranging from X-ray and therapy equipment to IBM mainframes.

Plan and conduct full system configurations, installations/de-installations and upgrades.

Acted as broker for used IBM equipment and repaired, upgraded and assembled PCs throughout the U.S., Europe, the Middle East and the Pacific Rim.

→ Install small networks and repaired printers and other peripherals.

→ Sell and market all services, including new business development and promotions.

→ Gained proficiency in LAN inter-working, routing protocols, TCP/IP configuration, modem technology, routers, ISDN and LANtastic.

→ Accurately diagnose failures and analyze/solve PCB, ICT and system-level problems.

<u>Datanon, Ltd.</u>, Carol Stream, IL   3/85-2/93
Contract Maintenance
Relocated to the U.S. and performed service contract administration and maintenance at Leggett & Platt, Carthage, MO.

Planned and managed the relocation of L&P's data center, including all daily maintenance and the repair of IBM Data Processing Equipment.

Provided full technical support and trained service engineers on mainframes and peripherals.

→ Upon transfer to Chicago in 1986, directly involved in research and development for upgrade paths on the IBM 3080 series of Mainframe Computers.

→ Performed upgrades at major corporations throughout the U.S., Europe, the Middle East, Africa and the Pacific Rim, primarily on IBM 3080, 3090, ES9000 and 9121 mainframes.

<u>IBM Corporation</u>, Johannesburg, South Africa   10/81-3/85
Senior Computer Engineer promoted from **Computer Engineer / Trainee**
In charge of all equipment repairs and upgrades for the full line of IBM computers and peripherals.

→ Responsible for all hardware in the data centers at South African Airways and the University of Witwatersrand at Johannesburg.

<u>Gilbarco</u>, Alberton, South Africa   2/81-10/81
Field Service Representative
Responsible for timely repair of the first Computerized Fuel Pumps in South Africa.

Assisted in organizing parts repair workshops and field repair service kits.

EDUCATION: <u>Vaal Triangle Technikon</u>, Van Der Bijl Park, South Africa   1980
Successful completion of two years of courses in Electronics.

* Currently studying for MCSE Certification.

PERSONAL: Enjoy scuba diving, outdoor sports, woodworking and home projects.

Sent two resumes; received one interview.

Melville Herman

441 Beer Street
Streamwood, IL 60107

emul@aol.com   630/555-7992

NETWORK OPERATIONS

PROFILE:

➢ Skilled in system design, network administration, and operations, including successful installation, troubleshooting, and management.

➢ Effectively configure, install and maintain LANS/WANS, Routers, and Windows NT systems, including documentation.

➢ Well-versed in TCP/IP, ICMP, and SNMP, as well as UNIX, C, Visual Basic, RAS (Remote Access Servers). and Total Control Hubs.

➢ Utilize Windows 95 and 98, DOS, LANtastic, ISDN, OSI Models, and Token Ring NICs; software includes AutoCAD R14, Visio 5.0, MS Word 97, Excel 97, PowerPoint 97, Lotus Notes 1-2-3, and Novell 3.12.
LAN: CSMA/CD; MAN: TCP, SPX, and NetWare; WAN: IP and RIP routing protocols.

EMPLOYMENT:

Jammen Electric Automation, Inc., Vernon Hills, IL   4/98-Present

QC Test Engineer

Responsible for a wide range of duties, including the design and use of in-house test programs and scripts for prototype products, as well as auto tester and system-level tests.

Personally set up user and group network access accounts; inscribe system test procedures.

Perform software upgrades and install and configure operating systems, including Windows 95/98, UNIX systems, and Windows NT.

Involved in escalation from Tier-1 support; work closely with managers, field engineers and application engineers regarding customer issues.

→ Gained proficiency in LAN/WAN interworking, routing protocols, TCP/IP configuration, remote access servers, modem technology, routers, ISDN, LANtastic, OSI models, and SNMP.

→ Effectively design, develop, and maintain test platforms including building test networks, evaluating test procedures, and testing equipment.

→ Document system installation, configuration, and optimization.

→ Accurately diagnose failures and analyze/solve PCB, ICT, and system-level problems.

→ Determine reliability of single-level piece parts, including testing, verifying, approving, and determining which vendors to utilize.

→ Provide technical support to customers and manufacturing staff; perform internal quality audits.

3Com Corporation, Formerly U.S. Robotics, Mt. Prospect, IL   7/96-4/98

Engineering Associate 3

Installed and maintained more than 20 LAN/WAN networks, including cabling and routing equipment.

Effectively installed and maintained 200-node high speed LAN/WAN networks, including routing equipment for system analysis and configuration.

Involved in the design, development, construction, and laboratory testing of a test station; configured Total Control Hubs, Edge Server pro, and Routers.

Installed and configured network hardware and software for 3Com products.

→ Provided staff training, leadership, and direction to less experienced associates; involved in lab meetings with other departments.

→ Designed and wrote a custom front-user interface, menus, batch files and micros; contributed new ideas for system improvements.

→ Performed extensive testing and debugging related to modems, total control hubs, Gigabit Ethernet, 10Base2, 100BaseT, Token Ring NICs, TCP/IP, Routers, and communication equipment, and analyzed results.

→ Gained an extensive knowledge of 3Com products, T1/E1 cards, Total Control Hub, system configuration, TCP/IP, ICMP, SNMP, R&D lab procedures, and new processes.

<u>Emro Marketing Corporation</u>, Hoffman Estates, IL   4/94-7/96
Assistant Manager
Effectively hired and supervised staff; constantly analyzed and reduced costs while maintaining a high standard of quality customer service.
Provided technical support to customers via telephone and solved higher-level problems.

<u>Silicon Systems</u>, Secunderabad, India   8/90-2/94
Hardware Engineer
Designed and developed RF circuits, including transceivers, oscillators, synthesizers, and filters.
Drafted high-density, multi-layer, mixed through hole and surface mount PCB's for dual refold and wave solder process.
Designed and created hardware specifications; generated engineering change notifications, bills-of-materials, and schematics.
Tracked new product releases and provided accurate and repeatable in-circuit tests of products off the assembly line.

→ Performed board-level debugging using high-speed scopes, multiple trigger space logic analyzers, and other development tools.

→ Worked with Ethernet Token Ring, NIC, asynchronous/synchronous data transmission, 32-bit microprocessors, and 100 mhz power amplifiers.

→ Handled quarterly projects and acted as liaison between engineering, planning vendors, and company personnel.

EDUCATION:

<u>Roosevelt University</u>, Chicago, IL
Master of Science Degree: Telecommunication Engineering.
Expected graduation: 12/99 with a GPA of 3.2/4.0.

* School Project: Set-up an IT department and a 300-node, high-speed LAN/WAN network.

<u>Osmania University</u>, India
Bachelor of Engineering Degree: Dual Major: Electronics and Communication Engineering

* Merit Scholarship from Nizam education and trust for securing First Division in all semesters. Graduated 8/90 with a GPA of 3.62/4.0.

PERSONAL:

U.S. Citizen; willing to travel.

resumes; received four interviews.

SATHER C. ROLL
478 Swell Road, #204
Marietta, GA 30062
cinnamon@pobox.com

Res: 770/555-1290   Cell: 770/555-0243

EXECUTIVE MANAGEMENT / OPERATIONS / CONSULTING

PROFILE:

◈ Comprehensive experience in business development, turnarounds and senior-level operations for multiple locations, including detailed analysis, consulting and the effective management of projects and revenue.

◈ Skilled in conceptual problem-solving in matters related to finance, budgets, revenue management, team building, hands-on leadership and computer system development.

◈ Plan and execute comprehensive plans for successful turnarounds in fast-paced industries; proficient in budget planning, forecasting, detailed performance modeling and financial analysis encompassing performance factors for individual business units.

◈ Human resource experience includes staff and management hiring, training, supervision and motivation; reorganize staff and management into cohesive, motivated teams, including assessment of management structures.

◈ Skilled in spreadsheet development, data processing and major corporate computer system upgrades; utilize Windows 95 and 98, Lotus, Excel, Access, PowerPoint, Outlook, Smartstream and MS Word; familiar with Novell networks.

EXPERIENCE:

Major Car Rental, East Coast Division, Atlanta, GA   11/96-Present
Senior Director of Operations
Promoted as part of a company restructuring, and to improve the P&L of a poorly performing division with more than $200 million in revenues.
Directly manage a staff of 11, indirectly responsible for 1,100.
Design and implement detailed plans to cease operations with a minimum of disruption, including a system to safeguard and redistribute company assets once operations had ceased.
Monitor pricing, reservations and utilization of automobiles to maintain effective fleet levels.
Travel 80% to establish, implement and conduct monthly operational review meetings with all branch managers. Personally provide training in all aspects of operations management, with a focus on how to manage branches to meet business plan goals.

♦ Successfully turned around 1996 divisional losses of more than $10 million to a 1998 profit of more than $10 million; 1998 was the first year this region ever showed a profit and the first time the division exceeded business plan.
♦ Created and directed a corporate task force to limit salvage losses nationwide; directed closing activities for 30 unprofitable locations.
♦ Through April 1999, company salvage losses are on a pace to be $7 million below 1998 losses of $35 million.

♦ Worked closely with each location to develop and oversee the implementation of customized, city-targeted business plans to improve bottom-line performance.

♦ Developed a profitability model used to determine an optimum business paradigm for any location, based on location specific factors.

♦ Responsible for divisional P&L and daily operations, including the design and implementation of strategic and tactical plans to improve all areas of performance.

♦ Devised and implemented yield strategies with the corporate revenue management group to support profitable revenue growth.

♦ Created margin analysis models to determine optimal fleet mix in all locations.

♦ Planned and executed fleet acquisitions and disposals to maximize profitability.

♦ Devised and implemented a new management training program to increase effectiveness of field management.

♦ Created and directed a corporate task force on limiting salvage losses.

♦ Implemented a division-wide field management restructuring process, which included determining staffing needs in all branches, assessing all management staff, and the final disposition of all salaried staff in the branches.

♦ Team leader for Automotive Rental Group Odyssey team responsible for coordinating development of enhanced computerized rental system, revenue tracking and analysis of safety and security issues.

General Manager of Operations, Jacksonville, FL   11/95-10/96
Responsible for P&L, daily management and operational functions for an operation with annual revenues of $7 million, a fleet of 750 vehicles and a staff of 35.
Location's monthly profitability exceeded prior year in 11 of 12 months, even with volume below prior year in most months.
Introduced a new marketing plan for a park-and-fly operation and increased revenues by 50 percent.

♦ Location exceeded profit budget all 12 months.

♦ Location exceeded customer service standard all 12 months.

Divisional Incremental Sales Manager
South Division, Fort Lauderdale, FL   5/95-10/95
Effective in supporting local management efforts in incremental sales in 45 locations in Florida, Texas and the Southeast.
Trained field management in incremental sales (fuel, insurance and upselling to larger cars).

♦ Determined branch sales budgets and monitored performance.

♦ Assisted branch management in day-to-day implementation of strategies to improve incremental sales and customer service.

Corporate Manager
Incremental Sales, Operations Planning, Fort Lauderdale, FL   10/93-4/95
Conceived and implemented programs to improve incremental sales performance in all locations.

Produced forecasts and budgeted incremental sales; closely monitored performance of strategies.

- Acted as Project Leader in a significant upgrade of a company-wide computer-ized rental system to improve performance.

Incremental Sales Manager, Seattle Rental Station, WA   6/92-9/93
Responsible for managing rental counter operations in a location with 40 rental agents.

- Devised and implemented a training program that increased performance and decreased turnover.

Time Critical Freight, Laurel, MD   6/90-12/91
President
Established and managed this distribution company, specializing in next day delivery services in the Washington and Baltimore area.
Performed all marketing, sales and business development.
Coordinated budgets, forecasting and finance functions.

- Selected and installed the company computer system for order entry, tracking, billing, manifests and bills of lading.
- Managed up to 50 employees and sold the company at a profit.

Michael's Courier Service, Chevy Chase, MD   1/81-5/90
Positions of increasing responsibility included:
General Manager, Sales Manager, Salesman, Dispatcher, Messenger
Eventually responsible for a team of 125 in all activities.

- Hired a computer programmer; instrumental in developing an online delivery tracking system using a Novell LAN.

EDUCATION: American Management Institute, Washington, DC   1989
Successful completion of a week-long class in Financial Analysis.

Client Development Institute, Reston, VA   1983
Successful completion of courses in Professional Sales

George Washington University, Washington, DC
M.A. Degree: English Literature   1980
B.A. Degree: English Literature   1979

Sent six targeted resumes; received four interviews and a new job.

Jackson Michaels
223 East View Drive
Bartlett, IL 60103
Jack@netcom.com

Res: 630/555-9223

Cellular: 630/555-8805

SENIOR MANAGER: CLIENT OUTSOURCING

PROFILE:

➤ Comprehensive experience in new business development, including full responsibility for program planning, staffing and highly profitable sales organizations.

➤ Well-versed in LAN and WAN systems, including SNA, frame relay and routed network architectures; coordinate budgets, systems, procedures and technical staff to quickly respond to new technologies.

➤ Effectively hire, train and supervise multiple high-impact sales teams in account acquisition and management.

➤ Skilled in market research, strategic planning and technical product development; handle market penetration and determine and meet specific client needs for technical product lines.

➤ Oversee P&L, successful turnarounds, long-term business growth and high product and service quality standards.

EMPLOYMENT:

All Technology, Inc., Lisle, IL   4/98-Present
National Team Manager
Directly responsible for the sale and implementation of IT management software and solutions for system, data and application management, primarily for productivity enhancement and cost reduction programs to major national accounts such as Sears, IBM and Andersen Consulting.
Personally recruit and motivate product specialists, including all interviewing and training.
Train and supervise a sales team in lead development, custom sales proposals, presentations and key account management.
Work directly with sales staff and clients to closely analyze their business procedures and create customized programs to lower cost and transaction time while expanding profitability.

◆ Projected to exceed annual sales quota of $4.3 million; currently 80% of 1999 quota.

◆ Exceeded 1998 sales quota in the first five months by 86%.

IBE, Schaumburg, IL   8/94-4/98
Project Executive
Directed all P&L and WAN outsourcing operations, primarily using SNA, frame relay and routed network systems.
Performed total project management, including full coordination of technical and sales teams.
Oversaw a team of 97 in sales, product configuration, installations, documentation and troubleshooting.
Developed and supervised delivery teams and prepared environments for ongoing operations.

◆ Specialized in account turnarounds, including detailed needs analysis and custom sales proposals and presentations.

◆ Accurately measured/tracked customer satisfaction and profitability.

- Designed and delivered mission-critical systems for operations at Sears, Zurich Insurance and Allstate.
- Responsible for an IBM business segment valued at $476 million at Allstate.

Digital Equipment Corporation, St. Louis, MO   1987-7/94
Sales Executive
Performed extensive account acquisition and sales, as well as project management for large, complex computer system installations.
Produced sales leads through strategic analysis of markets and industry trends; created and implemented custom sales proposals.
Established contacts and worked directly with top executives at major utilities.

- Reached 193% of targeted budget for FY 1993; exceeded 1994 goal by 200%.
- Designed production systems and custom integration programs to meet critical business needs.
- Earned the Circle of Excellence award in 1992; achieved 800% growth in six months in a single account.

Senior Sales Representative   1987-1991
As Account Manager for the Caterpillar Engine Division, planned and implemented sales campaigns in office automation, analytical analysis, CAD/CAM, quality systems, systems integration and customer services.
Directly involved in strategic committees; gained a detailed knowledge of corporate goals to formulate new applications for goods and services.
Produced highly effective sales campaigns for the engine division.

- Expanded market share from 30% to 65% and revenue growth from $2.8 to $8.1 million per year, FY 1986 vs. 1990.
- Increased consumption of goods and services by more than 50% for three out of four years, 1987-1991.
- Promoted to Sales Executive for strong performance, 1991.

Xerox Corporation, Peoria, IL   1980-1987
Senior Marketing Executive
Personally managed the Caterpillar account for Illinois, working directly with plants to target business opportunities and negotiate agreements.
Directly or indirectly increased sales for 85% of all product lines.

- Consistently promoted for strong sales performance; increases exceeded 140% each year.
- Member of Xerox's PAR/President's Club, 1976-1980.

EDUCATION: Eureka College, Eureka, IL
                  B.A. Degree: Business and Economics   1980
                  Concentrations in Speech, Theater, and Sociology.
                  President: College Alumni Board: 1992-1993; Elected Class President, 1976-1979.

                  Babson College, Wellesley, MA   1991
                  Advanced Consultant Training - Executive Education Program.

PERSONAL: Current board member of the Twinbrook YMCA. Fundraiser for The United Way, The Salvation Army and Eureka College.

Sent 33; received four interviews.

MAXWELL PANTHER
455 Argyle Road
Cheshire, CT 06410

catpeople@snet.net   203/555-3694

MANAGEMENT / OPERATIONS / VP

PROFILE:

➤ Comprehensive experience in new business development and operations management, including full P&L responsibility for capital budgets and sales at multiple locations.

➤ Coordinate a wide range of human resource functions; effectively hire, train and supervise sales staff and management in product lines, lead development, sales presentations and top-level client relations.

➤ Assist in marketing and promotions development, including advertising; skilled in new account acquisition and management, as well as contract and price negotiations.

➤ Skilled in cost-effective purchasing, financial analysis, forecasting and budget administration; negotiate contracts and coordinate major vendors and suppliers; design and utilize spreadsheets, status reports and correspondence using Excel, MS Word and PowerPoint.

EXPERIENCE:

<u>Velvet Fuel Service, Inc.</u>, Waterbury, CT   1988-Present
Gasoline Division Manager
In charge of divisional marketing, operations and the sale of more than 42 million gallons of motor fuel through 14 company facilities and more than 60 independent contractors in Connecticut and Massachusetts.
Train and supervise a team of four in sales and operations.
Indirectly supervise more than 100 for this independent distributor and marketer of gasoline and heating oil.
Perform vendor relations and align customers with suppliers in the setup of new combination convenience stores and gas stations.
Handle all human resource and employment issues for both the gasoline and oil divisions.
Research and write advertising and promotional materials for local media.

▷ Oversee $7 million in c-store sales through 12 company-operated sites.
▷ Coordinate marketing efforts for three brands of gasoline at all 70 locations.
▷ HR functions include troubleshooting for employee relations, including worker discipline, OSHA and government regulations, benefits and workplace issues to improve worker retention and morale.
▷ Personally established a compensation program for managers based on sales and efficiency; greatly improved worker morale and profitability.
▷ Chosen as the primary contact between this company and major oil companies, including retail and wholesale pricing and creative marketing efforts.
▷ Personally developed a new dealer business program, including direct mail, networking, lead development and sales, resulting in 30 new accounts and an increase of 10 million gallons annually, in a highly competitive industry with shrinking markets.

→ Implemented an on-site audio messaging system at gas stations to promote fuel and ancillary products.

<u>Getty Petroleum Corporation</u>, Philadelphia, PA   1982-1988
Regional Marketing Manager
Accepted full P&L responsibility for business development, marketing, and capital budgeting in Eastern Pennsylvania, Southern New Jersey, Maryland and Delaware.
Directed and expanded annual sales exceeding 113 million gallons of motor fuel through 200 retail outlets.
Effectively hired, trained, supervised and developed 14 sales representatives and marketing staff, as well as two field sales managers.
Worked closely with staff and managers in all departments, including legal, personnel, distribution, accounting, engineering and real estate.
→ Developed a corporate image program for this company.
→ Increased regional profitability by more than $1 million during the first two years in this position.
→ Created and implemented alternative uses for facilities, including c-stores and car washes, from site selection and economic analysis through construction and daily operations.
→ Promoted to this position from **Marketing Representative, Field Sales/ Operations Manager** and **New England District Manager, Power Test Corporation**: Developed and implemented training programs.

<u>A&R Getty</u>, Waterford, CT   1980-1982
Owner / Operator
Managed all marketing, sales and operations for a service station, including direct customer service, staffing and budgets.
→ Achieved annual sales of more than $750,000 and increased sales 30% in the first year of ownership; sold this business to pursue a corporate position.

Prior Experience as **Special Education Teacher**

EDUCATION: <u>Western New England College</u>, Springfield, MA
Masters Degree: Business Administration   1998

<u>The University of Connecticut</u>, Storrs, CT
Bachelor of Science Degree: Special Education   1979

COMMUNITY ACTIVITIES:
Member: Education Committees of the town of Cheshire   1995-1997
Director: Mercury Fuel MDA Golf Tournaments   1996-1997
Treasurer: Doolittle School PTA, Cheshire, CT   1994-1996

Sent 50; received 12 interviews.

JUAN VELDEZ
554 Hunter Court
Roselle, IL 60172
coffeeman@mailcity.com 630/555-2845

MANUFACTURING / PLANT MANAGEMENT

PROFILE:

- Comprehensive experience in total plant management, including full P&L responsibility for staffing, materials, and production line setup and streamlining.
- Skilled in the control of materials, plant safety, inventories, the latest assembly methods, and quality assurance for components and finished products.
- APICS Certified in MRP I and II; experience with ISO-9000, QS 9000, and SPC; constantly analyze production efficiency and reduce downtime.
- Effectively hire, train, and supervise staff and management teams; design and implement cross training, operational sequencing, labor reporting, and corrective action procedures.
- Fluent in Spanish, with a proven ability to reduce overhead and consistently meet deadline and production requirements.

EXPERIENCE:

Real Heavy Truck Products, Chicago, IL 12/98-3/99
Plant Manager promoted from **Manufacturing Operations Manager**
Responsible for all plant operations, including the management of up to 140 employees and seven supervisors.
Directed the setup and operation of production lines for truck parts, including vendor relations, job scheduling, tool maintenance, and quality control.
Communicated with customers, vendors, suppliers, and production staff in Spanish and English as required.
Oversaw a wide range of duties in shipping/receiving, manufacturing engineering, and tooling, as well as in the sewing, trim, rock guard, shield, and Tonneau Cover departments.

- Achieved 96% on-time shipping of products.
- Established a successful continuous improvement program.
- Created a preventive maintenance program and accepted oversight for plant safety.

Producers Financial Services, Hanover Park, IL 7/97-12/98
Loan Officer and Telemarketing Manager
Responsible for staff training and supervision to establish loans.
In charge of quality control, staff performance reviews, and disciplinary measures.
Personally processed loans to successful conclusion.

- Acted as this company's radio and TV spokesperson.

Merkle & Korff, Des Plaines, IL Freelance/temporary: 3/97-6/97
Manufacturing Consultant
On a consulting basis, conducted basic and motion/time studies.
Analyzed and incorporated more effective manufacturing processes; implemented procedures and trained personnel.

Admiral Tool and Manufacturing, Chicago, IL   3/96-2/97
Manufacturing Operations Supervisor
Effectively managed a first-shift metal stamping operation with a team of 35 union workers.
Conducted/oversaw quality inspections; ensured proper adherence to specifications, and implemented adjustments as required.
Instructed staff in safety and daily procedures.
Trained hourly workers in conformance to QS-9000 standards, including translation from English and Spanish.

➤ As Chairperson for the Productivity Improvement team, created a $305,000 potential annual cost savings resulting from a six-month study.

Olson International, Lombard, IL   10/94-3/96
Manufacturing Operations Manager
Directed a two-shift manufacturing operation with 56 employees and additional temporaries.

➤ Increased profit by $100,000 by reworking non-conforming material.
➤ Effectively met 95% of production requirements.
➤ Chaired the Manufacturing and Process Improvement Committee.
➤ Established and implemented lockout/tagout procedures; trained workers in those procedures.
➤ Conducted monthly safety inspections.

PSW Industries, Inc., Chicago, IL   2/93-10/94
Operations Manager - Pressroom
Managed a three-shift operation with 87 union workers for this independent lamination stamper producing electrical parts for motors and transformers.
Member of the Quality Corrective Action Team & Safety Committee Chairperson.

➤ Met and exceeded press production goals within a 10-month period.
➤ Implemented successful press-operator training programs; greatly improved raw material processes, work-in progress, finished goods, quality, and safety control.
➤ Reduced pressroom downtime and increased productivity.

Hako Minuteman, Inc., Addison, IL   10/90-2/93
Operations Manager - Assembly
Managed six assembly lines and trained/supervised 35 union workers for this manufacturer of residential cleaning equipment.
Scheduled workers' hours and compiled production and efficiency reports.
Performed hiring, training, and staff performance reviews.

➤ Conducted safety and right-to-know training in compliance with OSHA standards; Chairman of the Safety Committee.
➤ Redesigned the assembly operation and increased efficiency by 40%, productivity by 7%, reduced manpower by 67%, and saved the company $250,000.
➤ Decreased downtime over 450 hours per month in 1990 and 10 hours per month by 1992.

➤ Completed the redesign and tooling of assembly operations $60,000 under budget.

<u>Midas International</u>, Bedford Park, IL   7/89-9/90
Manufacturing Superintendent
Managed four supervisors and up to 85 union employees using MIII, Eaton/ Leonard Benders, and robotic, automatic, and manual welding cells.
Coordinated workloads using a Mapics 36 system.
➤ Translated the entire quality procedures manual from English to Spanish.

Prior Experience:
Plant Manager: National Marketing Services, Mundelein, IL,   1987-1989
➤ Converted a 28,000 s.f. warehouse to manufacturing use.
➤ Coordinated construction, material selection, permits, and capital purchasing.
➤ Hired trained union staff of 100; initiated manpower planning, policies, and benefits.
➤ Established setup and sub-assembly operations; assisted in estimating and pricing.
➤ Prepared expense reports and capital budgets.
➤ Developed computerized scheduling/inventory and implemented successful labor improvement programs.

General Foreman: Parts Division, Deere & Company, Waterloo, IA, 1975-1987
Supervised up to 75 in sheet metal production using 200- to 600-ton hydraulic presses.
➤ Maintained a 93% incentive average within an 89% plant goal environment.

EDUCATION: <u>Truman College</u>, Chicago, IL
Associate in Applied Science Degree

**ADDITIONAL
TRAINING:**

Completed several Deere Employee Education Programs, college-level courses in: Decision Processing, Data Processing/Control, MRP Concepts, Blueprint Reading, Group Communications, Production/Inventory Control, Labor Improvement, Wage Administration, Effective Interviewing, Supervisory Skills, Affirmative Action I and II, and Safety Training.

Acquired a **Manufacturing Engineering Degree** through the Deere Employee Education Program and completed 60 hours of MANMAN Manufacturing and repetitive VAX training from ASK Computer Systems, Inc.

Perform Geometric Dimensioning and Tolerancing, SPC, Gage Repeatability and Reproducibility from the American Supplier Institute, Inc., and Black & Decker.
➤ Trained in TQM and Windows 95 through Northern Illinois University, DeKalb, IL.
➤ Trained in Lotus through Elmhurst College, IL.

Thomas Jefferson

2256 Scott Drive #238
Roselle, IL 60172
630/555-7221

PRODUCT DEVELOPMENT

OBJECTIVE: **A position using proven creative talents and highly developed organization skills to bring to market new, successful products.**

PROFILE:

› Comprehensive experience in multiple aspects of new product design and development, including conceptualization, prototyping, project management, and marketing strategies.

› Proven ability to handle multiple tasks and effectively organize to achieve specific goals; spearhead projects, and work effectively in team environments. Exceptional follow-up and attention to the details to ensure that projects meet deadlines.

› Skilled in conceptualizing new item designs, including features, look, and appeal. Coordinate brainstorming sessions, artwork, marketing/ promotion development, prototyping, and the production processes; visit Asian facilities to organize new and existing product development.

› Actively seek new challenges and pursue specific objectives. Proficient in WordPerfect and Lotus, as well as production management on AS 400 to track status of prototypes and items in production.

EXPERIENCE:

Pottle Corporation, Itasca, IL
Senior Project Manager   1997-Present
Responsible for all aspects of new product and line development, including conceptualization, scheduling, art direction, and production for this large consumer giftware producer.
Interacted with overseas manufacturers to communicate item specifications, materials requirements, production schedules, and prototyping.
Inspected prototypes as well as final product to ensure complete compliance with design and quality requirements.
Supplied manufacturing department with packaging specs, artwork, copyright, and legal information.

→ Headed the development of the company's third most successful line; line promoted to collectable status.
→ Effectively worked with a variety of departments to launch successful products.
→ Recognized for team building skills and excellence of work.

Project Manager, New Product Development   1994-1997

Coordinated the design and production processes of more than 30 licensed and in-house direct mail programs, with revenues exceeding $39 million annually.

Directed total project management, including brainstorming, line development, product critiques, and production coordination for 10 core product lines.

Worked closely with licensed and freelance artists in the design of new lines and products.

➔ Visited Asian manufacturing facilities to gain understanding of production processes and work with site representatives on prototypes, new product ideas, and production requirements.

Project Manager, Licensing   1990-1994

Handled licensing and international distribution rights contract establishment, administration, and management.

Maintained extensive contact with international subsidiaries, and legal department to track contract and negotiation status.

Processed contracts, amendments, and financial agreements with licensed artists.

Acted as the primary liaison between Enesco and their international subsidiaries, and with the client base for copyright/trademark information.

➔ Maintained accurate contract files, including copyright/trademark and royalty payments/financial commitment updates.

➔ Promoted to position from Licensing Administrator.

Cheshire Company, Mundelein, IL   1989-1990

Administrative

Responsible for coordinating the receipt of incoming equipment orders, inventory control, and trade show support.

Worked with District Sales Managers in distributing sales leads, planning sales meetings, and preparing presentations for new dealers.

AWARDS AND DISTINCTIONS:

Outstanding Creative Support Person of the Year
Enesco Corporation, 1992

Above and Beyond Award
The Greater O'Hare Association, 1997

One of only four interviewed for a job that received 2000+ resumes; hired for the position.

HAROLD FIXIT
3248 Somerset Drive
New Orleans, LA 70131
504/555-3557

R&D / PRODUCT DEVELOPMENT
Willing to Travel or Relocate

PROFILE:

➢ Comprehensive experience in advanced R&D projects and new product development processes from concept to completion, with responsibility for risk analysis, change management, and cross-functional team performance.

➢ Skilled in product specification determination, concurrent design, quality control, budget administration, value analysis/re-engineering; read and interpret blueprints/schematics.

➢ Proficient in strategic planning, marketing research, sales management, lead development, new product introduction, and flagship customer service.

➢ Knowledge of intercultural business customs and practices; work closely with manufacturers and government agencies in the U.S., Canada, and Mexico on supplier agreements and legal matters.

➢ Well-versed in Apple and IBM systems, including AutoCAD 12.0, Excel, and Quick Books Pro; read and interpret blueprints/schematics; knowledge of production and inventory systems including MRP, JIT, and SPC.

EMPLOYMENT:

Cleary Laboratories, Inc., San Diego, CA   1992-Present (as required)
Consultant
Provide business management and technical assistance consulting services to this growing genetics testing laboratory in the Southwest.

→ Directly involved in restructuring the firm into a holding company, GenTest Laboratories, with three subsidiaries, from one centralized enterprise.

→ Develop and implement a strategic marketing plan to expand the human identification service and a specific market penetration strategy for the newly created tissue-typing department.

→ Interview consulting firms to create a bar coding chain-of-custody system.

Super-Damp, Inc., New Orleans, LA
A manufacturer of surge suppressors for the rail industry; in the process of becoming an ASTM AAR quality certified firm.

Operations Manager   12/92-Present
Responsible for the planning, direction, and administration of daily manufacturing and office management operations, including production scheduling, shipping/receiving, procurement, and materials management, AP/AR, and customer/supplier relations.
Hire, train, and supervise a five-person staff, including three sales representatives; supervise two machinists in utilizing standard digital readout lathes and adherence to customer specifications and design requirements.

→ Re-negotiated supplier pricing terms, resulting in a 7% cost reduction.

→ Reduced lead time for custom parts from eight weeks to two days by using JIT.

→ Currently in charge of two new products in service trials: a ruptured disk assembly and unique bolt for high-pressure chlorine tank cars.

Sales and Marketing Manager	6/88-12/92

In charge of the planning, logistics and supervision of market research, product positioning and introduction, publicity, and sales management.

Hired, trained, and supervised a five-person staff, including two independent manufacturer's representatives; negotiated the outsourcing agreements.

Conducted surveys and primary market research, performed data analysis, and assessed customer specifications and requirements.

Worked closely with advertising agencies on sales brochures/direct mail campaigns.

Coordinated participation in and introduced new products at trade shows, including the annual Hazardous Materials Trade Show in Dallas, Texas.

→ Created and implemented a two-prong strategic marketing approach to sell to manufacturers leasing tank cars and to firms constructing tank cars.

→ Directly acquired 175 major accounts, including chemical companies American Cyanamid, Dow Chemicals, IMC Fertilizer, Vulcan Chemicals, Noranda Chemicals, and BSAF, and tank car manufacturers Trinity Industries, ACF, Union Tank Car, Procor, and GATX Corporation.

→ Presented the Hydro-Damp product line to the American Railroads Tank Car Committee for approval as a new rail safety device.

→ Achieved an 11% increase in sales of $1.5 million from zero within the first year of Canadian government approval.

New Products Supervisor	4/86-6/88

Set up and directed all aspects of product development/management for this new company, with full technical, budget, and schedule performance responsibility from concept to delivery.

Selected and worked closely with patent attorneys to process international patent applications and streamline the product approval process.

Handled publicity activities, including national print advertisement placement, promotional brochure design, and direct mail campaign supervision; contracted a marketing/advertisingconsultant.

→ Gained product approval by AAR (USDOT), with legislative support from U.S. Representative Bill Tuazin, and, consequently, approval by the Mexican Department of Transportation.

R.W. Aviation, New Orleans, LA	1985-1986
Flight Instructor/Commercial Instrument Pilot
Graduated 10 students to private pilot license status; an additional 25 flew solo.

→ Hold single/multi-engine ratings and logged 1100 hours.

EDUCATION:

University of New Orleans, New Orleans, LA	Graduated 1992
Master of Business Administration

Louisiana Tech University, New Orleans, LA	Graduated 1985
Bachelor of Science degree in professional aviation

Sent about 25 resumes to ads and contacts; received 12 interview offers; accepted six interviews and a new job. Lionel followed up on all resumes with notes or phone calls.

LIONEL HUTZ
626 Camera Lane
Bartlett, IL 60103
630/555-3362

PRODUCT MANAGEMENT / PURCHASING

PROFILE:

➤ Comprehensive experience in new business development, cost-effective purchasing, and the total management of technical product lines.

➤ Design and implement systems and procedures for shipping, receiving, warehousing, product tracking, and prompt distribution to key accounts.

➤ Highly skilled in product sourcing, networking, pricing, and competitive analysis; handle strategic planning and long-term business development through personal client relations and strong contacts in the electronics industry.

➤ Coordinate and expedite purchasing with vendors, suppliers, and sales/marketing staff to anticipate and meet specific client needs on time and under budget; familiar with MRPII, JIT, ISo 9000, and various Windows software for status reporting.

➤ Plan and conduct staff training in sales, contract coordination, and state-of-the-art product lines.

CAREER BACKGROUND:

Zoller Electronics, Addison, IL   1995-1999
Promoted to various positions, most recent first:

Product Manager
Managed extensive vendor relations, purchasing, and business development for more than half of $23 million in semiconductor revenue for this component distributor.
Performed product sourcing through a wide range of vendors and suppliers for the best possible price.
Produced accurate price estimates and quotes; negotiated contracts within strict P&L parameters.
Responsible for expedites, registrations, deliveries, and debits, as well as account follow-up.
Planned and conducted presentations to internal sales staff and clients on marketing strategies, competitors, and product lines.

→ Increased gross profit from 17% to 21% on all designated product lines.
→ Recognized for the turnaround of unprofitable projects and deals.
→ Determined the reasons for lost sales; logged more than 2000 quotes and bids.
→ Responsible for a wide range of suppliers, including Actel, Altera, Analog Devices, Benchmarq, Fairchild, Harris, ICS, IDT, Intel, Intel Mass, Level One, and Xicor.

LIONEL HUTZ
Page Two

Project Manager

In charge of all business functions for a $20 million system account.
Recommended asset buying and negotiated pricing for field sales staff.
Worked closely with the corporate asset manager on forecasts, inventory turns, and bonded inventory issues.

→ Managed an order processing function for 12,000 personal computers; achieved 99% on time delivery, with DOAs of less than 1%.

→ Coordinated a margin enhancement program that increased margins from 3% to 17%.

Inside Sales / Marketing Representative

Developed and managed more than 50 OEM accounts, including contract manufacturers.
Produced and utilized a real-time price quoting system.

California Microwave, Bloomingdale, IL   1994-1995
Buyer / Expeditor

Purchased and expedited electronic components for high-volume producer of wireless communication systems.
Utilized MRP and JIT standards; gained familiarity with ISO 9000.
This company closed its doors in 1995.

→ Reduced stoppages by 95%; conducted and managed the daily shortage meeting.

Personalized Trucking Service, Chicago, IL   1992-1994
Sales Representative

Performed needs analysis and trucking sales to Fortune 500 accounts.

→ Produced $250,000 in new business; maintained a $5 million base.

Motorola, Inc., Cellular Group, Arlington Heights, IL   1990-1992
Supervisor / Dock Operations

Managed traffic, daily workflow, and outbound UPS shipments.

Fuji Photo Film U.S.A., Inc., Itasca, IL   1981-1990
Product Control Manager

Effectively purchased, managed, and promoted industrial film products.

→ Increased annual inventory turns from two to six.

→ Shipped 95% of orders complete and on time, up from only 70%.

Wells Lamont Corporation, Niles, IL   1976-1981
Regional Sales Administrator

Expanded sales through competitive analysis and interface with purchasing and production staff.

EDUCATION: Valparaiso University, Valparaiso, IN
B.S. Degree: Business Administration   1976
Emphasis: Management and Marketing

Sent about 20; received 15 interviews.

JAMES HENDERSON
3230 North Pembroke Drive
South Elgin, IL 60177
847/555-6822

PRODUCTION SUPERVISOR

PROFILE:

➢ Comprehensive experience and hands-on training in numerous aspects of production supervision, including scheduling, staff motivation, training, evaluation, reporting, and system troubleshooting.

➢ Extensive background in a wide variety of plant operations, including machine set-up, quality assurance, production reporting, custom molding, forklift operations, and conveyor systems arrangement.

➢ Proven ability to troubleshoot and resolve problems quickly. Skilled in injection molding, inventory and shop floor control, JIT, and RF; utilize IQMS and AS/400 systems, as well as MS Word for database updates and reporting.

EXPERIENCE:

Maurice Makers, Morris, IL   5/98-Present
Supervisor / Lead Process Technician
Responsible for production activities at this automated plant, including working with robotic and other automated systems; additional duties similar to Duraco, below.
Skilled in the commission and qualifying of injection molding machines.
Schedule orders and work directly with customers regarding product specifications.
Communicate with vendors and suppliers to order new equipment and supplies.
→ Gaining experience with closed and open-loop plant-process water systems.

Duraco Products, Inc., Streamwood, IL   1987-5/98
Lead Process Technician
Responsible for all plant operations, including quality assurance, staff supervision, work coordination, troubleshooting, inventory control, and system streamlining for this manufacturer of plastic consumer items.
Trained and evaluated employees in mold setting and injection mold troubleshooting. Supervised a team of process technicians and coordinated activities of mold setters.
→ Evaluated machine cycles and identified ways to improve productivity.
→ Performed job scheduling for up to 90 workers on machines, packing, and shipping.
→ Worked with quality control personnel to resolve any quality issues.

EDUCATION:

Elgin Community College, Elgin, IL
→ Successfully completed a range of technical classes including Heating and Refrigeration, Welding, Electrical Controls, and Sheet Metal Working.

High School Graduate

TRAINING:

Fred Pryor Schools **How to Supervise People** (certificate)

Sent "about" 60; received 20 interviews.

RALPH WIGGUM
4465 Cat Tail
Carol Stream, IL 60188
630/555-0194

PROJECT MANAGEMENT / ORACLE SYSTEMS

PROFILE:

➤ Comprehensive experience in the setup and management of complete ORACLE systems for MRP, including cost-effective procurement, inventory control and MRO expediting.

➤ Perform staff and management training and supervision in complete system integration, upgrades and utilization.

➤ Negotiate contracts with vendors and suppliers for reduced overhead and quick response; skilled in JIT, Y2K compliance, cycle time management and process improvement; coordinate production, purchasing and operations for multiple locations.

➤ Familiar with state tax regulations; coordinate budgets and procedures with programmers, technical staff and management.

➤ Handle full system documentation and the writing of manuals and procedures; skilled in Windows, Excel and Wings for spreadsheets and status reporting.

EXPERIENCE:

Village Office Equipment, Inc., Libertyville, IL
ORACLE System Administrator / Trainer   1993-1998
Responsible for virtually all aspects ORACLE system installation, debugging and use, including extensive staff training and documentation.
Effectively trained and motivated approximately 10 employees per month for six years in rules and procedures for purchasing.
Directly supervise three buyers and one clerk.
Researched and wrote an article for Motorola's procurement newsletter on FER.
Resident expert on special user tax issues with the State of Illinois.
Created and implemented numerous cost reduction methods and process improvements (documentation available) related to:

- Implemented autofax procedures and FER (Facility Engineering Requests) procedures.
- Payables, purchasing and problem-solving.
- American Express and Pro-Card.
- Return order procedures and further process procedures.
- Progressive payment.
- Saved more than $1.8 million with numerous suppliers through price negotiation and working with employees at cellular facilities in Illinois, Washington, Arizona, Florida and Texas.
- Chosen to debug and implement a complete ORACLE purchasing system for Brazil.
- Eliminated a costly, non-value procedure; worked with attorneys to develop an extensive, FER master contractor service agreement.
- Produced and updated a monthly and Y.T.D. cost-saving spreadsheet for management.

Ralph Wiggum
Page Two

- Developed and maintained purchasing guidelines, rules and procedures for ORACLE requisition users.
- Developed and maintained a detailed, preferred supplier list.
- Earned an award from the President of General Systems for outstanding achievement and cost reductions.

Production Buyer / MRO Buyer   1988-1992

Performed cost-effective purchasing of all commodities for specific end products, including the IMTS carrier phone.

Responsible for a wide range of special projects and monthly reports, including tracking of cost savings and variances.

Reported the status of ship plans to management.

- Handled extensive vendor sourcing and relations, including securing bids and quotes.

Production Buyer   1985-1988

Purchased a wide range of commodities for cellular phones, including injection molded parts, die cast items, sheet metal stamped items and other mechanical parts.

MRO Purchasing / Developmental   1982-1984

Primarily responsible for engineering procurement and a wide range of special projects.

Production Control / Planner / Scheduling   1979-1982

Recognized for highly accurate forecasting, including reading, interpretation and use.

Tracked and reduced inventory spikes, greatly lowering total inventory costs.

Receiving Supervisor   1978

Trained, supervised, scheduled and motivated a team of 10.

Supervisor   1975-1978

Supervised 25 material handlers, with waveline audit responsibilities.

Stockroom and Material Handler   1971-1974

Represented the material organization at daily staff meetings to expedite ship concerns and shortages.

- Meetings resulted in Motorola's meeting its financial plans for 11 consecutive years.
- Earned award for perfect attendance for 10 years straight, with no vacation time off.

PRIOR EXPERIENCE:

U.S. Army Medical Supply Specialist.
Earned Bronze Star Metal and other Awards.

EDUCATION:

W.R. Harper College, Palatine, IL
Material Management Certificate
Completed an additional 77 hours of business related study.

Selectively sent two and received one interview; hired for the position.

CALVIN A. BOSS
4414 Jammer Street
Rowlett, TX 22488
Double@cyberramp.net

Res: 972/555-6421   Ofc: 972/555-4850

PROJECT MANAGEMENT

PROFILE:

➤ Comprehensive experience in team leadership and motivation, including technical product development from schematics and CAD design to modeling and production.

➤ Familiar with ISO 9000 and complete quality control, as well as client relations, documentation, and budget administration.

➤ Analyze and streamline configurations and coordinate software applications, database management, and documentation updates; knowledge of materials and vendor relations.

➤ Skilled in CAD drafting and design and state-of-the-art applications including:

Software and Platforms:
Unix, Pascal, Oracle, Fortran, BASIC, and C.

Applications:
Autocad Rev 13, CV CADDS 6 and Parametric/Explicit, and CV CAMU VIEWLOGIC
Digital Equipment VAX 8800 and 11/780 Series Computers
PCs using Windows, DOS, and UNIX operating systems
Macintosh computers and application software packages

EXPERIENCE:

Partly / M-Systems, Garland, TX
Partly is a $10 billion, Fortune 600 Corporation in the Software Development/ System Integration industry.

Group Leader - Engineering Design Drafter   12/96-Present

Responsible for supervising a team of five in schematic capture, including all drafting, design, CAD work, and production for defense reconnaissance systems.

Perform extensive group and individual training, as well as job assignment and coordination with upper management and other technical staff.

Accountable for complete project quality and documentation for upper management.

Act as liaison to the engineering group, providing support, development, and drafting expertise on schematic diagrams, mechanical drawings, and printed wiring board drawings from engineering models.

→ Conducted meetings on ISO 9000 and implemented improvements, of which four out of five were accepted by upper management.

→ One idea reduced labor hours for a specific procedure from 100 to 10.

→ Act as VIEWLOGIC and ISO 9000 quality control administrator.

→ Advanced to Group Leader from zero experience in only one year.

Senior Engineering CAD Specialist   5/91-12/96

Directed the design of a 3D Solid Modeling project using Computervision's Product Visualization application. Produced a virtual reality walk-through of various floor configurations.

Generated software interaction diagrams using the Software Through Pictures application on a Sun/UNIX workstation.

Updated and maintained a database of more than 150 AutoCad files and a 20,000-record database using Oracle.

Scheduled and documented database updates to meet quarterly publishing requirements.

→ Planned and conducted extensive AutoCad training for peers and managers.

→ Updated and modified manager's floor plans, equipment rack elevations, and cable wire listings.

→ Supported baseline installation activities requiring overseas travel to sites such as Australia.

Engineering Drafter   9/83-5/91

Assisted in staff training and managed the revision of schematics, flow charts, block diagrams, and printed circuit board layouts in accordance with strict military standards such as 275E.

Updated and maintained floor plans CV CADDS 3 and 4x computer systems using a CVD digitizer and graphics workstation.

→ Captured microwave integrated circuits and produced silk-screen layouts on CV systems.

→ Maintained and prepared site floor plans for facility interface, control documents, and evolution floor plans.

SECURITY ACCESS:

Acquired Active Security Clearances following Special and Extended background investigations.

EDUCATION:

Amber University, Dallas, TX
B.S. Degree   May 1999
Major: Management: Information Systems, GPA: 3.7/4.0

Eastfield College, Dallas, TX
Associate's Degree   July, 1992
Major: Drafting and Design

Stephen F. Austin State University, Nacogdoches, TX
Major: Computer Science   Spring/Fall, 1982

Richland College, Dallas, TX
Major: Computer Science   1981, 1983-85 ,and 1993-94

• Total college credit hours completed: 156.

Sent 50, received 14 interviews and six job offers.

Saunders Zach
2250 Iris Avenue
Hanover Park, IL 60103
630/555-8951

PURCHASING / PROCUREMENT

PROFILE:

➢ Comprehensive experience in cost-effective purchasing, including extensive material sourcing, price negotiations, and distribution management.

➢ Background in manufacturing environments, including purchasing of raw materials, operating supplies, capital equipment, and outside/contract services.

➢ Develop domestic and offshore sources and control high-volume distribution operations and multi-step production operations.

➢ Knowledge of SPC, JIT, and MRP, as well as formal quality control programs; proven ability to improve inventory turns and overall profitability.

➢ Familiar with MRP II (BPCS 4.02 system); **Certified ISO/QS 9000 Auditor**; assist in QS 9000 Certification.

EMPLOYMENT:

<u>Area Jester</u>, Raceway Park, IL
Commodities Manager / Purchasing   1997-Present
Manage the sourcing and purchasing of $15 million in production materials, including steel, plastic resins, cold forgings, molded cloth, paper, and rubber speaker components, as well as packaging materials.
Train and supervise one planner/buyer and a purchasing assistant.
Utilize MRPII (BPCS 4.02 system) for inventory management, shop floor control, and prompt status reporting.

→ Through effective negotiations, achieved a $400,000 cost reduction in 2 1/2 years.
→ Trained in SPC and the automotive Production Part Approval Process (PPAP), as well as Failure Mode Effects Analysis (FMEA).
→ Chosen to travel to China and Taiwan to conduct audits of suppliers, 1997 and 1998.
→ Promoted to this position from:

Senior Buyer   1996-1997

<u>TLK Industries</u>, Palatine, IL   1994-1996
Project Coordinator
Responsible for new procedures and the supervision of concurrent projects, including ISO 9001 certification.
Directed the corporate quality management process, system documentation, and virtually all internal communications.

Saunders Zach
Page Two

Trained, supervised, and scheduled two employees in the quality department.

→ Revised and updated virtually all purchasing procedures.

→ Researched, updated, and re-wrote procedures for the quality manual to ISO 9001 specifications.

→ Updated bills of materials and organized material safety data sheets.

→ Documented the emergency response system.

→ Acted as Senior Advisor to management on process systems, redundancy elimination, hazardous materials, and preventive maintenance techniques.

ZI, Inc., Reedsburg, WI   1983-1994
Purchasing Manager
In charge of corporate purchasing, including the cost-effective buying of capital equipment, raw materials, components, packaging, supplies, and outside services.
Performed vendor sourcing, bid preparation, price/discount negotiation, and the review of vendor performance.
Worked closely with domestic and offshore sources; coordinated procurement planning and operations with manufacturing, engineering, finance, and marketing managers.

→ Played a key role in creating and implementing a quality management program.

→ Established and maintained a sophisticated cataloging system detailing product and vendor history.

→ Negotiated single-purchase contracts valued up to $80,000 for die cast molds and tooling.

→ Managed a major inventory and implemented JIT and MRP systems.

→ Joined this company as Production Control Specialist; gained experience in scheduling manufacturing and assembly operations, and advanced to management of shipping and receiving, before promotion to Purchasing Manager.

EDUCATION: W.R. Harper College, Palatine, IL
Certificate in Materials and Logistics Management, 1996.
Expected completion of Associate's Degree in Management, 2001.

Triton College, River Grove, IL
Completed training in Excel 5.0 and MS Word 6.0, 1996.

Sent or e-mailed about 200; received 25 interviews.

SANTO PROVENZANO

2201 Calib Avenue, #302   310/555-6459
Santa Monica, CA 90403   E-mail gath@aol.com

OBJECTIVE:

Product Management
A leadership position utilizing hands-on abilities in communications, project supervision, client relations, and business administration.

PROFILE:

- Extensive background in new product development and introduction, process re-engineering, strategic planning, target marketing, distribution operations, and successful team facilitation in international marketplaces.
- Manage product sales, key account maintenance, competitive analysis, pricing, market surveys, contract negotiation, quality control, inventory, and report generation.
- Successfully develop and implement innovative programs to increase market share, profit margins, and cost savings in rapidly shifting markets.
- Train and supervise staff in a wide range of industrial chemicals; participate on cross-division teams involved in business expansion and market identification.
- Extensive experience with international business practices and protocols, particularly in Europe and the Pacific Rim; fluent in English, German, Chinese (Mandarin), Filipino, Spanish, and French.

EMPLOYMENT:

The Uncle Group   1985-Present
Uncle Chemical Group Inc., Dallas, TX
Senior Sales Representative - West Coast   1995-Present
Responsible for sales, account maintenance, order processing, and product management for a $13.8 million territory in California and the Rockies, and part of the $108 million West Region.

→ Successfully maintain and upgrade major account sales volume in a highly competitive and decreasing market.

→ Oversaw cross-functional groups in identifying and accommodating logistical requirements to ensure timely delivery and client satisfaction.

→ Consistently recognized by management and clients for excellent skills in troubleshooting and problem resolution in high-pressure situations.

Financial Analyst   1994–1995
Provided extensive market and financial analysis to enhance long-term marketing and customer satisfaction strategies for the entire company.

→ Personally improved methods for generation of Slope and Scatter diagrams and analyses, which are now used company-wide.

→ Assisted in developing three marketing strategies, leading to increased earnings of almost $6 million for two separate divisions.

→ Served on a seven-man Customer Satisfaction Implementation team that used Malcolm Baldridge Assessment skills gained in an intensive training program.

Product Supervisor   1994
Coordinated production activities for VA/Acetyls and Formaldehyde at six plants in the U.S., Mexico, and Canada, including the largest acetic acid facility in the world in Clear Lake, TX.

SANTO PROVENZANO
Page Two

    →   Recognized by management for achieving a complete and profitable plant turnaround in only 34 days.

    →   Resolved a recurrent problem to better manage storage and production planning.

    →   Finished cross-training in sales techniques and product orientation, as well as Purchasing, Legal Liaison, Transportation, and Credit.

<u>Uncle AG</u>, Frankfurt, Germany   1991-1994
Product Manager
Coordinated new business development, marketing, order processing, and international client relations for up to $20 million in annual volume.

    →   Worked with a full range of products, including Acetaldehyde, Acetic Acid, Carboxylic Acids and NPG, and Butyraldehyde.

    →   Expanded internal client base by extensive market surveys and analysis for the Organic intermediates group.

<u>Uncle Singapore Pte, Ltd.</u>, Singapore   1985-1991
Management Assistant   1990-1991
Provided effective support to executives involved in contract negotiations, new office operations, and product development in Asian marketplaces.
Maintained close contact with Board of Directors and ZDA corporate planning group in Frankfurt, Germany, along with legal liaison and site inspections.

    →   Coordinated all construction activity and new business start-up for the regional technical center and rebottling/refilling facility.

Senior Sales Executive   1988-1990
In charge of chemical sales to a highly diverse clientele, including Refrigeration, Pharmaceutical, and Fire-fighting firms.

    →   Personally developed and introduced Frigen refrigerants into a completely new market; also managed a small-scale CFC mixing/filling facility and tank farm.

Medical Representative   1986-1988

    →   Consistently ranked as the best sales representative with highest gross profit and commissions.

Management Trainee   1985-1986

    →   Handled internal auditing for order processing and sales tracking, resulting in greater departmental productivity.

EDUCATION: <u>Singapore Institute of Management</u>   1988
                      Diploma in Marketing Management

                      <u>National University of Singapore</u>   1985
                      B.Sc. Degree in Chemistry

                      *   Received an ASEAN Merit Scholarship from 1982-1985.

Sent about 100; received six interviews.

TED E. WILLIAMS
5520 East Crystal Avenue
Crystal Lake, IL 60014

Res.: 815/555-8945   410@mc.net   Fax: 815/555-8984

PURCHASING / MANUFACTURING

PROFILE:

➤ Comprehensive experience in production operations and cost-effective purchasing, including full responsibility for manufacturing, quality, and successful turnarounds.

➤ Skilled in quality control and highly profitable turnarounds at multiple locations; manage production line setup, analysis, and streamlining.

➤ Proficient in vendor relations, product/component sourcing, and inventory control for domestic and foreign locations.

➤ Familiar with TQM, JIT, continuous flow manufacturing, and focused/cell manufacturing; accurately measure and reduce scrap, re-work, lost time, and inventories.

➤ Effectively train and supervise teams of engineers, supervisors, line workers, and support staff at all levels of experience.

EXPERIENCE:

Golfers, Inc., Crystal Lake, IL   1996-Present
Director of Manufacturing
In charge of virtually all operations at four plants, including cost-effective purchasing, inventory control, cost-reduction, and profit/loss functions.
Effectively train and supervise all plant managers and purchasing staff in purchasing, MRP, and team coordination for high-volume production of electrical products.
→ Currently purchase up to $20 million per year, including all price/contract negotiations with vendors and suppliers worldwide.
→ Save up to $800,000 per year in purchases through detailed planning, charting, and status reporting of all production operations.
→ Provide detailed documentation of production output to constantly compare and improve techniques, processes, and procedures.

Eaton Corporation, Various locations
Corporate Quality / Supplier Management - Carol Stream, IL   1994-1995
Personally developed a solid base of North American commodity suppliers for the Appliance, Automotive, and Lectron Divisions.
Established preferred supplier status and on-time deliveries.
Effectively interfaced with all department supervisors and purchasing staff.
→ Created, implemented, and met strict quality standards for 17 manufacturing facilities and eight purchasing departments.
→ Reduced suppliers from 15,000 to 8,000.

Plant Manager - Athens, AL   1993-1994

Effectively trained and supervised a team of seven in engineering, accounting, human resources, and quality management.

Products included hot and cold controls for various appliances.

Annual sales exceeded $20 million, with 350 employees in all major departments.

→   Through detailed research and negotiations, reduced inventory by $1.2 million, and eliminated the need for - and use of - a 60,000 sq. ft. off-site warehouse.

→   Implemented continuous flow manufacturing

→   Developed - and trained supervisors in - a very effective Focus on Quality operating system.

General Manager - Melbourne, Australia   1992-1993

Researched and documented all primary plant operations, including output, overhead, staffing, and quality.

Developed and implemented new Quality Operating systems.

Established quality improvement teams with customers.

Supervised six staff and managers to successfully implement all procedures.

This plant has a total of 150 employees and annual sales of $25 million, producing timers for washing machines, switches, automobile horns, and thermostats.

Focused on field failures and cost improvement, resulting in:

→   Greatly increased quality and profits, with reduced downtime and a letter of commendation from top executives of the Email Laundry Group Division.

Plant Manager - Wauwatosa, WI   1991-1992

Implemented quality operating systems, with a focus on reduction of defects shipped to customers, thereby regaining their confidence.

Greatly reduced scrap, re-work, customer returns, and unfavorable labor variance.

Employees: 350, with annual sales of $28 million.

→   Reduced defects from 27,800 ppm to 1000 ppm in just over a year.

Plant Manager - St. Thomas, Ontario, Canada   1989-1991

Developed and utilized a Quality Operating system with a focus on scrap, re-work, and labor reduction.

Products included drier receivers and accumulators for automotive applications; 550 employees and $32 million in sales CDN.

→   Turned around the operation from a $3.5 million loss to break even in nine months; on target to a $1 million profit within six months.

→   Lowered part defects from 22,500 ppm to 140 ppm over 14 months.

→   Earned the **Ford Q1 Award** for excellence.

Plant Manager - Crystal Lake, IL   1970-1989

Implemented major quality improvements and reduced costs, while increasing production from 6,000 motors to more than 50,000 daily.

→   Cost improvements offset 19 years of materials and labor cost increases.

Sent 38; received 10 interviews; accepted new position through a personal contact.

GEORGE B. STRAIT

221 Sheridan Drive
Joplin, MI 34801

Residence: 452/555-6154
E-mail: Georg@terraworld.net

GENERAL MANAGEMENT / MANUFACTURING
Quality, Engineering, or Plant Management

PROFILE: Comprehensive experience in plant management and operations, with P&L responsibility for total quality systems and process engineering, in consumer and light industrial markets.

➢ Advise senior management on emerging industry standards; formulate strategic quality management policies to achieve financial goals; effectively communicate ideas and technical information at all levels for a high-performance environment.

➢ Recruit and direct cross-functional teams to meet engineering, production, and customer requirements; skilled in customer needs assessment, competitive analysis, product development, benchmarking, supplier relations, facility layout, concurrent engineering, contract negotiation, and budget administration.

➢ Well-versed in lean manufacturing processes, including cellular manufacturing, TQM/SPC, JIT, PPAP, APQP, line balancing, and Design of Experiments; working knowledge of J.D. Edwards production control software; registered ISO 9000 auditor.

➢ Technical knowledge: grey/ductile iron casting, plastic molding, die casting, stampings, metal removal, heat treating, forging, sheet metal forming, painting, and product assembly; expert in metrology and metalography.

CAREER BACKGROUND:

<u>Appliance Company</u>, Outdoor Cooking Division, Neosho, MI ⸻ 1997-Present

Quality Manager ⸻ 11/97-Present

In charge of strategic and daily quality management functions for this $400 million plant manufacturing gas, electric, and charcoal barbecue grills, with 1,250 employees in peak production season.

⇨ Planned and launched a total quality management program to meet ISO 9000 requirements and customer-defined product specifications.

⇨ Initiated a program to reduce critical defects by 50% in the 1998 production year and to zero defects in 1999; decreased customer complaints to the Call Center by 30%.

⇨ Served as 1999-2000 ASQ local chapter Program, Education, and National Quality Month Chair.

⇨ Redesigned the facility layout to accommodate an outsourcing contract to manufacture PowerMate/Coleman consumer generators in unanticipated high demand.

Production Manager ⸻ 3/97-11/97

Directed all manufacturing operations, including product fabrication, finishing, assembly, and packaging, with responsibility for line balancing, daily production schedules, and quality craftsmanship in sheet metal forming, powder paint, porcelain coating, wire grid fabrication, and silk-screen printing.

⇨ Increased production volume from 7,000 ($1MM) units per day to a record 14,600 ($2.17MM) units per day, while reducing direct labor workforce by 200 employees.

⇨ Improved productivity from 40% to over 90% in actual vs. earned direct labor hours.

The Thermos Company, Freeport, IL   1995-1997
Director of Quality Assurance and R&D
Managed quality systems functions for North American operations, including the Consumer Customer
Service group and Return Materials Department, of this Nippon Sanso $250 million subsidiary
manufacturing gas barbecue grills, steel and glass vacuum insulated food containers, ice chests and jugs,
and school lunch kits.

⇨   Acquired the R&D group in December 1995.
⇨   Standardized engineering change order procedures, decreasing the turnaround time from 30 to
       10 days.
⇨   Introduced a fastener standardization program and generated a savings of $300,000 on
       implementation.
⇨   Redesigned the thermos barbecue grill line for a $2.9 million cost savings.
⇨   Commercialized several houseware products, including Steel Commuter Travel Mug, 56-Quart
       Split Lid Cooler, and the TAZ Lunch Kit, to achieve $3 million in additional sales revenues.

The American Tool Companies, Inc., DeWitt, NE   1990 to 1995
Director of Product Standards   1/94-11/95
Set up and managed external/internal product reliability testing facilities serving plants in the U.S.,
Europe, and Brazil, for this $300 million privately-held manufacturer of hand tools and power tool
accessories for the do-it-yourself and industrial markets.

⇨   Produced corporate quality manuals, detailing procedures for quality system documentation,
       product quality planning, quality data retention, and warranty returns.
⇨   Member of various corporate teams, including the New Product Development Committee and
       ISO 9000 implementation; contributed to the rollout of 14 new products.
⇨   Developed testing policies, procedures, and methods for new and manufactured product lines,
       including Vise Grip Locking Pliers, Quick Grip Bar Clamps, Marathon Saw Blades, Prosnip
       Metal Shears, Unibit Step Drills, Chesco Hex Keys, Turbo Max Drills, Hanson Drills and Taps,
       Straight Line Chalk Boxes, Irwin Auger, and Speedbor Flat Bits.
⇨   Designed and implemented a supplier certification process to meet ISO 9000 requirements.
⇨   Promoted from **Director of Quality Assurance**, 11/90-1/94.

Prior Positions/Employers   1980-1990
         Senior Quality Control Engineer, The Trane Company, Tyler, TX
         Quality Control Engineer, Compressor Assembly, The Trane Company, Tyler, TX
         Quality Control Engineer, Purchased Parts and Process Control Die Cast, The Trane
         Company, Tyler, TX
         Assistant Plant Metallurgist, Republic Steel Corporation, Union Drawn Division, Gary, IN
         Management Trainee, Metallurgical Department, Republic Steel Corporation, Akton, OH

TRAINING: Numerous seminars completed include:
                       Lead Auditor Training/RAB ISO 9000 Certification.
                       ASQC Stepping Toward Quality.
                       Juran - The Last World Tour.
                       Quality Management by Deming.

EDUCATION: University of Cincinnati, Cincinnati, OH
                       B.S. degree in metallurgical engineering

Sent 50; received 15 interviews.

Mary T. Zidek
4405 Sword Place #45
Bloomingdale, IL 60108
630/555-4397

OPERATIONS / MANAGEMENT

PROFILE:

➢ Skilled in the management of customer service, sales, and business operations, including responsibility for staffing, procedures, and cost-reduction.

➢ Coordinate inventories, promotions, and status reporting for multiple locations; handle internal audits and analytical problem-solving in fast-paced situations.

➢ Familiar with international business practices; handle top-level presentations in a professional manner; conversant in French.

➢ Analyze and reduce payroll and capital expenses; reduce shortages and negotiate with vendors and suppliers; knowledge of Windows 95, Lotus 1-2-3, WordPad, Groupwise, and MS Publisher for sales reports and correspondence.

➢ Effectively hire, train, supervise, and motivate staff and management teams; well-versed in human resource issues and regulations.

EMPLOYMENT: <u>Lores & Tony</u>, Schaumburg and Oak Brook, IL
Operations Manager 1997-Present
Responsible for virtually all operations for this $30 million location, including the hiring, training, and/or supervision of 250 staff and managers.
Manage all aspects of housekeeping, stocking, and inventory control; oversee detailed audits of all products and sales records.
Coordinate functions of the cash office, as well as alterations and the purchase of all supplies.
Ensure maintenance and repair of numerous POS registers, telephones, and computer systems.
Oversee petty cash and constantly track and reduce expenses.
In charge of maintenance issues related to facilities, such as landscaping and interior lighting for maximum promotional effect.

→ Increased gift certificate sales by 5% for FY 98.
→ Earned $25,000 in corporate credits for reducing chargeback claims to zero.
→ Reduced general workers' hours by 23% for FY 98; ranked #19: up from #72 of 73 stores.
→ Physical inventory: achieved provision of 2% for three consecutive seasons.
→ In charge of all store hiring; achieved a major reduction in payroll.
→ Exceeded goals for new accounts in the last three seasons.
→ Plan all vacations and schedules for 250 workers.
→ Resolve all customer service problems as Senior Executive Representative.

Mary T. Zidek
Page Two

Regional Control Manager   1995-1997
Central Shortage Control, Manhattan, NY
Regions: Chicago, Dallas, Houston, and New Orleans   1995-1996
Regions: New Jersey, New York, and Connecticut   1996-1997
→   Trained two successful Regional Control Managers.
→   Trained an entire region in the Physical Inventory Process.
→   During inventory reconciliations, worked closely with staff and managers
    in loss prevention, profit improvement, price management, and buying of-
    fice procedures.
Successfully reduced shortages in six target stores.
Inventory Control Representative for four seasons.
Internal Auditor: Responsible for the cash office, safe room, sign placement, pric-
ing, and reduction of losses, as well as for receiving.
Completed formal corporate training in a wide range of issues.

Manager of Support Services, Woodfield, Schaumburg, IL   1994-1995
Directed housekeeping, stocking, supply expense reduction, and inventories for
annual sales volume of $25 million.
Assisted operations managers in all duties, including staffing issues and the flow
of merchandise in and out of the building (averaged three trucks per week and
500 receipts per truck).
→   Assisted in the liquidation process; converted the old Woodfield store to a
    virtually new location; worked with numerous truck lines and contractors.

Area Sales Manager, Woodfield   1992-1994
Developed a sales volume of $2.5 million in men's furnishings, clothing, intimate
apparel, hosiery, and children's wear.
→   Increased sales growth over plan for six consecutive seasons.
→   Achieved passing shortage and pricing audit scores.
→   Conducted accurate, quality physical inventories within merchandise areas.

EDUCATION: Illinois State University, Bloomington/Normal, IL
                        Bachelor of Science Degree   1991
                        Major: International Business; Minor: Management
                        GPA: 3.0/4.0
                        Member: Alpha Delta Pi Sorority.
                        Panhellenic Delegate and Treasurer.

                        Bristol Polytechnic University, Bristol, England   Spring, 1990
                        Completed courses in International Business
                        GPA: 4.0

Posted on various Internet databases; received at least 50 interviews.

Ann Klepacz
P.O. Box 3047
Newport Beach, CA 92659

714/555-5772
Ann@msn.com

SAP CONSULTING

Comprehensive skills in SAP consulting and data warehousing, including complete business analysis and custom solution development for SAP users. Proven ability to build alliances with systems integrators and SAP partners to solve problems on time and under budget.

* Accurately translate theory and training into practice; re-engineer business processes and develop software implementation plans that clients can effectively realize and apply.

* Interface with IT executives, management, and staff, including MIS Directors, CEOs, CFOs, and Comptrollers, in the analysis of business operations and IT requirements.

* Experience in personal networking and intelligence gathering. Establish strategic alliances and personally manage relationships with accounts, resulting in additional sales.

* Specialize in IT Marketing and Business Development, with diversified experience in marketing, information management, and accounting for competitive, high-growth, and start-up companies.

* Skilled in research and writing; created training manuals, software documentation manuals, persuasive graphical presentations, and newsletters.

ENTERPRISE SOFTWARE EXPERIENCE
Consulting Project Manager – Great Getter, Inc. - 1997 to present
- Design and implement data warehouses, including data requirements analysis and tools selection.
- Determine migration/extraction requirements for SAP R/3 and Oracle applications software.
- Trained in Data Modeling, Methodology, Prism Warehouse Executive, Prism Quality Manager, Prism Warehouse Directory, Prism Schedule Manager, and Prism Web Access.

SAP Director of Marketing, Systematic Systems Integration - 1997
- Created marketing collateral for SAP data extraction interface. Provided pre-sales technical support.
- Defined data access/extraction requirements for SAP projects. Specialized in extraction requirements for bar-coding and RF terminals at manufacturing plants, particularly during upgrades of SAP versions.
- Developed an extensive lead tracking system from involvement with SAP user groups, referrals, and contacts met at numerous conferences. Cultivated customer-focused vendor/client relationships.
- Built alliances with vendors marketing complimentary products to enable collaboration and increased market intelligence. Extensive contact with Big Five, DEC/COMPAQ, HP, and Intermec representatives.

SAP Consultant - KPMG - 1995-1996
- Analyzed business process re-engineering, workflow, and SAP data requirements.
- Configured FI/CO/SD/MM. Demonstrated SAP functionality and provided technical answers.
- Explained SAP options regarding accounts payable and credit limit choices to clients.
- SAP Partner Academy Training included: Introduction to Sales and Distribution, Shipping, Billing, Conditions and Pricing, Configuration and Organization, Introduction to Materials Management, Purchasing, Inventory Management, Aris Toolset, SAP Fundamental Hierarchy, SAP Navigation, SAP EDI, and SAP Security Authorizations.

Ann Klepacz
Page Two

CONSULTING EXPERIENCE - 1982-1998

Marketing, Sales and Seminar Consultant – Apple, Microsoft and Oracle
- Consultant to Oracle during the planning of Financial Applications seminars. Advised them on target audience, speakers, presentation materials, and prospect and lead tracking systems. 1997
- Contracted by Microsoft, Apple, Times Mirror, RIA, and 30 other companies to produce conferences on CD-ROM for tax research and technology for accounting firms. Contracted nationally known speakers. Maintained attendee profiles for use by clients' sales representatives. 1991-1993
- Contracted by Apple to create reports on accountants' influence in the selection of Macintosh for their practices and their clients. Focused on accountants' buying behavior, business software for Macintosh vs. PC, and suggestions on increasing use of Macintosh. 1992
- Conceived, outlined, and implemented tax software seminar series at hotels and CPA firms. 1991-93.

Software Implementation and Training
- Created Web sites, provided consultations, maintenance, and promotion to increase traffic. 1997-1998
- Revised accounting/medical billing software procedures, dramatically increasing cash flow. 1997-1998
- Provided cost/benefit analysis of various software/hardware options, training, and related business costs and changes needed during software implementation. Responded to numerous RFPs. 1982-1998
- Instructor for Microsoft NT, Novell Netware, and numerous desktop applications courses. 1989-1995
- Implemented accounting software modules, documented customization, and trained users. 1989-1995
- Converted data from competitive tax software for numerous CPA firms. 1989-1992

Accounting and Business Reporting Analysis
- Licensed to practice before the IRS for audits since 1991. Specialized in high-income clients.
- Successfully convinced the IRS of client's net operating loss, exceeding $400,000, due to fire, without normal documentation. Reconstructed loss from secondary sources. 1996
- Tax preparation for partnership and corporations including consolidated corporations, with related sales tax, property tax, and business tax reporting for federal and states. 1991-1995
- Contracted by economist for complex litigation procedure involving over 20 groups of real estate partnerships to provide analysis of conflicting financial data dating back 20 years. Reconstructed financial records, prepared spreadsheets, and presentations for litigation. 1994

EDUCATION

MBA, University of San Clemente, 1982. Concentration in Marketing and International Business.
BA, University of East Florida, 1978. Extensive Business and International Studies Courses.

Professional Conferences attended: SAP TechEd '98, SAP ASUG User Conference '97, Microsoft SAP Customer Workshop, SAP Year 2000 Seminar, SAP/Microsoft/DEC Seminar, Microsoft Tech-Ed, Microsoft Professional Developer Conferences, and Microsoft Sitebuilder Conference.

Sent about 24; received eight interviews and a new job.

DANIEL BURKE

231 Rosati Road   Residence: 580/555-5101
Enid, OK 73703   E-mail: pizza@ionet.net

QUALITY MANAGEMENT / COMMERCIAL INFORMATION SYSTEMS

PROFILE:
- ➢ Comprehensive experience in senior-level management of corporate commercial information systems and quality assurance functions, with P&L responsibility for technology policies, standards, and budgets in a deregulated environment.

- ➢ Skilled in strategic planning, policy formulation, product development, risk analysis, change management, implementation logistics, and budget administration; proven ability to lead organizations through restructuring and process re-engineering.

- ➢ Hire, train, and supervise project teams and independent contractors in quality and federal/state regulatory compliance; nearly certified PMI project manager and BSI Lead ISO Auditor; well-versed in ISO 9002, JIT/EDI, and continuous improvement processes.

TECHNICAL KNOWLEDGE:
- ➢ *Software:* Windows/DOS and mid-range turnkey and company-developed accounting, office productivity, and dispatch/freight forwarding systems.
- ➢ *Network/Communication Software and Languages:* Novell, TCP/IP, NFS, leased line T-1, and Frame Relay WAN.
- ➢ *Hardware:* IBM AS/400, SCO UNIX servers, Novell, and Qualcomm two-way truck satellite communication systems.

CAREER BACKGROUND:

<u>Nolan Transport, Inc.</u>, Enid, OK   1987-Present
A $101 million privately held, tractor/trailer over-the-road bulk trucking firm.
Vice President, Information Systems and Quality   7/94–Present
In charge of the planning and direction of information systems and quality assurance functions, including all telephone and communication systems, with P&L responsibility.
Hire, train, and supervise 11 direct staff and four managers, with oversight management of 12 project team members, on $100,000 to $750,000 projects.
Administered a $1.4 million annual operating budget, with capital acquisition determination and approval authority.

- → Analyze, interpret, and apply lane/market data and emerging trends to demand forecasts.

- → Modernized the company technologically from a high-cost job shop environment to low-cost, standardized operations; completely replaced every application with networked, online systems and methods.

- → Acquired and transformed the Quality Department into a driving force for cost containment and avoidance, focusing on costs of quality and ISO certification.

- → Initiated and developed a middle management training program; involved in the setup, staff training, and opening of all new offices.

→   Orchestrated the ISO 9002 certification process in 50 offices nationally; certified 12 locations and corporate headquarters by end 1995.

Director, Information Systems   8/92–7/94

Responsible for all aspects of daily company-wide information systems operations, with a budget of $1 million; supervised three data processing managers.
Determined and managed technology capital acquisitions, installations, and maintenance.

→   Upgraded the IBM System 38 to an AS/400 system, interfacing with AR/AP, general ledger, and payroll functions for the first time in the history of the company.

Manager, Communication Systems   5/87–8/92

Directed multiple projects to support AT&T UNIX communication systems for order entry applications, including software development and post-installation troubleshooting, working closely with clients to assess and adhere to project specifications, requirements, schedules, and budgets.

→   Purchased over 50 UNIX-based computers, networked with home office computers, for field dispatchers to place orders and monitor equipment resources.

<u>Computer Applications Ltd.</u>, Oklahoma City, OK   1984–1987
Software Development Project Leader

Managed a team of system analysts/programmers in order entry system development and maintenance for clients of this privately-held, Sperry value-added reseller.

→   Provided direct sales force with technical evaluations of clients.

→   Negotiated consulting/development contracts with companies ranging in gross revenues from $3 million to $12 million.

→   Management liquidated the company as of the Sperry/Burroughs merger.

TRAINING: <u>Seminars completed include:</u>
                            Project Management, Project Management Institute
                            ISO/Quality Management, British Standards Institute

EDUCATION: <u>Oklahoma State University</u>, Stillwater, OK
                            B.S. degree in computing and informational sciences

Sent three; received two interviews and a new job.

JOHN R. CROCKER

446 Spring Drive, #315
Roselle, IL 60172

630/555-1363

SYSTEM ANALYSIS / DESIGN / PROGRAMMING

OBJECTIVE: A position where skills in project management will be of value.

PROFILE:
- Extensive background in business application design, coding, testing, documentation, staff training, post-installation evaluation, and technical assistance.

- Proven ability to communicate technical/complex information in understandable terms to non-technical and technical personnel; plan and conduct presentations, and write proposals, system documentation, and client reference materials.

TECHNICAL KNOWLEDGE:
- Proficient in Tandem languages, software, and operating systems including Tandem TAL, COBOL, Pathway/SCOBOL, Enable, Enscribe, DDL, and Tandem Guardian.

- Knowledge of IBM PL/1, Basic Assembler Language, COBOL, IMS DB-DC, and MVS.

CAREER BACKGROUND:

No Problem Data, Inc., Itasca, IL   8/96-Present
Lead Programmer / Analyst
Perform detailed system analysis, design, programming, testing, documentation, and installation of this company's wireless dispatching system for utility customers.
Develop and customize systems to meet specific customer needs; modify TAL and COBOL pathway servers for multiple customers and write server programs for new customers.

Quickie Computing Corporation, Elk Grove Village, IL   1987-1992
Senior Programmer / Analyst
Responsible for all aspects of analysis, design, programming, testing, documentation, and installation of online check authorization systems for retail food service businesses.
Determined customer specifications/requirements working closely with client/company personnel including engineers and systems trainers.
Estimated project schedules and costs; prepared job quotes for sales proposals and bids.
Trained and supervised junior programmer/analysts.
Interfaced with the Project Coordinator to produce reference and training manuals.
→   Received a letter of commendation and bonus for consistently high performance.
→   Innovated the "driver's license on-the-fly" access method for check authorization systems, and provided the undergirding documentation for multi-merchant systems design.

Major Projects
- *Eagle Foods, Appletree Foods, F&M:* Lead analyst assigned to check authorization programs and the CRT system.
- *Safeway Foods:* shared Lead Analyst assignment and backup Analyst for the CRT system.
- *Walgreen's, Sunrise, Schnucks, and National Stores:* backup Systems Analyst.

JOHN R. CROCKER
Page Two

<u>Control Data Corporation (CDC)</u>, Park Ridge, IL   1983-1987
3M purchased the health care system and closed this facility.
Senior Programmer / Analyst, CDC   2/85-3/87
Retained to integrate the CDC and Sentry Data software.
→   Selected to write the interface between the CDC registration system and Sentry Tandem-based patient accounting system for full integration.
→   Upgraded and maintained the Sentry Data registration system under pre-existing contracts.

Senior Programmer / Analyst, Sentry Data, Inc.   5/83-2/85
Managed the Tandem-based health care system for hospitals, including module customization in accordance with client specifications.
→   Specialized in the patient registration subsystem.
→   CDC purchased the rights to Sentry Data's software.

<u>First National Bank of Chicago</u>, Chicago, IL   1980-1983
Senior Program / Analyst, International Systems Group
Provided technical assistance to the Bank's New York Edge Act office, including business application design, development, and implementation, and module enhancement and modification.
→   *Applications:* accounts payable/receivable, cash management, international cash letter, profit allocation, and financial statement functions.
→   Primary resource for worldwide support of the International Banking pay-receive system.
→   Developed main customer account statement programs to provide clients with reports from the SWIFT 950 and the International Balance Reporter cash management systems.
→   Created the ability for the New York office to make international clearing house payments in New York; increased payment transaction capability to a peak volume of 2,000 payments per day from 600 daily payments.

<u>Northern Trust Company</u>, Chicago, IL   1978-1980
Senior Programmer, Information Systems and Services
Performed a wide range of programming activities, including business system analysis pre-planning, feasibility reports, functional specification, and DDA system interface design.
→   Supervised year-end testing of the Savings system.
→   Chaired the DDA ad hoc committee to develop system maintenance procedures.
→   Served as Training Coordinator for the Retail Banking Division of the IS Department.

TRAINING: <u>Numerous seminars and courses completed include:</u>
■ Tandem seminars in Concepts and Facilities, TAL, GUARDIAN, Data Communications, and System Manager.

EDUCATION: <u>Roosevelt University</u>, Chicago, IL
B.G.S. degree candidate in Computer Science; Focus: Business Information Systems

<u>University of Wisconsin</u>, Madison, WI
B.A. degree candidate in Journalism

Sent 50; received seven interviews and a new job.

SUSAN BRIGHTER
2242 Hampton Street
Naperville, IL 60565

Res.: 630/555-1547   Brighter@xnet.com   Fax: 630/555-2569

TELECOMMUNICATIONS / IT PROJECTS

PROFILE:

➤ Comprehensive experience in telecommunications, including networking routing, administration, account updating, and system debugging/maintenance.

➤ Effectively troubleshoot IRQ and I/O conflicts; map Novell networks; familiar with NT application servers, including backups, monitoring, anti-virus work, and documentation.

➤ Skilled in MS Office and Macintosh systems, as well as Lotus, Office Works, and cross-platform functions; familiar with staff hiring, training, and supervision.

➤ Utilize and/or install modems, network interface cards, memory, power supplies, scanners, fax servers, local/network printers, and programmable telephone equipment.

➤ Knowledge of general accounting, including accounts payable/receivable, general ledgers, budgeting, forecasting, tax preparation, and status reporting.

EMPLOYMENT:

Barley Technical Corp., Wheaton, IL   1996-Present
Ranked #123 among the Inc. 500, with employees in 20 states.
Office Manager / System Administrator
Reporting directly to the President, administer and maintain Novell 3.12/NT 4.0 Servers, a 24-node Ethernet network, and all related hardware and software.
Personally maintain and administer network and local printers, scanners, and a fax server.
Supervise two employees in accounts receivable, payroll, and general reception, including employee relocations.
Effectively train employees on new software installations.

→ Assisted in construction buildouts, including contractor relations and loan negotiations.

→ Acted as Project Accountant for the build-out of three offices.

→ Administer 401K, profit sharing, and medical plans.

→ Responsible for all Human Resources and Accounting functions; procure international visas for consultants; coordinate job fairs and special occasions.

Midwest Fertility Center, Ltd., Downers Grove, IL   1995
Eight locations in two states with 50-60 Employees.
Controller: Reported to the President
Saved more than $70,000 in commissions created by software design problems.
Performed extensive research and troubleshooting to correct problems using analytical skills.
Responsible for financial accounting, reporting, and analysis, as well as A/R, A/P, payroll, job costing, and inventory control.
Located and negotiated with vendors and suppliers; handled cost-effective purchasing and contract supervision.

→ Acted as project coordinator for a Surgi-Center build-out and construction.

→ Consulted with owners regarding business endeavors in real estate and joint ventures.

227

St. Petronille Church, Glen Ellyn, IL   1992-1994
Bookkeeper
Performed all essential bookkeeping functions and reported to the chairman of finance. This church consisted of 2,300 families, a school of 400 students K-8, and a religious ed. program with more than 600 students.
Responsible for all accounting functions, including contributions, A/P, A/R, general ledger, payroll, budgeting, bank reconciliations, and financial statements.

→ Setup a peer-to-peer system for four computers.

→ Proposed, researched, purchased, and installed an 11-module, integrated accounting and management system by Omega C.G. Ltd.; wrote the program to convert member data.

→ Uncovered an embezzlement scheme involving over $70,000 annually of a total budgeted income of $2.1 million.

→ Prepared and consolidated financial statements for reporting to the Diocesan controller.

→ Streamlined procedures for expeditiously paying over 600 vendors with a minimum of paperwork and additional approval requirements.

→ Implemented policies for 50 to 65 full-time and part-time employees, in compliance with state and federal labor laws, and maintained all personnel files.

→ Analyzed, monitored, and consolidated budgets for 15 departments; prepared the salary budget for 13 staff managers according to Diocesan guidelines.

CJ's Accounting and Taxes, Naperville, IL   1990-1991
Self-employed: Public Accountant and Consultant
Compiled monthly financial statements for corporations and year-end financials for six corporations, two partnerships, two sole proprietorships, and approximately 35 individuals.
Utilized a Macintosh computer with Peachtree Insight G/L software and after-the-fact payroll processed on an Excel spreadsheet.

→ Filed all necessary tax forms, including 941, 940, 1120, 1065, 1040, ST1, IL501, Worker's compensation, and union reports.

Carpetland USA, Munster, IN (Headquarters)   1988-1989
Office Manager - Reported to the Regional accounting manager.
Responsible for the accounting department, including general ledger maintenance and analysis, account reconciliations, labor and material variances, and overseeing A/P, A/R.

→ Uncovered a scheme by the sales manager to alter figures on the computer.

→ Recovered $20,000 of charge invoices never processed because of a fire.

Malibu Interiors, Downers Grove, IL   1985-1988
Home Furnishings retailer with annual gross sales of over $4,000,000.
Accounting Office Manager - Reported to the President.

PRIOR EXPERIENCE:
* Accounting instructor for Omega Software Corporation (temporary assignment).
* Air Traffic Controller. * Internal Revenue Collector.

EDUCATION:
Associate's Degree: Computer Information Systems, College of DuPage   1994
Associate's Degree: Accounting, College of DuPage   1991
CURRENTLY STUDYING for CNE Certification.

Sent about 40; received four interviews and numerous inquiries from Internet distribution.

NELLIE SPEAKER
2253 Sofar Court
Bartlett, IL 60103

630/555-1276
E-mail: Whale@cdnet.edu

CORPORATE TRAINING / DEVELOPMENT

PROFILE:

➢ Comprehensive experience in training and communications, including program planning, administration, and human resource development.

➢ Skilled in creative public relations and promotions; effectively plan, implement, and track the performance of market research, strategies, and community outreach.

➢ Utilize Internet resources, databases, and various software for such applications as Web site development, job market analysis, applicant testing, career matching, and the publication of findings.

➢ Experience in staff hiring, training, supervision, and motivation; handle performance reviews and all key aspects of employer/employee relations.

➢ Perform group and individual counseling for virtually all ages; determine aptitudes and career goals and define methods to reach those goals.

EMPLOYMENT:

<u>Peterson College</u>, Gilberts, IL   1989-Present
Career Services Manager
Responsible for all major career services at this community college, the largest in Illinois, with more than 20,000 students.
Personally hire, train, and supervise a team of three office staff and five student aides in program creation/administration, media relations, student testing, and job placement assistance.
Through research and analysis, provide and interpret data on the local employment outlook and on future staffing needs of national and global industries.
Plan and conduct seven to 10 presentations for up to 400 at-risk students per week to encourage further education and skill development to meet changing employer needs.
Handle extensive public and media relations to promote COD educational and career services to the public at large.
* Developed a highly successful, $60,000 computerized job matching system called AIMS: the Automated Industry Matching System. This is now linked to more than 20,000 employers and matches more than 2,000 students per week. AIMS was eventually adopted by four other community colleges.
* Compiled data on local, national, and global job trends and wrote/published *Jobs and the Economy.*
* Designed a Web site featuring COD career services, classes, and special programs.
* Recently co-chaired a conference of the Midwest Association of Colleges and Employers, with a guest list including John Callaway, Lynn Martin, and numerous CEOs.

NELLIE SPEAKER
Page Two

Elgin Community College, Elgin, IL   1984-1989
Admissions and Registration Supervisor
Directed all admissions and registration activities at ECC to increase enrollment
and improve service to full- and part-time students.
Worked closely with the Dean of Student Services and acted as liaison to foreign
students.
* Responsible for writing and implementing a script for touch-tone registration,
  resulting in greater enrollment.
* Chaired the Nursing Selection Committee and updated/maintained entrance
  records for all nursing candidates.

Illinois Technical College, Chicago, IL   1982-1984
Admissions Counselor
Provided advice and assistance to students in the selection of academic programs
to meet their needs.
Counseled and worked with students throughout the enrollment process.
Evaluated high school transcripts, administered entrance exams and assisted students in applying for all types of financial aid.
* Edited and wrote articles for the school newspaper: *Tech Talk.*

PRIOR
EXPERIENCE: Chrysler Learning Service Center, Detroit, MI
                  Intake Specialist
                  Administered interest inventories and job skill ability tests to people who had
                  been incarcerated or institutionalized, or who had experienced long-term
                  unemployment.
                  Tested candidates and recommended training programs based on findings.
                  Updated and maintained weekly progress reports on all clients.

EDUCATION: DePaul University, Chicago, IL
                  Pursuing a Master's Degree in Career Counseling
                  Expected graduation: 12/02.

                  University of Illinois at Chicago, Chicago, IL
                  Bachelor of Arts Degree: Psychology

MEMBERSHIPS: **Member of Two Boards of Directors:**
                  The Naperville Community Career Center for Downsized Executives.
                  DKIN: Disabled Kids In Need.
                  * Affiliated with ACE: The Midwest Association of Colleges and Employers.

Sent about 50; received 10 interviews.

ANDREW TAYLOR
452 Cedar Court
Dunwoody, GA 30350
TaylorA@aol.com

Res: 770/555-9797   Ofc: 770/555-3513

MANAGEMENT / OPERATIONS

PROFILE:

> ➤ Comprehensive experience in staff training, supervision, and operations management, including full responsibility for team leadership, customer service, and quality control.

> ➤ Trained in project management and system setup and administration; consistently track call center volume and measure needs and capacity for effective staff scheduling.

> ➤ Experience in sales support and troubleshooting, including pricing, contract negotiations, budgeting, and forecasting.

> ➤ Communicate with customers, vendors, suppliers, and fellow workers with professional yet personal written and oral communication skills.

> ➤ Utilize MS Office 95 and 97, as well as MS Word, Excel, Access, Outlook, WordPerfect, Internet Explorer, and Netscape PC for spreadsheets and correspondence.

EXPERIENCE:

<u>Computers By George</u>, formerly All Electronics Corporation, Alpharetta, GA
Call Center Supervisor   9/93-Present
Effectively train and supervise a team of 15 in call center operations and the dispatch of service technicians to client locations nationwide.
Work closely with district managers and staff in telecommunications, including call routing and the analysis/streamlining of service calls, including routing and logging of calls to engineers.
Work directly with contractors and ensure quality of work; compile and present monthly reports on contractor quality.
Utilize a relational database to register, profile, and track customer and call status; maintain four different screens/nodes.
Provide mission-critical support for desktop hardware and applications, UNIX, VMS, premium services, Windows NT, server teams, and Internet/multi-vendor support.

→ Earned Trail Blazer award for three years due to highly professional, personal involvement in ensuring excellent service delivery and a positive attitude.

→ Assist in staff hiring and the constant updating and support of this 24 x 7 call center with top management.

Contract Administration 5/90-9/93

Handled established accounts for upgrades, renewals, and contract changes.
Sold supplemental services, including upgrades and add-ons; negotiated prices
with customers.

→ Maintained a large database of major accounts, sales leads, and multi-
   vendor relations.

→ Instrumental in conversions, updates, renewals, warranties, and
   supplemental services.

Service Delivery 9/88-5/90

Worked extensively with major accounts to track performance measures and
responses.
Coordinated/allocated vendor resources and subcontractors for quick problem
resolution.

→ Implemented action plans by effectively managing installations and
   outages.

Office Manager, Chicago, IL 6/85-9/88

Effectively planned and implemented office procedures for internal support,
including work order expediting.
Closely tracked and reported expenses and inventories.

→ Performed group and individual cross-training of technical staff in
   general reception, customer relations, and office procedures.

Receptionist, Chicago, IL 3/82-6/85

Managed a wide range of tasks for complete administrative support, including
call answering and expediting.
Communicated with customers and staff in a professional manner.
Handled a variety of general office procedures and paperwork.

EDUCATION: Harry S. Truman College, Chicago, IL
Successful completion of courses in Business.

New Horizons Learning Institute, Atlanta, GA
Completed courses in various Microsoft applications.

Sent five; received two interviews.

PAMELA L. ELFIN

2225 E. Madison Street
Chicago, IL 60661

Pamie@aol.com   312/555-4557

TRAINING / DEVELOPMENT

PROFILE:

➤ Plan and conduct group and individual training programs and seminars, including full responsibility for written and oral presentations to groups and individuals.

➤ Experience in promotions, public relations, special events, and meetings to train and motivate staff, management, and potential customers.

➤ Skilled in the writing of newsletters, brochures, and instructional aids; familiar with various desktop publishing software, including Microsoft PowerPoint, for promotions and creative correspondence.

➤ Strong knowledge of financial products including stocks, bonds, and mutual funds; utilize Excel for spreadsheets, graphs, and charts.

EXPERIENCE: Old Tabby Investments, Chicago, IL   1997-Present
Investment Executive
Responsible for new business development by presenting seminars, networking, and conducting informational programs to the general public.
Conduct interviews of potential clients and create custom investment programs for people in a wide range of situations.
Analyze individual portfolios to determine asset allocation, employing stocks, bonds, mutual funds, and annuities for personal and retirement accounts.
Work closely with clients to determine and meet their specific investment goals.
Perform product research, spreadsheet development, and status reporting on stocks and business development.

→ Utilize research skills and a strong knowledge of investment instruments and tax codes related to personal investing.

→ Winner of a free trip for Outstanding Contribution to Sales.

Smith Barney, Chicago, IL   1992-1996
Financial Consultant
Planned and conducted numerous presentations on investment topics for investment clubs and community groups.
Acted as consultant for fee-based, money management programs.
Conducted training on such topics risk tolerance, needs, asset allocation, and rollovers for retirees.
Helped in strategic planning, defining investment goals, and building investment portfolios.

PAMELA L. ELFIN

Page Two

→ Responsible for more than 300 accounts.

→ Additional topics included projecting financial needs for retirement, funding college education, and maximizing retirement plans.

Gruntal & Company, New York, NY   1990–1992
Account Executive / Assistant to a Certified Financial Planner
Performed customer service and problem-resolution on a daily basis.
Assisted clients in retirement planning.

→ Advised and monitored investments for a small, personal group of clients.

→ Assisted in producing a quarterly newsletter with an emphasis on investment strategies.

Woodlawn Foundation, New York, NY   1988–1990
Fundraising Coordinator
Involved in designing a successful volunteer program to raise capital for an educational foundation.
Recruited, trained, and motivated up to 75 volunteers involved in networking and fundraising.

Produced and constantly updated donor lists.

→ Monitored and computerized records.

→ Chief writer, producer, and editor of a quarterly newsletter.

Dean Witter, WI and IL   1981–1988
Account Executive
Responsible for selling and marketing investment services to a wide range of clients.

→ Promoted from various positions, including:
   Branch Manager's Assistant, Registered Sales Assistant, and Account Executive.

Prior Experience as:
Secretary to the President of a Business Consulting Firm.
Secondary English Teacher.

LICENSES: Series 7, Series 63, and N.A.S.D. Registration (1982).
                  Series 65 (1992).

EDUCATION: Boston College, Boston, MA
                  Bachelor of Arts Degree
                  * Graduated Cum Laude.
                  * Major: English; Minor: Secondary Education.

Sent 50; received eight interviews.

RANDALL B. SEMANTIC
220 Summer Lane
Toronto, Canada, M4T1B4
Randy@interlog.com   416/555-0874

TELEVISION PRODUCTION / BROADCASTING

PROFILE:

➢ Comprehensive experience in television broadcasting and production, including full responsibility for national broadcasting of live and taped sports and special events, entertainment, informational, and news programs.

➢ Extensive experience with the Canadian Broadcasting Corporation (CBC), the Olympic Games, the NHL, Major League Baseball, Imperial Life, White Rose, and special how-to programs.

➢ Perform research, writing, and development of corporate training and sales videos.

➢ Coordinate all aspects of video and broadcast production, from talent coordination and set design to lighting, camera placement, editing, and special effects.

➢ Proficient in all standard and state-of-the-art production techniques, including non-linear computer editing and digital technologies.

EMPLOYMENT:

<u>Ambrose College of Technology</u>, North York, Ontario, Canada
Instructor   9/98-Present
Responsible for training 18 students in all aspects of TV production and studio operations, including related theory and lab work.
Plan and implement all lab activities and tests; work closely with students and track individual performance.
Lab subjects include: scripting, floor plans, crew positions, studio camera use, ENG/EFP cameras, angle of axis, lighting, video editing, graphic layout, video switchers and systems, character generators, audio boards, set design, and direction.

→ Create and supervise a wide range of practical exercises; all students must write, block, and shoot a 30-second commercial.

→ Provide experience in camera operations, switching, lighting, computer graphics, and all editing functions, including inserting text and graphics.

<u>Rob Francis Productions</u>, Toronto   1986-Present
Independent Producer
Effectively manage corporate video productions and broadcast and freelance work, including marketing and training videos, as well as other instructional programs.
Hire and coordinate writers and assist in script writing; manage creative personnel at all levels.
Locate and hire all talent, including actors, commentators, announcers, and researchers.

Key accounts include:
McDonald's, KFC, AMC, CBC Enterprises, Imperial Life, the NHL, Proctor & Gamble, Schenley, and the Roy Thomson Hall.

Sports Broadcast Productions include:
The XV Commonwealth Games, Victoria, 1994; Isolation Director at athletics venue for host broadcaster; originated international video and audio production feed to world broadcasters.
The XVV Olympic Winter Games, Calgary, 1988; Associate Director at the ski jumping venue for host broadcaster.
CBC TV News: Producer in charge of satellite news gathering and dissemination, as well as on-air coordination.

Red Rose Crafts and Nursery Sales, Ltd., Unionville, Ontario   1989-1997
Executive Producer / Communications Specialist - Red Rose Productions
Responsible for all aspects of production and management for *The Hobby Garden*, a 65-episode, national TV series with broadcast sales to Global, Life, and TVO Networks.
Oversee a. $450,000 budget and supervise all staff and crew.

→   Managed budgets and media promotions, while personally selling commercial time to underwrite production costs.

→   Coordinated marketing departments of program sponsors; prepared and produced a wide range of commercials.

Producer and Manager for Red Rose Productions, producing training videos for staff and how-to demos for in-store customer use.
Created and produced craft video titles for retail sale, from concept to package design.
In charge of producing all French versions of Red Rose projects.

→   As Co-Chair for the Canada Blooms flower show, produced a profit of $150,000.

Canadian Broadcasting Corporation, Toronto, Montreal, Halifax   1968-1985
Television Producer / Director
Performed full management of sports productions, including the XI Commonwealth Games in Edmonton; directed boxing venue coverage and originated international AV production feed to world satellite feed.
For the XXI Olympic Summer Games in Montreal, directed basketball coverage for ORTO and earned the **1976 TV Award.**

Other projects included (full details on request):
Sports of the XXI Olympiad, Montreal; Montreal Expos Baseball, Hockey Night in Canada, Montreal; World Cycling Championships; the Canada Summer Games, and Universiade in Turin, Italy.
Entertainment productions such as: From Our Family to Yours; New Years Eve Live!; Front Page Challenge and the Bob McLean Show.
News and special events: The Journal and The Papal Visit.

RANDALL B. SEMANTIC

EDUCATION:
Ryerson PolyTechnic University, Toronto
Radio and Television Arts Diploma
Graduate: Landscape Architecture Certificate Program

McGill University and Concordia University, Montreal
French as a Second Language

COMPUTERS:
Skilled in various computer systems: Adobe Premiere for Digital Audio and Video Editing, Microsoft Word, Excel for spreadsheets, Access for database management, and PowerPoint and Netscape for presentations and Internet access.

MEMBERSHIPS:
GWAA: Garden Writers Association of America.
Civic Garden Center and the YMCA.

Sent to five internal postings; chosen as one of three among 56 applicants for interview.

MARK CHECKER
2306 Dover Drive
Hanover Park, IL 60103
630/555-8916

QUALITY / INVENTORY / ADMINISTRATION / SUPERVISOR

PROFILE:

> Comprehensive experience in a wide range of business operations, including staff management, quality control, inventory management, and management reporting.

> Proven ability to build teams and motivate associates to achieve peak performance. Skilled in problem analysis and resolution; identify the root causes, develop answers, and implement solutions.

> Superior communication skills to coordinate various activities between departments. Handle multiple priorities and projects effectively.

> Proficient in Excel, PowerPoint, Word, and e-mail on a Macintosh system. Develop spreadsheets, format reports, and create graphs to present data in clear/meaningful ways.

EXPERIENCE:

Clarity, Inc., Itasca, IL   1993-Present
Manufacturing Quality Coordinator / Analyst   11/96-Present
Responsible for all aspects of quality control, including inspections, documentation, staff supervision, and quality reporting for the packing division.
Coordinate the activities of the quality auditors and monitor results; train and motivate personnel.
Document all inspection data; utilize various spreadsheets to format reports as well as graphs of inspection results.
Establish and implement action plans to eliminate quality defects.
Conduct regular meetings with packing group, auditors, supervisors, and managers to discuss quality issues.

→ Worked with the corporate Quality Department to develop the proper links for data retrieval from the field.
→ Wrote the quality auditing MPS for the Packing group.
→ Championed a TCS / Problem Solving team to attack and resolve issues such as cycle time, cost reductions, and quality.
→ Showed a 20% decrease in defects (1997).

Quality Auditor   1/96-10/96
Performed random inspections of packed crates to determine the quality level of the department.
Documented inspection results on hard copy and entered into UNIX Wingz spreadsheets.
Investigated and identified the root causes for defects created in packing.
Worked with the management team to develop action plans to correct quality mistakes.

MARK CHECKER
Page Two

Participated in weekly meetings with the quality department to discuss quality concerns.

→   Represented Motorola on multiple client visits to China and India.

→   Championed a quality TCS Team that was responsible for a 50% decrease in defects within 5 months.

→   Worked with clients to identify and correct quality problems.

Field Team Leader / Refurb Inventory Control   12/94-1/96

Traveled to client warehouses to lead the inventory, packing, and quality evaluation of refurbishing equipment.

Led Motorola associates in preparing shipments for return back to consolidation warehouses.

Consolidated all refurbishing equipment in appropriate warehouses. Created a showroom atmosphere for customers to view and evaluate merchandise for possible purchase.

→   Recognized and rewarded for exceptional performance and commitment to job while running an outside packing firm to handle critical customer orders.

Team Leader   11/93-12/94

Directed a group of 12 to 15 associates in sorting, verifying, and packaging of ancillary and warranty equipment.

Coordinated with planners and schedulers on work load capacities.

Worked with crate vendors and Motorola engineers to develop more reliable crates for our clients.

→   Installed a Productivity Metric that resulted in increased productivity through greater visibility and ownership.

→   Implemented the first Attendance Metric that focused on improving cycle time and workload capacity.

→   Installed a department Reward and Recognition program that resulted in increased morale and productivity.

→   Represented the department on a TCS team that streamlined processes to improve cycle time.

Packer   5/93-11/93

TRAINING: Completed a wide range of Motorola university courses including:
Macintosh Excel Introduction, Intermediate and Advanced

Macintosh PowerPoint	*MPC Wingz*
The Six Steps to Six Sigma	*Alternative Thinking*
Continuous Improvement Tools	*QSR Training*
Advanced Manufacturing Processes	*Emergency Evacuation*

EDUCATION: College of DuPage / Northwood University

→   Currently pursuing a Bachelor's Degree in Business Administration with a Minor in International Business.

Sent about 50; received 10 interviews; accepted a new position.
Received many more interviews from Internet distribution.

ALBERT H. KINSEY

7777 Pecan Drive
Oakland, NJ 07436

Ofc: 201/555-0857
Res: 201/555-0636

OBJECTIVE:

Executive Management - Sales / Marketing
A senior leadership position utilizing entrepreneurial talents for an advanced technology company, requiring team building, client relations, needs analysis and growth.

PROFILE:

- Comprehensive hands-on background in all aspects of change management, process re-engineering, new business development and strategic planning in diverse technology environments.

- Manage P&L, budgeting, territory expansion, new product introduction, data/network consolidation, outsourcing, contract negotiation, competitive analysis, market research and account maintenance.

- Extensive systems experience with WANs, LANs, client-servers, disaster recovery operations and consulting services; proficient in TQM, ISO 9002 and other quality programs.

- Hire, train, mentor and coach management and staff in company product lines, policies and procedures.

- Work at the executive-level with Fortune 500 clients such as Citicorp, Bank of New York, Chemical Bank, MetLife, Prudential, Paine Webber, Chubb, Morgan Stanley, ADP, Bell Atlantic, Nynex and UPS.

- Recognized by corporate management for consistently exceeding all objectives and for skills in troubleshooting and problem resolution in high-pressure situations.

EMPLOYMENT:

<u>Total Network Techfolks</u>, Oakland, NJ   1993-Present
An $85 million company with consistent growth since 1984, providing mainframe connectivity through innovative application of channel networking, as well as Gateway and client-server hardware/software solutions.
Area Sales Director
Responsible for sales, marketing and customer support for 11 states in the United States' Northeast corridor.
Hired, trained and supervised seven new sales representatives and six SCs, resulting in exceptional performance.
→   Increased sales by 300% in only three years with 40 new accounts; personally closed the largest transaction for 1995.
→   Directed the most profitable sales area in the company.
→   Achieved extensive market exposure for this firm with all IBM Metro trading areas.
→   Created a structured marketing plan for all national and major accounts.
→   Maximized account coverage and maintenance through unique territory assignment methods.

J.D. Edwards and Company, Secaucus, NJ   1992-1993
A privately held $250 million company specializing in financial software for
AS/400 platforms; named "Best of Breed" for G/L, payroll, financials and manu-
facturing/wholesale distribution.

Large Account Executive
In charge of sales and maintenance of domestic accounts, specializing in IBM
and AT&T, as well as key clients in the NY metropolitan area.
→   Personally positioned this firm as a strategic partner with IBM/ISSC.

AT&T - Paradyne, Oakland, NJ   1983-1992
A high-growth, WAN communications company tasked with development and
implementation of innovative communications technology, including the in-
vention of Channel Extension and high-speed modem technology.

Senior Account Executive - Large/National Accounts
Managed sales, marketing and customer relations with clients in the NY metro,
PA and New England areas for the Channel Extension product line.
→   Personally responsible for the IBM account worldwide.
→   Positioned this firm as a strategic partner with IBM/ISSC; established
         a greater market share nationwide.
→   Assisted ISSC in winning and fulfilling the first public outsourcing
         contract.
→   Nurtured additional partnerships with other sales forces.

Assistant to the Executive Vice President
Coordinated highly successful efforts to completely reengineer field sales and
service worldwide through strategic sales, marketing and long-term planning
with a global perspective.
→   Achieved 130% of annual project objectives on time and within budget.
→   Increased field sales productivity through streamlined operating pro-
         cedures and resource allocation.
→   Facilitated cross-functional partnerships between departments, along
         with new goals and job models.
→   Developed and implemented unique approaches to enhance manage-
         ment and staff performance in sales, customer service and quality.

District Manager
Assumed sales, marketing, system engineering and administration for a NYC
and Long Island non-performing territory.
→   Improved sales by 300% in 18 months and staff performance to 132%
         of goal from 37%, resulting in five of six candidates for the 100% club.
→   Successfully sold the first jointly marketed transaction with AT&T.
→   Oversaw the reorganization into two districts, along with a doubled
         staff and team-based goal setting.
→   Spearheaded a joint marketing effort after acquisition by AT&T.

Senior Account Executive

Managed sales and marketing in northern NJ in a variety of sales positions with increasing responsibility.

→   Improved sales of Channel Extension products by over 30%; won 20 different awards for performance and leadership.

→   Also served as Senior Account Manager; mentored six other Account Managers.

<u>Commerce Clearing House - Computax Inc.</u>, New York, NY   1980-1982

A $50 million division, specializing in tax services and in-house systems for accountants; formerly RJ Software Systems.

Assistant Division Manager

In charge of sales/marketing strategies for services and systems in the NYC area.

Hired, trained, motivated and supervised a professional staff in product lines and company policies.

District Sales Manager

Created an effective sales team of three field representatives in client training, field support and excellent customer service in a NY metro, PA and New England territory.

Area Sales Manager

Personally grew the assigned sales territory in the above area with four sales representatives.

<u>Burroughs Corporation</u>, Paramus, NJ   1978-1980

A multi-billion computer company with leading edge products in close competition with IBM.

Zone Manager

Handled sales and marketing efforts of mini-computer systems to a diverse business clientele.

→   Created the first targeted branch for computer sales to a professional niche, i.e., accountants.

Marketing Representative

Coordinated new product introduction, lead generation and sales presentations.

→   Successfully sold a record number of minicomputers in one year, resulting in a new vertical branch.

EDUCATION: <u>Fairleigh-Dickenson University</u>, Teaneck, NJ   1978

B.S. Degree in Accounting

*   Completed corporate seminars and workshops in Process Development, Management Principles, Successful Sales Techniques, Executive Imaging, Effectiveness Training and Managing Organizational Change.

Chapter 13

At Last:
The
Interview

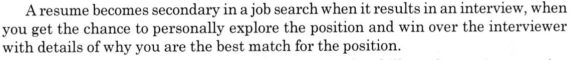

A resume becomes secondary in a job search when it results in an interview, when you get the chance to personally explore the position and win over the interviewer with details of why you are the best match for the position.

The interview is your chance to elaborate on the skills and experience you've showcased in your resume—and to make a personal connection with the person you hope to work with. It's your opportunity to go for the close. Therefore, it's absolutely essential that you enter the interview with the information and skills you need to make that close.

Entire books have been written on interviewing, but following are a few key tips for a job-winning interview.

Research the company and position

I stressed in the previous chapter the importance of learning as much as possible about job opportunities you are pursuing *before* developing and sending your resume and cover letter. I emphasize again, even more strongly, how important it is to walk into the company with a clear understanding of the environment you may soon be working in.

Not only do you want to know such facts as the size of the company, annual revenues, locations, chief activities, and plans for the future, you'll also want to know about the culture of the company. Why? Because if you walk into the interview knowing that the company is very traditional, you'll present yourself as more conservative, perhaps focusing on your steadfastness, and reliability, and long tenure at previous jobs. You'll probably avoid talking about the value of radical change and how you pushed for cutting-edge management changes in a previous job.

Practice your answers

While it's true that you cannot predict exactly what you'll be asked in the interview, you should have some idea of the types of questions to prepare for. Examples: "Tell me about yourself." "What is it you like best about the work you do?" "What are your weaknesses?"

At the very least, prepare a response to the question, "Tell me about yourself." Often, what interviewers are assessing with this question is your ability to communicate what's *important*. If you go off on a tangent about where you were born and what your hobbies are, you're not really focusing on your interviewer's interests (unless, of course, they bring this up first). Prepare a brief speech, no more than a couple of minutes long. It should sum up the most important skills and attributes you can bring the company, as well as your work experience in relation to its needs.

If you feel you need help in preparing for other commonly asked interview questions, check the Appendix at the end of this book for some great books on the topic.

Job Search Tip

Timing is everything

When's the best time to book an interview? Believe it or not, it can make a difference. An AccounTemps survey, published in the *Chicago Tribune*, polled 200 executives. It found that job applicants who interview in the morning may be viewed more favorably than those with interviews later in the day.

A full 83 percent of those responding said they preferred to interview candidates between *9 a.m. and 11 a.m.* No other time of day even came close. In general, hiring managers said they dislike interviewing near their usual break times. I think it's also because early in the morning hiring managers are less overwhelmed with work and their busy schedules.

Present a professional image

This is another case in which your research of the company and job will come in handy. Is it a casual corporate climate? It may be true that in some cases, dressing more casual for an interview will be entirely appropriate, but as a rule, it's always safe to wear a suit (whether you're a woman or man) to an interview, no matter what the position.

Arrive on time

This is basic. Your punctuality is an important measure of your reliability. Do whatever you have to in order to arrive at the interview on time. In fact, work to get there about 10 minutes early. This will give you time to collect yourself, review your notes and resume, and enter into the meeting with a calm and positive attitude.

Be positive

No matter what—you were given horrible directions, the office was hard to find, traffic was terrible—start off your interview with a positive attitude. Your interviewer wants to talk to someone who conveys enthusiasm, optimism, and eagerness. No matter what sort of day you've had, keep that smile on your face and think positive!

Don't be nervous

Although it may seem that way at first, an interview is not a life-or-death situation. Relax and try to be yourself. The employer may be interviewing other candidates who come across more relaxed and confident but who don't have the skills and experience you have. *Don't let them get your job.*

The interview is another chance to discover and market your potential while learning more about what the employer really wants. The way I see it, you're there to interview the company, as well. You shouldn't feel as if the burden is all on *your* shoulders to make a good impression.

Any decent interviewer understands that you may be nervous. He or she should know how to put you at ease right from the start with some light conversation, rather than to put you on the spot—but don't count on it.

Some interviewers actually enjoy intimidating candidates with out-of-this-world questions or impossible situations to see how you react under pressure. Just keep in mind that it's all a show to see what you're made of. Retain your composure as much as possible, thoughtfully consider your replies, and maintain eye contact with the interviewer when responding.

Job Search Facts

Speak up! An Accountemps/Robert Half survey polled 150 executives from the nation's 1,000 largest companies. Fully one-third said that during interviews, applicants are often *too humble* in recounting their own achievements. The lesson: Don't take anything for granted or assume employers already know how great you are. When you're called in for an interview, don't overwhelm the listener and brag about yourself, but by the same token, don't downplay your abilities.

Downplay personal information

Interviewers are prohibited by law from asking certain questions about your personal life. Questions that attempt to ascertain your ethnic background, marital status, sexual activity, physical or mental health are off-limits.

Be careful not to *offer* too much personal information. Feel free to talk briefly about your favorite leisure activities (golf, etc.), if prompted, or any other personal attribute or activity you share with the interviewer. Just keep in mind that the interview is not the place to talk about how excited you are about your upcoming wedding or how you're eager to supplement your income so you can buy a new yacht.

Of course you're not perfect, and employers don't expect you to be. Sometimes they just want to hire someone who seems to have the right kind of skills, the right type of background, and whom they think they can get along with and train in their way of doing things.

A company can always train you in a specific task or procedure, but it can't change your personality and make you fit in to its work environment. As a former corporate recruiter, I can guarantee that employers are more interested in hiring someone who seems reliable, trainable, and a good fit with its company culture.

Job Search Resource Materials

Web sites, books, listings, and catalogs

Many of the books listed below cross-reference companies by industry and provide insight on company size and products, as well as names of human resource personnel and key managers.

Check the resources and support materials on my favorite Web sites:

- **TopSecretResumes.com** (For a free resume analysis from myself and my company)

- **Execunet.com** (Executive networking and resources for postings at $75,000 and above)

- **CareerMagazine.com**

Here are some of the most popular Web sites that can help you in your job search:

- **www.monster.com**
  Lists more than 250,000 jobs in many fields, but no postings from headhunters.

- **www.careerpath.com**
  Carries classified ads from the 90 largest newspapers in the United States.

If you have a job and are looking for a better one, try a site that has a job agent. A job agent is a program that shops for jobs for you. These sites protect your confidentiality, search for your dream job and send you a private e-mail based on the profile you provide. Here are some of the best:

- **www.nationjob.com**
- **www.careerweb.com**
- **www.joboptions.com**

You can also put your credentials before a World Wide Web audience. Be sure to use the text, online, digital format explained by Wayne Gonyea earlier in this book.

Here a few of the sites, most of which are free:

- **www.careermosaic.com**
- **www.headhunter.net**
- **www.careerbuilder.com**

Remember that using the Internet is not a substitute for traditional job-hunting techniques. It should supplement, not replace, them and everything you post on the Internet is a public document.

- **Books:**

Rites of Passage at $100,000+. By John Lucht. Lucht maps out a career marketing strategy that may work for you. Covers the recruitment business and how to make it work, personal and non-personal networking, direct mailings, interviewing, and more.

America's Corporate Families, Vol. I, and *America's Corporate Families and International Affiliates, Vol. II.* By Dun's Marketing Services. Two hard-cover volumes updated annually. Information on more than 11,000 U.S. parent companies and their 60,000 subsidiaries and divisions.

Commerce Register's Geographical Directories of Manufacturers. Numerous directories for specific regions. Organized by city, this book provides information on manufacturers with more than five employees in the state or region, including addresses, telephone numbers, products, and sales figures.

Corporate 1000 Yellow Book, International Corporate 1000 Yellow Book, and *Over-The-Counter 1000 Yellow Book.* By Monitor Publishing Co. Each lists names, titles, and many direct-dial numbers for key officers, plus outside board members and their companies.

Directories in Print. By Gale Research, Inc. Published every two years. Companies are organized by industry. Describes the contents of 10,000 publications, including directories, professional and scientific rosters, and other lists and guides.

Directory of Corporate Affiliations. By National Register Publishing Company, Inc. Subtitled *Who Owns Whom.* Lists 40,000 divisions/subsidiaries of over 4,000

U.S. public and private companies. Gives assets, liabilities, net worth, income/ earnings, and approximate sales. Indexed by geography, (state and city), S.I.C. (Standard Industry Code), and professionals affiliated with the company, with a cross-reference index of divisions, subsidiaries, and affiliates. Also summarizes recent mergers, acquisitions, and name changes.

Directory of Executive Recruiters. (Kennedy Publishing). Updated each year, lists thousands of executive recruiters; indexed by industry specialties, with information on recruitment industry methods. The book and its lists of recruiters are also available on disk for an extra fee.

Dun's Europa. By Dun's Marketing Services. Profiles top 35,000 European manufacturing, distribution, financial, and service companies. Listings in both English and indigenous language.

Electronic Resumes. By Wayne and James Gonyea (McGraw Hill, 1995). Includes a disk for creating an electronic resume.

Employment Agencies. By American Business Directories. Lists thousands of employment agencies around the country.

Encyclopedia of Associations. By Gale Research, Inc. Four volumes in three books, with detailed information on more than 22,000 U.S.-headquartered nonprofit associations and organizations of all kinds.

Encyclopedia of Business Information Sources. Gale Research, Inc. More than 20,000 information sources on 1,280 highly specific subjects ranging from abrasives to zinc. Lists encyclopedias, dictionaries, handbooks, manuals, bibliographies, associations, societies, etc.

Success 2000 and *Getting Hired In The '90s.* By Vicki Spina and Corporate Image Publishers. Job search tips and strategies to increase your motivation.

Guide to American Directories. By B. Klein Publications. Updated every two years. Describes content, frequency, and cost (if any) of 7,500 directories in a variety of fields (over 300 classifications) with phone numbers.

International Directory of Company Histories. By St. James; available from Gale Research, Inc. Volume 2 published in 1990. Gives basic information and histories for about 1,250 companies in the United States, Canada, the U.K., Europe, and Japan.

International Directory of Corporate Affiliations. National Register Publishing Company, Inc. Vol. 1: Non-U.S. holdings of U.S. Parent companies; Vol. 2: U.S. and worldwide holdings of foreign enterprises.

Job Hunter's Resource Guide. By Gale Research, Inc. Annual, one volume. Lists reference materials for 150 specific professions/occupations. Also has a "how-to" section.

Job Seeker's Guide to Public and Private Companies. Gale Research, Inc. Information on more than 25,000 companies, including corporate overviews, specific job titles, and estimated number of openings for each, hiring practices, personnel contacts, employee benefits, application procedures, and recruitment activities.

Million Dollar Directory Series. Dun's Marketing Services. A five-volume series listing 160,000 public and private U.S. companies. Includes key facts on decision makers, company size, and lines of business. This may be hard to find, considering its $1,250 annual lease fee.

Million Dollar Directory of Top 50,000 Companies. Dun's Marketing Services. Covers the top 50,000 companies from the *Million Dollar Directory Series.*

Moody's Industrial Manual and News Reports. By Moody's Investor's Service. Annual, two volumes. Provides full financial and operating data on every industrial corporation on the NYSE and ASE, plus more than 500 on regional exchanges. Twice-weekly news reports update developments.

Moody's International Manual and New Reports. Moody's Investor Service. Full financial data on more than 5,000 international corporations. Twice-weekly news reports update developments.

The National Directory of Addresses and Telephone Numbers. By General Information, Inc. Great for your mailing list. Provides addresses and phone numbers for U.S. corporations, both alphabetically and by S.I.C. category.

Standard & Poor's Register of Corporations, Directors and Executives. Three volumes with just about everything on major U.S. and Canadian companies and those who run them.

Standard Directory of Advertisers. National Register Publishing Company, Inc. More than 25,000 U.S. advertiser companies with addresses, phone numbers, sales, number of employees, and primary businesses.

Thomas' Register of American Manufacturers. Thomas Publishing Company. Annual profile of 150,000 manufacturers and their major products and services. Includes 12,000 pages of catalog material and 112,000 registered trade/brand names.

Ward's Business Directory of U.S. Private and Public Companies. By Gale Research, Inc. Annual, four volumes. Provides demographic and financial business data on over 85,000 companies. Includes alphabetical and ZIP code listings.

Who's Who in America or *Who's Who in Finance & Industry.* By Marquis Who's Who, Inc. These books profile thousands of leaders and innovators from fields including business, government, art, law, science, medicine, and education.

▸ **Here's a sheet we give to our customers:**

10 Strategies for Planning and Executing the Job Hunt

1. Write/get a professional resume and solid base of operations.
   When your resume is perfect, consult books on interviewing and get access to an answering machine, computer, laser printer, fax machine, and copier for custom cover letters.

2. Develop a "big world" outlook.
   Enhance your peripheral vision. Look at any and every opportunity to get your foot in the door. If you're going after a select few companies and agencies, you face tremendous competition. Broaden your search and *network, network, network.*

3. Target your audience.
   Make your target group as large as possible, but remember the 80/20 rule: focus most of your efforts on the 20 percent of your target group of greatest interest. Customize/personalize correspondence and, when possible, tailor your resume to the job.

4. Be strategic.
   Create a marketing plan for your job hunt. You're the product. Share the plan with those you meet. Refine the plan as you go along.

5. Adjust your search to the market.
   Concentrate your search on high growth markets. Make yourself available for freelance or contract work.

6. Don't be afraid to phone first. Be assertive, yet considerate of the other's time. Persistence pays. Your goal is to get your name into the employer's head, to extract information, and/or schedule an information interview. Thrive on rejection. Stay positive no matter what happens. Things change—sometimes quickly.

7. Develop outside interests, but put in regular hours for your search.
   If your life is well balanced, finding your next position is less stressful. You'll need endurance. Eat smart, get your sleep, and get plenty of exercise.

8. Be realistic.
   It can take up to one month for every $10,000 in salary to find a job. Be prepared to start at a lower-paying position if required to supplement your income.

9. Get attention.
   Expand your network by joining a chamber of commerce or professional groups in your industry. Attend luncheons, seminars, dinners, and after-hour meetings when possible. Meet new people and develop a network of contacts.

10. Enjoy the hunt.
    Job hunting can be a complex, challenging game with great payoffs for those with drive and stamina. Finding a job is probably the toughest job you'll ever have—and you don't even get paid for it—but you will become stronger for the experience.

Free
Resume
Analysis

With expanding use of the Internet, my career books, fax, and e-mail, we've written resumes for clients all over the U.S., and in just about every country in the world. I'll be happy to review your resume, give basic feedback, and quote an exact price for writing your custom resume. We conduct a personal interview with you over the phone (the call's on us within the U.S.) and write a high-impact resume for you in one to three working days. After you proofread and finalize the content, we can mail you 10 laser prints on quality paper, and/or send it out on disk, or e-mail directly to your home.

For your free resume price quote and feedback, simply fax, mail, or e-mail your resume to us, then call at the numbers listed below and we'll discuss your options. Here's how to reach us:

A Advanced Resume Service, Inc.
850 E. Higgins Road #125-Y
Schaumburg, IL 60173
Phone: 630/582-1088
24-Hour Fax: 630/582-1105

E-mail: ADVRESUMES@aol.com
Web site: TopSecretResumes.com

We accept Visa, MasterCard, American Express, and Discover.

Index